INTERNATIONAL POLITICAL ECONOMY SERI...

General Editor: Timothy M. Shaw, Professor of Political Science and International Development Studies, and Director of the Centre for Foreign Policy Studies, Dalhousie University, Nova Scotia, Canada

Recent titles include:

Pradeep Agrawal, Subir V. Gokarn, Veena Mishra, Kirit S. Parikh and Kunal Sen
ECONOMIC RESTRUCTURING IN EAST ASIA AND INDIA: Perspectives on Policy Reform

Solon L. Barraclough and Krishna B. Ghimire
FORESTS AND LIVELIHOODS: The Social Dynamics of Deforestation in Developing Countries

Kathleen Barry (*editor*)
VIETNAM'S WOMEN IN TRANSITION

Jorge Rodríguez Beruff and Humberto García Muñiz (*editors*)
SECURITY PROBLEMS AND POLICIES IN THE POST-COLD WAR CARIBBEAN

Ruud Buitelaar and Pitou van Dijck (*editors*)
LATIN AMERICA'S NEW INSERTION IN THE WORLD ECONOMY
Towards Systemic Competitiveness in Small Economies

William D. Coleman
FINANCIAL SERVICES, GLOBALIZATION AND DOMESTIC POLICY CHANGE: A Comparison of North America and the European Union

Paul Cook and Frederick Nixson (*editors*)
THE MOVE TO THE MARKET? Trade and Industry Policy Reform in Transitional Economies

Mark E. Denham and Mark Owen Lombardi (*editors*)
PERSPECTIVES ON THIRD-WORLD SOVEREIGNTY: The Postmodern Paradox

Frederic C. Deyo (*editor*)
COMPETITION, POWER AND INDUSTRIAL FLEXIBILITY: Social Reconstructions of the World Automobile Industry

John Healey and William Tordoff (*editors*)
VOTES AND BUDGETS: Comparative Studies in Accountable Governance in the South

Jacques Hersh and Johannes Dragsbaek Schmidt (*editors*)
THE AFTERMATH OF 'REAL EXISTING SOCIALISM' IN EASTERN EUROPE, VOLUME 1: Between Western Europe and East Asia

Noeleen Heyzer, James V. Riker and Antonio B. Quizon (*editors*)
GOVERNMENT–NGO RELATIONS IN ASIA: Prospects and Challenges for People-Centred Development

George Kent
CHILDREN IN THE INTERNATIONAL POLITICAL ECONOMY

David Kowalewski
GLOBAL ESTABLISHMENT: The Political Economy of North/Asian Networks

Laura Macdonald
SUPPORTING CIVIL SOCIETY: The Political Role of Non-Governmental Organizations in Central America

Gary McMahon (*editor*)
LESSONS IN ECONOMIC POLICY FOR EASTERN EUROPE FROM LATIN AMERICA

David B. Moore and Gerald J. Schmitz (*editors*)
DEBATING DEVELOPMENT DISCOURSE: Institutional and Popular Perspectives

Juan Antonio Morales and Gary McMahon (*editors*)
ECONOMIC POLICY AND THE TRANSITION TO DEMOCRACY: The Latin American Experience

Paul J. Nelson
THE WORLD BANK AND NON-GOVERNMENTAL ORGANIZATIONS
The Limits of Apolitical Development

Archibald R. M. Ritter and John M. Kirk (*editors*)
CUBA IN THE INTERNATIONAL SYSTEM: Normalization and Integration

Ann Seidman and Robert B. Seidman
STATE AND LAW IN THE DEVELOPMENT PROCESS: Problem-Solving and Institutional Change in the Third World

Tor Skålnes
THE POLITICS OF ECONOMIC REFORM IN ZIMBABWE: Continuity and Change in Development

John Sorenson (*editor*)
DISASTER AND DEVELOPMENT IN THE HORN OF AFRICA

Howard Stein (*editor*)
ASIAN INDUSTRIALIZATION AND AFRICA: Studies in Policy Alternatives to Structural Adjustment

Sandra Whitworth
FEMINISM AND INTERNATIONAL RELATIONS

David Wurfel and Bruce Burton (*editors*)
SOUTHEAST ASIA IN THE NEW WORLD ORDER: The Political Economy of a Dynamic Region

Post-Socialist World Orders

Russia, China and the UN System

Robert Boardman
Professor of Political Science
Dalhousie University, Halifax, Nova Scotia

Published in Great Britain by
MACMILLAN PRESS LTD
Houndmills, Basingstoke, Hampshire RG21 6XS
and London
Companies and representatives
throughout the world

First edition 1994
Reprinted (with corrections) 1996

A catalogue record for this book is available
from the British Library.

ISBN 0–333–55236–9 hardcover
ISBN 0–333–66475–2 paperback

First published in the United States of America 1994 by
ST. MARTIN'S PRESS, INC.,
Scholarly and Reference Division,
175 Fifth Avenue,
New York, N.Y. 10010

ISBN 0–312–10671–8

Library of Congress Cataloging-in-Publication Data
Boardman, Robert, 1945–
Post-socialist world orders : Russia, China and the UN system /
Robert Boardman.
p. cm.
Includes index.
ISBN 0–312–10671–8
1. Russia (Federation)—Foreign economic relations. 2. China–
–Foreign economic relations. 3. International cooperation. 4. Post
–communism. 5. United Nations. I. Title.
HF1558.2.B63 1994
337.47—dc20 93–31342
CIP

---

10 9 8 7 6 5 4 3 2 1
05 04 03 02 01 00 99 98 97 96

Printed and bound in Great Britain by
Antony Rowe Ltd, Chippenham, Wiltshire

For Emma

Contents

Acknowledgements

Studying constantly moving targets is never easy, even when the pace of change is not on the scale of that in Russia and China in the 1980s and early 1990s. The aim of this book is to assess the significance of the changing relationships of these countries with the intergovernmental organisations of the United Nations system during this period, and to draw from this record observations about the utility of IGOs in the context of contemporary world-order debates.

I am grateful to the many individuals who helped me in this task. At Dalhousie University I benefited in more ways than it is possible to remember from conversations with four Killam post-doctoral Fellows, each of whom was present for several months at various times of the research: Dr Alexei Izyumov, Dr Ludmila Nemova and Dr Vladimir Drebentsov from the Institute of United States and Canada Studies, Moscow, and Dr Zou Keyuan from the Department of International Law, Beijing University. During the course of my three visits to Moscow, researchers and staff at the Institute for World Economy and International Relations and the US–Canada Institute in particular gave invaluable assistance. I should also like to thank Dr Leonid Leshchenko of the Institute for Social and Economic Problems of Foreign Countries for help during my stay in Kiev, and officials of the Ministries of Foreign Affairs in Moscow and Kiev. In Beijing in 1991 staff of the Chinese Academy of Social Sciences made possible valuable meetings with scholars and officials from the Beijing Institute for International Strategic Studies, the China Institute of International Studies, the Centre of International Studies of the State Council, the Institute for Strategic Studies of the National Defence University, the National Environmental Protection Agency and other institutions. Thanks are also due to staff of the Guandong Provincial Academy of Social Sciences for much appreciated help during my visit to Guangzhou the following year.

I should also like to thank Dr Paul Marantz, University of British Columbia, and Dr James Tang, University of Hong Kong, for suggestions on various aspects of the study, and Dr Sanjay Yadav for assistance in the early stages of the project. None of these people, of course, bears any responsibility for what may have been done with their advice.

Research for the book would have been impossible if I had not been able to exploit the resources of several libraries, and the time and patience of their staffs. These include the Dag Hammarskjoeld Library, New York, the Joint IMF–World Bank Library, Washington, the libraries of the World Health Organisation, the International Labour Organisation and GATT in Geneva, the Soviet Studies collection of the University of Glasgow Library, and the Centre of Asian Studies, University of Hong Kong.

Funding support for the research was gratefully received from the Social Sciences and Humanities Research Council, the Canadian Institute for International Peace and Security, and the Research Development Fund at Dalhousie University. A CIIPS fellowship awarded through its exchange programme with the US–Canada Institute allowed me to undertake a productive visit to Moscow.

Chester Basin ROBERT BOARDMAN

The author and publishers are grateful to the following for permission to reproduce the two maps in this book: International Monetary Fund for the map of the former Soviet Union; and Macmillan Publishing Company, New York, for the map of China from *Comparing Political Systems: Power and Policy in Three Worlds*, fourth edition, by Gary K. Bertsch, Robert Clark and David Wood – Copyright © 1991 by Macmillan College Publishing Company, Inc.

List of Abbreviations

AFL-CIO	American Federation of Labor–Congress of Industrial Organizations
CFC	Chlorofluorocarbon
CIS	Commonwealth of Independent States
CMEA	Council for Mutual Economic Assistance
COCOM	Coordinating Committee for Multilateral Export Controls
CPE	Centrally planned economy
CSCE	Conference on Security and Cooperation in Europe
EBRD	European Bank for Reconstruction and Development
EC	European Community
ECE	Economic Commission for Europe
ECOSOC	Economic and Social Council
FAO	Food and Agriculture Organisation
FLS	Front-Line States
GATT	General Agreement on Tariffs and Trade
IBRD	International Bank for Reconstruction and Development
IDA	International Development Association
IFI	International financial institution
IGBP	International Geosphere–Biosphere Program
IGO	Intergovernmental organisation
ILO	International Labour Organisation
IMF	International Monetary Fund
ITO	International Trade Organisation
MFA	Multifibre Agreement
MFN	Most-favoured nation
MNC	Multinational corporation
MSC	Military Staff Committee
NAM	Non-Aligned Movement
NGO	Non-governmental organisation
NIC	Newly industrialising country
NIEO	New International Economic Order
NWICO	New World Information and Communication Order
OAU	Organisation of African Unity
OECD	Organisation for Economic Cooperation and Development

PHC	Primary health care
PLA	People's Liberation Army
PLO	Palestine Liberation Organisation
RSFSR	Russian Soviet Federated Socialist Republic
SDI	Strategic Defense Initiative
SDR	Special Drawing Right
SEZ	Special Economic Zone
SWAPO	South West African People's Organisation
TDB	Trade and Development Board
UNCED	UN Conference on Environment and Development
UNCTAD	UN Conference on Trade and Development
UNDP	UN Development Programme
UNEF	UN Emergency Force
UNEP	UN Environment Programme
UNESCO	UN Educational, Scientific and Cultural Organisation
UNFICYP	UN Force in Cyprus
UNICEF	UN International Children's Emergency Fund
UNIFIL	UN Interim Force in Lebanon
UNPROFOR	UN Force in Bosnia
UNRRA	UN Relief and Rehabilitation Administration
UNTAG	UN Transition Assistance Group
UNTSO	UN Truce Supervision Organisation
WHO	World Health Organisation
WTO	Warsaw Treaty Organisation

1 Introduction: Political Economy and Institutional Order

INTERNATIONAL ORGANISATION AND THE CRISES OF LATE SOCIALISM

For most states, most of the time, membership of the intergovernmental organisations (IGOs) of the UN system is a routine fact of life. It is as natural a feature of formal statehood as national airlines and postage stamps – if less prestigious than the former, perhaps, and not so consistently useful as the latter. There have been exceptions. Cold War disputes blocked the route to early UN membership for a number of states in the 1950s. Indonesia's frustrations with the UN took it temporarily out of that body in the mid-1960s. Those of Singapore and the United States with UNESCO had similar consequences in the early 1980s. A few states have interpreted aloofness from IGOs as both a symbol and a partial guarantee of their ability to protect their independence. Some lack the resources to justify extensive participation in a large number of agencies. Normally, however, what is more intriguing is what states choose – and have the capacity – to do with their membership cards.

During the 1980s the Soviet Union and China were among the countries that significantly extended their ties with the UN system. The Soviet Union's reform programme of the late 1980s was structured in part with a view to its gaining membership of the World Bank (IBRD) and the International Monetary Fund (IMF). Once the Russian Federation had secured this in 1992, these and other institutions continued to occupy a prominent place in Moscow's economic planning. A guest at, and firmly implanted on the agenda of, Group of 7 meetings in the early 1990s, Moscow indicated that it saw membership of this grouping too as a goal. The new outlook on IGOs formed a crucial part of the Gorbachev reform programme. It was a key element both in domestic restructuring and in the pursuit of a less confrontational world order inspired by the emphasis of the 'new thinking' on the concepts of common security and the interdependence of the world economy. Stress on the UN also served other purposes in the late 1980s, including the revitalising of party and governmental structures.

Similarly, the course and the details of China's programme of economic modernisation came to be shaped more and more in association with international financial institutions (IFIs). Like Russia, China also developed supportive attitudes towards the UN's peacekeeping and conflict-resolution role during this period. However, China's more cautious stance was reflected in its resort to abstention or non-participation in Security Council votes that taxed too strenuously its willingness to be carried along by Western-led consensus positions.

There were elements of novelty in both cases. Earlier Soviet responses to the UN were moulded among other things by an ideologically grounded antipathy, the adversarial relationship with the United States, a sense of responsibility to its socialist civilising mission and its minority situation in the institution. These factors nursed a diplomatic style characterised, for some Western critics, by sullen obstructiveness, propagandising, and a calculating eagerness to politicise issues. This image, inadequate though it had always been as a depiction of the Soviet presence in the UN, lost its remaining shreds of realism in the radical turns of policy initiated by Moscow in the Soviet Union's final years. Hostility to the government's pro-Western posture, especially in relation to IFIs, became one of the defining features of Russian domestic political turbulence and ideological diversity in the early 1990s.

For its part, China in the early 1980s had had relatively few years of experience of taking part in UN affairs. It was allowed to join the institution – or, more accurately, its government took over China's seat – only in 1971, some twenty-two years after the establishment of the People's Republic. Shortly before the changeover, serious interest in international institutions had been one of the many casualties of the Cultural Revolution. The modernisation programme initiated by Beijing in the late 1970s welcomed these, in contrast, as valued agents in the construction of China's economic future. Restraints imposed by prevailing ideological interpretations of the principle of self-reliant development eroded. China declared that it was ready to receive aid and technical assistance, as well as to act in the role of donor in relation to other developing countries.

Comparing the two countries for purposes of analysis does not assume the existence of structural or behavioural similarities between them. There are profound differences between the economies of Russia and China, as there are between their political cultures. These features were conspicuous even when both were communist countries; and structural and ideological differences then marked their respective approaches to democratic centralism and socialist economic development. Russia and China occupied differing positions in relation to nineteenth-century European colonial expansion. The ethnic cleavages that mark Russia, and still more those that characterised the Soviet Union, have some but minimal parallels in the case of China. Russia is part of Europe as well as of Asia. From the late 1940s to the late 1980s its economy functioned as the dominant element in a regional division of labour for which there was no equivalent in the case of China. China in the 1990s has the unusual distinction of retaining a political and governmental structure still dominated by a communist party.

Comparative study is nonetheless useful.[1] It requires appreciation of both similarities and differences in the conditions of the two countries. Both states have been engaged in ambitious market-oriented economic reform programmes that have had significant implications for their relations with international institutions. The governments of each have had to contend with, and have responded in different ways to, forces demanding and resisting greater democratisation. Economic policies were framed in the case of Russia in the early 1990s, however, in a context of explicit repudiation of any lessons to be learned from the socialist past. The Chinese Communist Party, in contrast, continued to situate its own planned course formally within a socialist framework of economic development and, more forcefully, to insist that this be implemented according to socialist concepts of democracy.

More specifically, from the vantage point of this study, Russia and China are each not only members of most bodies in the UN system, but also, within the UN itself, permanent members of the Security Council. Both are central players in the formulation of approaches to the resolution of post-Cold-War world-order issues during the 1990s, including debates on the reform and future of the UN itself.

Whether, to extrapolate from the Soviet collapse, they are also likely to share similar futures – perhaps as large ex-socialist states with chronically troubled economies and a disposition to domestic political turbulence – remains to be seen. Many of the problems confronting China in the 1990s are arguably similar to those faced by the former Soviet Union. So too are the structural contradictions inherent in the long-term project of reconciling the Marxist–Leninist goal of perfecting socialist society with the controlled unleashing of market forces. China has outperformed the Soviet Union economically, however, and lacks many of the basic ethnic and nationalist cleavages that fractured that country in the 1980s. Its ruling elites have kept a tighter clamp on domestic political dissent, and, the temporary international sanctions following the 1989 suppression of the prodemocracy movement notwithstanding, have maintained relatively intact a powerful and supportive external constituency of Western states and multilateral institutions.

Awareness of the circumstances of the other was an intriguing feature of both Russian and Chinese commentary in the late 1980s and early 1990s. Chinese observers engaged in intense speculation about the likely impacts of the Gorbachev reforms and later about the lessons and significance of the Soviet road to disintegration for their own country. Russian analysts, too, investigated the roots of Chinese economic successes. Some saw these as increasingly relevant to the conditions of Russia in its reduced straits as a member of the ranks of large developing countries like China and India.

THE NATURE OF INSTITUTIONAL ORDER

What intergovernmental organisations are able to do for, and to, countries depends on a number of factors. States differ widely in economic, military and diplomatic capabilities. They are situated differently in relation to the main forces of the international economy. Internally, governments and the actors of civil societies vary considerably in their respective stakes in the existing international institutional order. IGOs reflect these disparities of power in the internal political dynamics of interactions among member-states; the degree to which in their range of membership they are representative of international society; and in their formal structures and processes of decision-making.

Viewed in this sociological context, international institutions are clearly not indispensable. Governments could tackle problems of the environment, regional conflict, the international protection of human rights or other matters without formal intergovernmental bodies of the type found in the UN system. States can and do cooperate with each other in a multitude of ways outside the frameworks of IGOs. During the Cold War the US and the Soviet Union engaged in various kinds of cooperation in security and other areas as a result of such factors as the constraints of nuclear weapons technology, the political and economic structures of bipolarity, perception of the risks of escalation of local conflicts, and the cumulative effects of learning from crises.[2] Bilateral and multilateral forms of cooperation among states and other actors outside IGOs are less intense at the global than at regional levels, but are still a conspicuous feature of world society.

Indeed for this reason a distinction is useful between politics inside IGOs and the more widespread phenomenon of institutionalised forms of interstate cooperation. Multilateral cooperation of this more general kind has been defined as comprising 'institutional arrangements to define and stabilise the international property rights of states, to manage coordination problems, and to resolve collaboration problems'.[3]

Further, the kind of institutional order generated by IGOs is only one element of the broader structures of economic, political and legal order present in the international system. States, like members of any set of social relationships, have throughout history made rules to govern their interactions with each other. Such orders may be inimical to, or may actively encourage, the development and maturation of formal institutional intergovernmental arrangements. These in turn vary in the degree to which they can be considered relatively autonomous actors. Evidence of the usefulness of IGOs is nonetheless provided by the extent to which collaborative processes of interaction among states, at both regional and world levels, have tended increasingly to become institutionalised.

There are many reasons why governments and other actors may see such institutions as useful, or why in particular cases they may base their judgments more on the perceived marginal disutilities of IGOs. The opportunity costs of contributing financially to the upkeep of costly secretariats, infrastructures and programmes enter such calculations. So can inertia: there may be few incentives for a government to change direction. It is often useful for governments to be present in multilateral forums just in case something happens which, negatively or positively, might affect their countries' interests. And there are a variety of kinds of interest in IGOs inside governments, from the higher calculus of definitions of 'the national interest' to the bureaucratic stake of a forestry, trade or education agency in protecting its territorial right to take part in international meetings. States may through IGOs seek economic advancement or the erosion of externally created structural disadvantages. They may aspire to global solutions to common problems or the expedient tempering of the visionary plans of others, dominance over fellow members or the multilateralising of strategies of resistance to powerful neighbours or would-be hegemons.

Puzzling over the significance of international institutions has been a feature of empirical and normative theorising about international relations for at least several centuries. The kind of regional or world order an academic observer or a foreign-service officer assumes to exist affects their respective attitudes towards IGOs. Quite different judgments flow from a Westphalian statecentric model or a Mitranyian functionalist model.[4] This historical profusion of interpretations has produced diverse transformationalist, instrumentalist and pluralist approaches to understanding IGOs.

First, *transformationalist perspectives* have judged these institutions according to their potential, in conjunction with other forces, to alter fundamentally the basic structures of international politics or the world economy. This thread connects various types of nineteenth- and early twentieth-century idealism, especially the liberal internationalist perspective on law, cooperation and institution-building, with more recent policy debates on issues of the global commons. Just as realist critics of the 1930s and 1940s found this approach wanting, so some of the regimes literature of the 1980s has been criticised for concealing a hidden idealist agenda.[5] Socialist theorists have generally been skeptical about IGOs, often detecting in their workings the manipulative capabilities of capitalist states, and preferring instead to look to forces outside them for transformative potential. However, assumptions about the capability of some types of IGOs to serve as catalysing agents of structural change can still be discerned in analyses in socialist states, for example in both Soviet and Chinese approaches to the New International Economic Order (NIEO) agendas of the 1970s.

Secondly, IGOs can be viewed as *instruments* – of states, or of the economic forces states may be seen as representing. In the classical, and especially the realist, tradition of theorising, states are assumed to be the dominant actors in international relations, security issues to be paramount, and anarchy to be the characteristic feature of the international system.[6] Institutions are from this perspective marginally useful adjuncts to the mechanisms governments devise for themselves in their dealings with others. As tools of foreign policies they may facilitate attempts by states to fashion rules to promote their interests. They may affect the shifting balance of relative gains and losses of states in international arenas. Though a powerful tradition in international relations theory, this perspective has been challenged from a number of different directions, including that of normative theorising.[7] A variety of structuralist and other political economy approaches would also view IGOs as instruments. These depart from the path of realist analysis, however, in the identification of the clients on whose behalf bodies such as the World Bank or the IMF are presumed to be acting: not states, but rather the interests of transnational capital in a globalising economy.

Thirdly, IGOs can be appraised from the perspective of various *pluralist views of world society*. Grotian assumptions about the possibilities latent in the international community for cooperation among states have influenced some of these approaches. The range of phenomena to be studied is large: non-governmental organisations (NGOs) as well as IGOs, multinational corporations (MNCs) as well as multilateral institutions, the multiple connections between societies as well as those between governments, revised as well as conventional interstate agendas. Processes of quasi-governance within these complex systems of interaction have become so consolidated that some observers have detected the existence and growing significance of broad regulatory regimes, and of policy communities transcending national boundaries.

The orientations states develop towards IGOs depend on a number of factors. These include the issues involved, the institutional maturity of a regime or institution, the competitive interactions among national bureaucratic actors and the impact of constitutional structures such as federalism.[8] Some governments are relatively more prone to support multilateralism, others to be more suspicious of the constraints and loss of sovereignty this may imply.

First, governments can adopt *proactive initiating strategies* in international institutions, or they may incline towards more *reactive and passive postures*. Depending on the issues, they may resort to variations of either in the same institution or conference. Secondly, the policies of governments and the votes of delegations may be aimed at securing *paradigm shifts* in the mandate and programmes of the organisation, or just *incremental improvements in performance*. This can be combined with the first dimension in various ways. Revolutionary calls for radical change, for example, may be pursued reactively through established organisational procedures. Thirdly, governments vary considerably in the extent to which IGOs are seen as having an impact – desirable or otherwise – on their *domestic policies and national economies*. Compliance with IGO decisions may involve not only an investment of political will on the part of governments, but also complex bargaining among domestic actors. Support for conference resolutions does not necessarily imply a readiness to initiate such processes. Especially if it is the result of external pressures, a government's tilt towards IGO policy preferences – for example on the structural adjustment of national economies – can also generate domestic social and political costs.

To the question 'Do IGOs matter?', there is thus no easy answer. Such theoretical perspectives on their significance are important not only as a prelude to more detailed study. A diversity of views, implicitly held or explicitly formulated, can also be found in practice among the governments and domestic political actors that deal with IGOs and attempt, directly or indirectly, to influence them.

These attitudes have some bearing on the policies adopted by states. Such views were developed more formally and rigorously in the Soviet Union, as in other socialist states, especially with the rise of interest in the UN from the early 1960s. Others prevailed in the 'deideologised' conditions of the early 1990s. Statements of viewpoints are not necessarily, of course, a reliable indication of beliefs. Speeches and articles may be designed to sustain or change the viewpoints of others (domestic as well as external), to deflect influence attempts or simply to provide more attractively value-laden and intellectually coherent rationales for actions. Used carefully, however, such sources can help us locate and assess the definitions of interest, underlying attitudes and perceptions of specific conjunctures that shape the approaches of states to IGOs.

This study analyses the changing relations of Russia and China with the IGOs of the UN system. The focus is primarily on the years spanning the early 1980s and the early 1990s, a rich period for study which encourages exploration of the many connections between economic development and foreign policy, and the external and domestic policies of governments. The aim is to examine the character of the changes that took place during these years, identify their causes, analyse their significance in terms of both the IGOs and the countries themselves, and, finally, to discuss the implications of these developments for future institutional order.

The comparative framework examines Russian and Chinese policies in three broad kinds of UN arenas: economic and financial policy-making, particularly in relation to issues of economic development; cooperation and conflict in technical and functional issue-areas; and approaches to questions of international peace and security and the role of the UN in the settlement of conflicts. This is not a historical study, but where it appears important to do so for purposes of understanding developments during this period, comparisons and contrasts are also drawn with the earlier historical experiences of the Soviet Union and China with international institutions.

This classification is not intended to be exhaustive. Nor can we hope to treat systematically the many issues and organisations characteristic of each of these three broad areas. Within each, rather, the approach has been selective and institutional. Where appropriate, too, the relevant contexts of foreign policy, economic policy and domestic politics are examined. Thus the first set of questions focuses attention on IFIs, particularly the World Bank and the IMF. For the second, two specialised agencies – the World Health Organization (WHO) and the International Labour Organisation (ILO) – have been chosen as case studies, together with the United Nations Environment Programme (UNEP). The third examines Russian and Chinese approaches to issues on the agenda of the Security Council. Following a preliminary historical overview in the case of each country (in Chapter 2 for the Soviet Union and Chapter 6 for China), policies in each of the three areas are discussed in turn (Chapters 3–5 and 7).

Part I
Russia

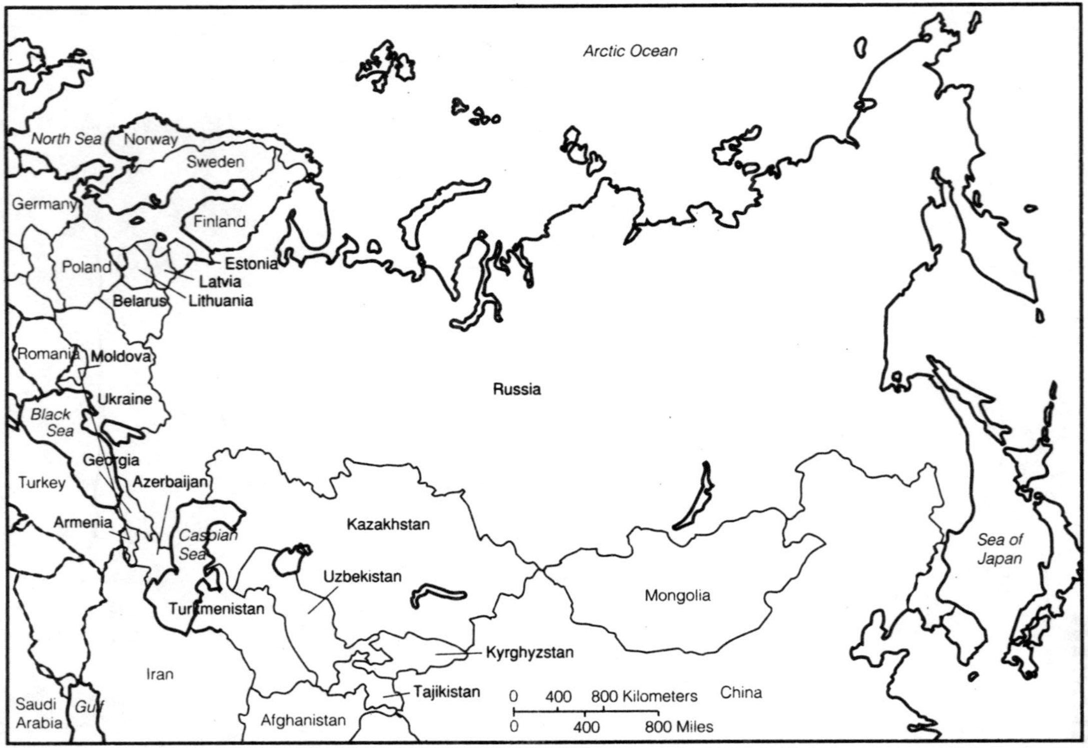
Arctic Ocean
North Sea
Norway
Sweden
Germany
Finland
Poland
Estonia
Latvia
Lithuania
Belarus
Romania
Moldova
Ukraine
Black Sea
Russia
Georgia
Turkey
Azerbaijan
Armenia
Caspian Sea
Kazakhstan
Uzbekistan
Turkmenistan
Kyrghyzstan
Mongolia
Sea of Japan
Iran
Tajikistan
Saudi Arabia
Gulf
Afghanistan
China
0 400 800 Kilometers
0 400 800 Miles

2 Historical Ironies: The Gorbachev Moment and the (Re)Emergence of Russia

Russian attitudes towards international institutions have been marked by periodic bouts of enthusiasm. In the late 1980s, as in the mid-1930s, suspicions about the character of these organisations, and about the Western countries which appeared to dominate many of their activities, were largely cast aside. The UN, like the League of Nations before it, came to be viewed as a potentially significant instrument for stabilising the country's external environment. By the beginning of the 1990s the Soviet Union itself was heading for collapse. As the former republics moved quickly to take up UN membership (with the exception of Ukraine and Belarus, which already had this status), Russia emerged in the Security Council and in other multilateral forums as the clear successor of the USSR. At the 1992 Security Council summit President Yeltsin said that it was a 'historical irony that the Russian Federation, a State with centuries-long experience in foreign policy and diplomacy, has only just appeared on the political map of the world'.[1]

This chapter looks at the course of these events and the changing theoretical perspectives on international institutions that accompanied and helped shape them. It begins with a brief review of the Soviet experience with the League of Nations and with the UN before the changes of the mid-1980s.

REVOLUTION AND SECURITY: SHOCKWAVES FROM THE PAST

The new, and still precariously placed, Soviet regime did not view developments at the Versailles conference as a high priority. Nor did it take seriously the early years of the League of Nations. It was preoccupied with pressing domestic matters: the recovery of the economy, the building of socialism, coping with civil war and intervention, and extensive security problems, both domestic and external. The first response was the almost automatic reflex of dismissing the Geneva body as an antirevolutionary, and anti-Russian, coalition. The League was something to be ignored so long as it remained immersed in obscure diplomatic niceties, but to be watched carefully whenever it threatened to interfere in the turbulent affairs of the new state.

Several factors reinforced this attitude. First, the ideological framework still being crafted by Lenin counselled a deep suspicion of the motives of the capitalist interests represented in the formal structures of the League.[2] The Paris peace talks and planning for the covenant were portrayed in Soviet commentary as a thinly disguised cloak for defending and promoting capitalism, and for supporting political and military intervention in Russia. In particular, Article 16, the covenant's sanctions provision, was viewed as a menacing element that could one day be turned against Russia itself. The League, moreover, was linked constitutionally and politically with the International Labour Organisation. The latter was a blatant device, in the emerging Soviet view of international institutions, designed both to perpetuate the oppression of workers in capitalist countries and to deny the legitimacy of the changes brought about by the October revolution.

Secondly, cooperation with international bodies was a practice tainted by association with the old regime. The Tsar's active dabbling with the European experiments of the 1890s in international mediation and dispute settlement machinery ensured a bleak reception for the League's mechanisms in the Moscow of the 1920s. As in the US, ironically a comparable case, Soviet hostility to the League was grounded in a deep-seated fear of entangling alliances and suspicion of the hidden agendas underlying the diplomatic codes of Western European chancelleries.

Yet, thirdly, this same caution also sprang from an older Russian diplomatic style: that observed by Curzon in the nineteenth century of 'waiting upon events, of profiting by the blunders of others, and as often of committing the like herself'.[3] When its security circumstances changed in the early 1930s, the Soviet Union waited no longer and jumped vigorously into the balance-of-power politics of the League.

It is possible that some kind of accommodation between Moscow and Geneva could have been found earlier than 1934. There was a widespread sentiment in pro-League circles in the West for Soviet membership.[4] One early attempt failed, however. An ILO commission set up in 1920 to investigate industrial conditions in Russia did not meet an implacable wall of hostility. The initiative was formally welcomed in Moscow as a sign that some members of the League were at last beginning to change their attitude towards the Russian people. Delays in making the arrangements, however, combined with a deteriorating situation in Ukraine following a Polish advance, led Moscow to declare that the timing of such a venture was not appropriate.[5]

Even if some form of relationship had been established at that time, however, it is unlikely that it could have survived continuing Soviet ideological condemnation of the ILO. Russian suspicions of the League were further clouded by the organisation's setting in Switzerland, where public opinion was not sympathetic to a Soviet presence. The murder of the Soviet delegate to a Lausanne conference in 1923, and the acquittal of the alleged murderers, led to a break between the two governments and an angry declaration from the Soviet Union that it would not attend any future conference held in that country.[6] A modest level of technical cooperation between Soviet authorities and international health bodies flourished in the 1920s and the Soviet Union joined a variety of arrangements such as the International Metric Union, but all this was contained within firm limits set by both sides.

Thus the League was viewed from Moscow in light of the criterion of the security of the Soviet state. Ideological opposition did not mean that membership was ruled out. Rather it implied that a calculation of Soviet security interests suggested either the irrelevance or the excessive risks of membership in a given set of circumstances. Such calculations veered more towards the option of membership in the late 1920s. The rapprochement between Germany – the other great European outsider – and the League was taken in Moscow as evidence of a more threatening international environment, and denounced routinely as a sign of Berlin's newfound alliance with anti-Soviet forces. The protracted issue of diplomatic privileges for Soviet officials in Geneva was finally resolved in 1927. Soviet officials were also actively participating from the mid-1920s in the preparatory talks that led to the world conferences on disarmament and on the world economy. The Soviet decision to join the Kellogg–Briand Pact put it for the first time within the framework of a collective security arrangement.[7]

The changing Soviet outlook on the League was signalled by Stalin in an interview with the *New York Times*' Moscow correspondent at the end of 1933: 'if the League were to turn out an obstacle, even a small one, that made war more difficult, while it furthered, even to a small extent, the cause of peace, then we would not be against the League'.[8] The precipitating event was the announcement by the new regime in Berlin of Germany's withdrawal from the League. The provisions of the covenant took on fresh significance in Moscow. Article 16 could be the basis for a collective security response to a future threat, direct or indirect, from Nazi Germany (or, later in the decade, to a possible Japanese threat to Siberia). Even so, the path to Soviet membership was not smooth. Some League members, including Switzerland and the Netherlands, were alarmed at the prospect; Ireland and others saw religious persecution in Russia as an insuperable obstacle; several had suffered financially as a result of the Russian revolution and still had claims against the Soviet state.[9] Working in Moscow's favour, however, were the longer-term strategic assessments of France, whose leaders were even more concerned than those in Moscow about German developments.

Inside the League from 1934, the Soviet Union was transformed into a staunch, articulate and at times creative advocate of the covenant's collective security provisions. Delegates argued the case for sanctions against Germany, Italy and Japan. Indeed this Soviet position was maintained more consistently, and over a longer period of time during the 1930s, than was the case with the League's traditional defenders. Many of these had concluded earlier either that the institution was incapable of mounting an effective response to aggression by a major power, or that the League's ambiguous answers on such occasions reflected accurately the complex realities of inherently ambiguous situations. With the aim of buttressing the League's importance in international affairs, Russia also continued and strengthened its premembership interest in the many international technical activities that surrounded League bodies. It simultaneously remained loyal, however, to its ideological duty of exposing the 'wilful lies concerning the position of Soviet labour' perpetrated by the ILO.[10]

The Soviet Union's attack on Finland in November 1939 was thus as consistent with this evolving definition of its security interests as was its consternation at its subsequent expulsion from the League. By the turn of the decade, however, events in Geneva had once again become irrelevant for Moscow.

THE UN IN SOVIET FOREIGN POLICY: THE POLITICS OF CREATION AND USE

The experience of League membership and memories of its abrupt termination went a long way towards shaping Soviet thinking about the United Nations. Gromyko later wrote about the Soviet view at the Dumbarton Oaks conference: 'We were determined to create such an organisation and we were determined that it should be effective'.[11]

The record of the League suggested several lessons. Any international organisation was bound to be at best a relatively weak guarantee of Soviet security. It would remain so so long as the Soviet Union was in a minority position as a lone socialist state in a world of powerful – even if ultimately vulnerable – capitalist states. Nonetheless the years at Geneva also indicated the advantages to Moscow of participation in this kind of enterprise, provided that Soviet core interests could be protected. Thus in the Soviet view the postwar United Nations was to be primarily devoted to issues of peace and security; its executive body, comprising the great powers, should have the final decision-making authority in these crucial areas; and each of these powers should have a veto over council decisions. As logical corollaries to this emerging Soviet perspective, economic and social questions were to be seen as marginal (especially given their awkward potential for legitimising interference in Soviet internal affairs); the proposed assembly of all nations should remain, in the final analysis, relatively powerless; and moves by Western, or smaller, states to undermine these fundamental working principles, particularly the veto, were to be strenuously resisted.

Recollection of the dismal fortunes of the League remained a starting-point for Soviet analyses of the UN for many years. This was, as Deutscher has described Stalin's view at Yalta, 'the same League that had never lifted a finger against Hitler and never done anything against any act of aggression.... No, Russia would not allow herself to be so treated in the future'.[12] The Western states in the League, a Soviet jurist wrote later, had been governed by 'anti-Soviet' policies, and had adopted 'reactionary and high-handed' attitudes towards the USSR.[13] The theme of the League's failures and 'its inglorious end' was developed at length by Gromyko in the UN General Assembly in the late 1940s.[14] This vein of commentary was reminiscent of much of what came out of Moscow in the 1920s and 1930s, though it glossed over the stance of active support of the organisation that Soviet delegations maintained in practice after 1934. Thus in a sense the UN, in its core international security role, was to be for the Soviet Union not so much a revived, and appropriately corrected, form of the League of Nations, but rather a modified extension of the practice of great power wartime collaboration.[15] Departures from this model, particularly verbal attacks against the Soviet Union in the General Assembly as the US 'unleashed' and stepped up its Cold War, prompted instant Soviet recollections of the worse features of the League.

The UN was not seen, that is, as a body that might help promote the breakdown of the basic 'two-camp' structure of the world. The Soviets' view was presented at the Moscow meetings in 1943 and developed at Dumbarton Oaks. There they proposed essentially a straightforward security organisation, one free of the economic and social clutter of the kind that had distracted the League. The veto in the council remained the crux of the issue throughout. Unanimity of the great powers, guaranteed by the institution of the veto, was for Stalin the 'basic condition' of UN effectiveness.[16]

The ingenious Soviet attempt to secure membership for each of the 15 Union republics was a much lower priority in practice. Held to be justified by recent constitutional change in the USSR, and by analogy with the British Commonwealth, the proposal bore little relation to Soviet political reality. President Roosevelt was nonetheless sympathetic to part of the Soviet case, particularly to the argument that the stability of the USSR might be threatened by a failure of the UN to accept Ukraine as a member, and that multiple membership would be a way to guarantee support for Soviet participation in the UN among members of the Politburo and Central Committee. However, this 'X-matter', as it came to be known, was for American officials one of extreme delicacy. Congressional and public opinion could easily have shifted back into the isolationist posture that had kept the US out of the League if it had gone through, or even if it had become a subject of public debate.[17]

The compromise – membership for the USSR and for the Ukrainian and Byelorussian republics – gave Soviet participation in the UN in subsequent decades an odd look. In practice the three delegations adopted identical approaches to the UN and to other institutions in the UN system.[18] The device arguably had some significance in the long run, even though it required the breakup of the Soviet Union itself before the other republics were able to join the UN. The nationalist view in Ukraine, for example, consistently viewed UN membership as justified by that country's political importance, and by its role in the Second World War. Participation in a group of organisations in the UN system was moreover tangible evidence of activity by the Ukrainian and Byelorussian foreign ministries, and one that was denied to their formal counterparts in the other Union republics (even to the RSFSR). Ukrainian diplomatic experience in the UN thus built upon its active participation, especially in 1945–6, in the work of UNRRA and the contacts this afforded with officials from Canada, the US and Britain.[19] In the official and academic Ukrainian view during the Soviet period, this potentially constructive relationship was thwarted from 1947 by America's Cold War against the USSR.

There was little room in this Soviet view of the ideal form of the UN for economic and social policy. 'Lonely and peculiar in a bourgeois world', as Emerson and Claude wrote in the early 1950s, the Soviet Union and other socialist states 'had little incentive to join its economic and social arrangements, and had reason to be cautious about undertaking obligations to open their books to or to be guided by the policies of international agencies to whose basic orientation they were opposed and in whose good will they had no faith'.[20] The Soviet Union did agree to the economic and social provisions of the UN charter at San Francisco in 1945, however, and had already reconciled itself to the fact that pressure from the smaller and middle powers made these unavoidable. This suspicious stance did not, however, constitute a rejection by Moscow of the idea that international organisations could play useful roles in economic policy areas. It seems more likely that the Soviet view was in practice in favour of functional specialisation. The UN was judged almost exclusively in the mid-1940s in terms of international security objectives, whereas at the same time the Bretton Woods design was seen as the appropriate vehicle for postwar economic and financial cooperation.

Praise of the UN charter became a remarkably consistent theme in Soviet commentary in succeeding decades – indeed for as long as the Soviet Union existed. If failings were evident in the UN, as they frequently were, then these could be attributed to the intransigence and deceit of a few easily identifiable culprits. The Soviet Union, after all, had a stake in the 1945 deal. It was a member of the UN from the outset, and a permanent member of the Security Council. It did not, as in the first half of the League's life, have to sit on the sidelines enduring the indifference or overt hostility of a complacent West. Not surprisingly, defence of the charter's constitutional principles and collective security arrangements was an almost unshakeable reference point in Soviet foreign-policy statements from the 1940s to the 1980s. This formal posture concealed at times both a smug assumption of socialist superiority and an unwillingness in practice to discuss seriously practical steps that might improve the workings of the UN. It did not, however, reduce the Soviet Union to inactivity. Apart from some notable exceptions, as in the socialist states' boycott of UN bodies in the early 1950s over the issue of Chinese representation, the Soviet presence at the UN was often characterised by a hankering for the right initiative: the well-timed appeal to a grand vision that would prove to be a turning-point in the history of the UN's consideration of a matter, whether disarmament, environmental protection or a Middle East settlement.

This context of insistent declaratory support for the UN, and especially for the charter, is important for assessing the significance of Gorbachev's discovery of the UN in 1987 and the much more actively pro-UN posture that followed. Thus as early as 1946 Stalin was able to defend the UN as 'a serious instrument for the preservation of peace'.[21] The tone was echoed by Brezhnev in the early 1970s: 'We want to see the UN an effective and authoritative organisation, concentrating its efforts on the maintenance of peace and security'.[22]

From the late 1940s, however, such statements, though they continued to be made, were qualified by important reservations. As one writer put it in 1972, the 'weaknesses and shortcomings' of the UN were not due to the organisation itself or its charter, but rather to 'the acts of some states which undermine the principles and cut across the basic provisions of the

Charter'.[23] Further, formal support for the UN and for charter objectives also has to be seen in relation to broader theoretical interpretations of the nature of international relations. These tended to marginalise the UN, both in theory and in practice, in the overall foreign-policy perspective of the USSR. This ambivalence in the Soviet outlook on the UN system – the oscillation between the enthusiastically promoted initiative on the one hand, and the 'suspicious, guarded and defensive' diplomatic style familiar to Western observers on the other[24] – reflected ideological predispositions, domestic political structures and broader foreign-policy objectives. But it was also a product of Moscow's situation, and self-image, as an outsider. The expanded membership of the UN and UN organisations from the 1950s eased this predicament, but never fully eradicated it. As Third World states took more control of General Assembly agendas in the 1970s, many became critical of Soviet and other socialist-state responses to international economic issues. Moscow's defensive denial that it was part of an exploitative industrial North served to isolate Soviet delegations still further from the main currents of UN politics.

This formal pro-charter lens also provided the Soviet Union with a valuable gauge for judging UN developments. The General Assembly's 'Uniting For Peace' resolution of 1950, designed by the US in the immediate circumstances of the Korean War to shift some of the Security Council's responsibilities to the General Assembly in the event of council deadlock, was held to be a clear violation of the UN's constitution. A similar reasoning was adopted to oppose the peacekeeping role of the UN, in the form this took from the creation of the UN Emergency Force in 1956. Such developments, according to the Soviets, signalled a potentially dangerous expansion of the authority of the UN secretary general, and ignored (and violated) important provisions of Chapters VI and VII of the charter. In the early 1970s Soviet delegates maintained that there was no need for the UN to spend time trying to define, or redefine, aggression: the charter contained 'sufficiently well balanced criteria on which any definition of aggression should be based'.[25] Revisions to the charter were accepted – for example, the expansions of the size of both the Security Council and ECOSOC – but only where consistency with original charter objectives could be unequivocally defended, and also where pursuit of Soviet foreign-policy goals (in these cases alignment of G77 with Soviet positions, portrayed as Soviet defence of the interests of small states in the UN) suggested the wisdom of expediency.

In addition to protecting the Soviet stake in the 1945 contract, this broadly conservative position served other useful purposes. Support for the UN was an indispensable, if double-edged, instrument for cultivating relations with developing countries. It formed an integral part of the peace rhetoric of Soviet institutions targeted at domestic and selected foreign audiences. Given the nonconvertiblity of the rouble, moreover, even financial support of the UN could be dispensed relatively cheaply, since moneys disbursed for UN technical activities normally remained within the USSR to fund international conferences, workshops and other activities on Soviet soil. Further, even small changes in the UN, however powerless that body might be thought in practice, could, when analysed in a wider context, translate into significant and threatening shifts in the international correlation of forces. In the late 1980s Gorbachev took the same logic, but reversed it. UN reform, now seen in a positive light, could have a multiplier effect and help bring about both global restructuring and domestic Soviet renovation.

Like any multilateral forum, then, the UN and the specialised agencies were for the Soviet Union arenas within which the larger struggles of mankind were played out. Such organisations presented opportunities to gain ground, as well as threats to favourable balances of forces achieved outside. Many Soviet statements in the Security Council and General Assembly from the 1960s to the 1980s have to be seen in the context of rivalry with China, or of attempts to dislodge the US from its self-defined role as defender of UN principles and protector of the interests of weaker states. Thus the Soviets never failed to highlight signs of weakening US support for the UN, as in the Kassebaum amendment for restricting its budgetary contributions.[26]

Appreciation of US power in the UN led to Khrushchev's much-publicised denunciation of the organisation as simply an instrument of the State Department. In the UN, the ILO and other organisations, Cold War struggles were often reduced to contests over the filling of secretariat positions. Outside the UN itself – where it had, among others, a guaranteed under secretary-general position – the Soviet Union followed a determined path of securing, and seeking to expand its allocation in, agreed formulae for the geographical sharing of such posts. The context of struggle in international politics also served to legitimise for Moscow the raising of 'political' issues, such as tensions in southern Africa or the Middle East, in technical bodies usually regarded by Western states as constitutionally barred from discussing these questions.

The Soviet Union's use of its personnel in UN bodies, both in missions and secretariats, occasionally became a matter of contention. Until the changes instituted under Gorbachev in the late 1980s, all such individuals, regardless of whether their formal duties were national or supranational, were officially viewed as Soviet citizens in the service of the USSR.[27]

Indeed there is a long list of Western, especially US, complaints of Soviet officials on both sides of this formal line overstepping the limits of accepted diplomatic behaviour. For some critics the Soviet presence in a variety of international organisations was no more than an extended arm of its intelligence agencies. The World Health Organization, for example, was described in the 1980s as 'the nerve centre of Soviet espionage in Europe'.[28] Links were argued to have been fostered by Soviet state-security officials with some NGOs aiming to secure accreditation and consultative status with UNESCO.[29] By the mid-1980s US officials, and senators, had concluded that the size of the Soviet mission to the UN in New York was unacceptably large. In the resulting negotiations on numbers, the Soviet side returned to its standing complaint of the 1970s (in the context then of Jewish human-rights' groups demonstrations) that the US, through interference and neglect, was failing to fulfil its obligations in international law as host state of the UN.[30]

The Cold War also extended into Soviet–American (and in the case of Bangladesh in the early 1970s, and Vietnam and Cambodia later, Soviet–Chinese) disputes over candidates for UN membership. Until 1955, when a package deal of entries by new states was negotiated with Washington, the Soviet Union tended to favour a more restrictive interpretation of the charter's 'peaceloving' criterion for membership.

Yet the Soviet Union was not blind to failings in the UN itself. Especially from the 1970s, delegations to the UN and to specialised agencies warned of the dangers of inflated secretariats, undisciplined spending habits and the proliferation of bureaucratic units. As in the acceptance of constitutional change in the size of the Security Council and ECOSOC, the Soviets were also capable of adapting to changing circumstances.

This flexibility was less evident, however, in response to practices and policy areas consistently viewed as lying at the core of the UN. Noting that many problems were to be discussed at the thirtieth session of the UN General Assembly in 1975, for example, *Pravda* maintained that 'the heart of the agenda is composed of problems of disarmament and the strengthening of peace and security'.[31] On this, the Soviet Union remained true to its 1945 vision of the role of the UN. A constant stream of grand initiatives characterised the Soviet style in this area. In the mid-1970s, for example, the Soviet Union called for a reduction of the military budgets of the permanent Security Council members by 10 per cent, and for part of the saved funds (said to be equivalent to $2 billion) to be used to provide assistance to developing countries. During the visit to Moscow in 1982 of Secretary General Perez de Cuellar, the Soviet Union urged support for a special high-level Security Council session to consider ways to strengthen the UN's collective security system.[32]

There were also some shifts in the Soviet view of the main UN organs. While the old predilection for the Security Council remained,[33] there was growing recognition of the value of the General Assembly. Indeed at times in the 1970s and early 1980s the 'wide range of the problems being discussed' by UN bodies – including environmental and economic development questions as well as disarmament – was cited as a positive virtue.[34] In the final analysis, however, the General Assembly was secondary. To the degree that smaller countries represented in it needed protection from imperialist powers, they were better advised to rely on the Soviet Union's watchful eye and veto power in the Security Council. As this was explained by *Pravda* in 1972: 'The cornerstone of the UN Charter is the principle of unanimity among the permanent members of the Security Council.... Without this principle both the creation and the viability of the UN would be unthinkable, given the existence in today's world of states with different social systems. [It] has repeatedly helped to avoid hasty decisions that could have had serious consequences for the cause of peace [and] has particular meaning for the young developing states, small countries and peoples fighting for independence'.[35]

POWERS AND *PREYEMNIKS*: CONTINUITY AMID COLLAPSE

Was the Soviet position on the utility of the UN genuine? Did it lead to practical actions, including a readiness to negotiate and compromise, directed towards the achievement of stated objectives? To both questions, Western states at the time tended to answer with a resounding negative. So did the Russian Federation from 1992. It also painted the short-lived Gorbachev experiment with UN reform with the same brush of condemnation. We will examine in succeeding chapters the changes and continuities that characterised various phases of Soviet, and later of Russian, UN system diplomacy in a number of different policy areas. In this section the focus is on the crucial period from 1985–93 that saw both the Gorbachev changes and the transition from the Soviet Union to Russia and the other successor-states.

Early references to the UN after March 1985, when Gorbachev emerged as head of the Politburo, tended to echo the standard pronouncements of the Brezhnev and post-Brezhnev era. More particularly, the UN was viewed in the mid-1980s primarily as an instrument that might have a bearing on the Soviet Union's strategic nuclear relationship with the US, especially in the context of the Reagan administration's Strategic Defense Initiative (SDI). Soviet delegations placed a high priority on securing agenda items on disarmament and seizing opportunities to denounce the spread of the arms race to outer space, both in the UN itself and in other agencies. General assessments of trends in world politics tended, as before, to pay lip service to the value of international organisations in the UN system, to condemn US and Chinese manipulations of these organs, to treat them as peripheral to the main forces driving international politics and the world economy, and to portray them as microcosms of, and factors within, the world correlation of forces.

The package of foreign-policy ideas produced by the twenty-seventh Congress of the CPSU in early 1986 established the conceptual and ideological groundwork for change, but did not in itself highlight the significance later placed on the UN. Indeed the 'new thinking' fitted comfortably within many of the intellectual and policy constraints of earlier paradigms. Questions about the imminence of the collapse of capitalism and the inevitability or otherwise of war remained central, as did attempts to elaborate the theory of peaceful coexistence. A more decisive break with the past, and one with significant implications for Soviet orientations to international institutions, came with emphasis on the common interests of states. This had formerly been suspect as a product of bourgeois globalist thinking. The idea that the Soviet Union could itself reap tangible rewards from cooperating with Western states on common world problems such as the oceans or the environment was no longer, as it had tended to be under Brezhnev and his immediate successors, castigated as a trap to inveigle it into milieux in which capitalist states could manipulate and marginalise it. This kind of argument posed many theoretical problems, and had to be reconciled with basic principles of class analysis applied to the international level. This process of theoretical adaptation will be examined later in the chapter.

The altered argument drew heavily on analyses of the risks inherent in nuclear confrontation between the two superpowers that were already a feature of Soviet strategic and foreign-policy thinking before Gorbachev. In elaborating on the ideas of *common security*, however, the Soviet Union significantly expanded concepts of security in two directions: firstly, through emphasis on the interdependence between the security concerns of individual states, and secondly through the exploration of a variety of non-military areas – primarily economic and environmental – that were increasingly held to be vital components of a dramatically broadened view of the late twentieth-century security predicaments of states. It was out of this radical change of outlook, as well as the more immediate pragmatic goals of deepening integration of the USSR in the world economy, that there grew the revitalised drive to enhance the utility of 'intersystem' international organisations that marked Soviet approaches to the UN and the specialised agencies from mid-1987.

Change had by then already been signalled by Soviet revisionism on the UN's peacekeeping role. Moscow agreed to contribute to the funding of the UN force in Lebanon. A declaration of intent to clear accumulated Soviet UN debts followed in 1987. The decisive event of that year, however, was more in the realm of declaratory policy. In an article published in September on the theme 'Reality and Guarantees of a Secure World', Gorbachev linked evolving Soviet ideas of common security with a call for the strengthening of international institutions across a wide span of policy areas, including the International Court of Justice as well as more traditional foci of Soviet interest such as the Security Council.

The article drew on previous Soviet thinking; indeed it was described officially as a logical extension of the January 1986 plan, approved at the twenty-seventh Congress, for the elimination of nuclear weapons and other weapons of mass destruction.[36] Its breadth of scope, however, clearly put it in a quite different category. As such it was widely circulated and commented on at the forty-second session of the UN General Assembly then beginning in New York. Gorbachev expanded on the same line of thinking in his own address to the subsequent session in December 1988. Soviet appreciation of the potential role of the UN had by then been underscored by the secretariat's role in fostering the 1988 Geneva agreements on the termination of hostilities in Afghanistan. The General Assembly resolution of November 1989 on the strengthening of international peace and security, jointly sponsored by the US and the Soviet Union, was viewed by Moscow as a high point of this period of intense diplomatic activity in the UN.[37]

Soviet proposals for renovating UN structures came fast and furious in the late 1980s. Peacekeeping by UN forces was accepted as a valuable role of the organisation. Defunct bodies such as the Military Staff Committee were reexamined with a fresh eye. The Soviet Union proclaimed its commitment to a moderate, nonconfrontational and deideologised stance in the ILO. It began to pursue actively the goal of membership of the World Bank and the IMF. These and other developments will be discussed in Chapters 3–5.

This revisiting of older Soviet concerns was increasingly joined in 1988–9 by attention to *global ecological issues*. As the threat of ecological catastrophe began to share centre stage in Soviet pronouncements with speculations about nuclear war, so too the capabilities of the UN system came still more sharply into focus. Foreign Minister Shevardnadze made plain the Soviet view of connections between environmental and security agendas at the 1989 General Assembly session. 'Political ecology requires urgent planetary decisions at the highest political level and an internationalisation of national efforts through the UN.... [It] requires the involvement of the Security Council in solving problems and activating such tools as transparency and monitoring'.[38] He developed the theme in a variety of speeches and articles.[39]

This mounting emphasis on world environmental matters served several purposes. As an incontestably 'common' area, the international ecological focus fitted perfectly into the increasingly dominant Soviet notions of common security and the interdependence of states. It was thus a useful weapon in UN battles against the US arms build-up. As a 'new' area, the ecological issue reinforced the growing corpus of the new thinking. It also served the theoretical objectives of Gorbachev, as a still young and vigorous party leader, of the redefinition and conceptual enrichment of Marxist–Leninist thought on international relations. With the Chernobyl disaster in the background, too, the globalising of Soviet environmentalism highlighted Moscow's somewhat belatedly found eagerness to deepen international cooperation in these areas. The strategy was also aimed at deflecting outwards the relentless pressures from environmental groups in Ukraine and other Union republics in the late 1980s, which were increasingly engaged with the issue of the Soviet Union's own looming ecological catastrophe.

The apparent Soviet change of heart on the UN prompted a mixture of consternation, skepticism and puzzlement among Western governments. Heroic initiatives, after all, were to be expected of new Soviet leaders. Dramatic calls for new means of injecting life into the UN charter, and into the UN's dormant disarmament efforts, were standard features of Soviet UN agendas. Many specific proposals seemed, moreover, to lack realism to Western observers. The frequently astonishing contrast between Gorbachev's and earlier Soviet positions on many issues sometimes gave the impression of a desperate but essentially directionless search for change. The newfound Soviet enthusiasm for the UN also failed to touch a receptive nerve among Western governments accustomed to viewing the UN with indifference or annoyance, especially in view of the dominance of neoconservative thinking in the US and Britain.

Evidence of a lack of Western responsiveness was not lost on Moscow. Deputy Foreign Minister Petrovsky commented favourably on the intensification of UN disarmament activity in 1987, for example, but pointed to a 'dearth of interest in international efforts' on the part of the US.[40] The reaction was to blame the West and to warn of the consequences for Moscow – domestic as well as international – should other countries ignore the momentous changes taking place in the USSR. Moscow also reacted to Western hesitation by stepping up the pace of its calls for a revitalisation of the UN system. The Soviet Union continued as before to be active in the

World Federation of UN Associations, for example, and hosted the 1989 session in Moscow. It also effected practical measures of its own. The old treatment of its nationals in the UN Secretariat ceased. Soviet citizens were permitted to sign long-term contracts to become officials of international organisations. More significantly, towards the end of 1990 the Foreign Ministry announced that these individuals would no longer be forced to hand over a large part of their salaries (in some cases up to two thirds) to Soviet missions. The practice, it was argued, had accented the 'insincerity' of Soviet reform efforts in the UN.[41]

This pattern was temporarily fractured by the tumultuous events of 1991. Yet despite the upshot of the failed coup attempt of August, the ban on the Communist Party, and then the disintegration of the country itself, a studied continuity marked Moscow's links with UN bodies. The US and other Western governments were already implementing in effect a dual diplomatic strategy of dealing with the emerging reality of Russia at the same time as maintaining formal relations with the USSR. Inside the Soviet Union an uneasy parallelism governed relations between the 'two Moscows' during the late summer and early autumn. It was far from clear what would be the foreign-policy role of the government of the successor state (then seen as the Union of Sovereign States), and what would be its position in the UN if individual republics sought to take up the option of membership. Soviet statements and commentary continued nonetheless to emphasise the importance of the UN, the significance of its 'renaissance' and the need, in view of the Gulf crisis, to build new structures of international security.[42]

In the event Russia secured unequivocal recognition as the Soviet Union's successor, and as the state, therefore, which would take over its seats in international organisations. Huge problems persisted in relations among the former Soviet republics, not least in the areas of nuclear weapons and external debts. Relations with other CIS states, and the still highly uncertain legal framework within which these were to develop, were from early 1992 defined as a first priority of Russian Federation foreign policy. However no room was left for doubt on the crucial diplomatic question of succession and UN representation. The other states could join Ukraine and Belarus and take up their own UN memberships, but Moscow made it clear that it was the Russian Federation which inherited the trappings of the former Soviet state in international law. Nor was there any objection to these assumptions in the West or in UN bodies.

The January 1992 CIS summit, moreover, gave a powerful signal of the determination of each former republic to cling strenuously to its newfound independence. To defuse possible unease on the part of the other ex-Union republics on this question (which in fact did not materialise) the Russian government made intriguing use of a distinction between the concepts of successor (*preyemnik*) and 'continuer' (*prodolzhatel*) states. All the former republics were successor states, said Foreign Minister Kozyrev in a January 1992 interview. Russia, however, was the continuer state. This 'means that the thread of communication with the outside world has passed to Russia'.[43] In late December 1991 the Russian flag was raised at the permanent mission in New York; President Yeltsin formally proclaimed the changes in a letter to the UN secretary general; and the Russian Federation took part in its first Security Council session. The same month also saw the culmination of steps in the UN General Assembly, with Soviet support, to abrogate the 1975 resolution equating Zionism with racism.

The role of continuer, however, contained an obvious dilemma. It could not be held to imply full continuity with the recent past. Thus the main Russian theme in commentary on the UN during 1992–3 was twofold. On the one hand Russian diplomacy at the UN was defined as having fundamentally the same task as that of the old Soviet Union: 'To ensure the external conditions for reform and entry into the world community'.[44] On the other hand a sharp contrast was drawn between the new and serious attitude of Russia towards the UN and the old, half-hearted and fundamentally duplicitous approach adopted by Gorbachev. The new Russian diplomat, at the UN and elsewhere, was said to be a world apart from his predecessor: as Kozyrev described the image of the latter, a 'morose and impenetrable bureaucrat, blinkered by rigid ideological guidelines and ready to serve the nomenklatura elite'.[45] At the start of the 1992 UN General Assembly session, he argued that the Soviet Union had been 'essentially in confrontation with the UN, since totalitarianism is incompatible with UN ideals'. There had been movement towards these ideals, 'but with reservations, halfway measures and loyalty to the socialist option'. The Russian policy, in contrast, was 'to go over to the other side. We want Russia to be on the side of the UN. We want to be directly on the side of democracy..., not develop rapprochement between two opposites'.[46]

This level of declaratory commitment to the UN has to be seen in the context of the fragmented and multipolarised internal political debates taking place in Russia in the early 1990s. Continuities in practice between Soviet and Russian Federation foreign policy – on the matter of IMF and World Bank membership, for example, and support for the UN's peacekeeping role – reflected an unbroken line of Foreign Ministry thinking between the late Soviet and the Russian Federation periods. The ministry in Smolensk Square, however, was itself the target of domestic attack from a variety of quarters in the early 1990s. It was criticised for meekly deferring to orthodox Western and IMF neoliberal policy preferences. Conservatives blamed it for purging, and others for failing to eliminate more thoroughly, personnel from the old regime.

The breakup of the Soviet Union thus opened up several fractures in the apparently smooth surface of pro-UN continuity. Even under Gorbachev, what appeared to be the ceaseless harping on the topic of the UN had provoked mixed reactions in the Soviet Union. One was puzzlement: the UN had long been thought 'so boring'.[47] Another was mounting indignation. Ossified sloganising about world institutions seemed to some critics to bear little relation to the real economic needs of the Soviet Union.[48] Environmentalists increasingly saw Gorbachev's UN adventurism as a digression from the country's own huge problems. A variety of critiques of the betrayal of socialism were launched by party loyalists. Underlying these debates, Soviet and Russian Federation attitudes towards the UN were intimately bound up with theorising about the nature of international organisations and of international politics. These analyses are the focus of the final section of this chapter.

METAPERSPECTIVES: THEORETICAL TURBULENCE

The UN was never a prominent feature of traditional Soviet views of international politics. Among academic studies of the 1970s and 1980s, for example, Lynch notes the 'relative paucity of Soviet theoretical and analytical work on international organisation', a gap which he attributes to the Soviet view of such institutions as 'a peripheral adjunct of the broader currents of world politics'.[49]

Attention to IGOs is more evident if we broaden the span of sources tapped. Soviet views of international institutions were often implicit in more general theoretical perspectives, such as treatments of the concept of peaceful coexistence, or of the hypothesis of the avoidability of wars. Further, Soviet observers oscillated in their response to international institutions between disinterest and periodic bouts of optimistic rediscovery. While US dominance of many UN bodies chilled the outlook from Moscow, other trends – particularly the entry of new states from the 1950s – prompted more favourable appraisals of the relevance of the UN to Soviet foreign-policy interests. The UN was also an unavoidable component of Soviet propaganda, domestic and external, and of the theoretical elaborations on which this was based. The rhetoric of peace and internationalism habitually associated with the world role of the first socialist state was incomplete without at least some kind of nod of tolerance in the direction of the UN charter.

Before examining the transition from Soviet to postsocialist Russia, it is useful to identify the general theoretical themes which had major implications for Moscow's view of IGOs from the 1940s to the 1980s. All were crucial aspects of the bipolar logic of the period. Four are of special significance: the theory of peaceful coexistence, the analysis of the nature of war and of its inevitability, the methodology of the correlation of forces, and the structural hypothesis of the division of the world into two camps.

An old topic in Soviet thinking about international relations, Lenin's writings on *peaceful coexistence* were given fresh prominence as a result of Khrushchev's famous speech to the twentieth CPSU Congress in 1956. Later formulations went on to emphasise the requirement of cooperation among nations in political, cultural and economic fields in a nuclear age. The underlying objectives were tied to the motivating vision of a peaceful socialist world, the goal of restraining the inherently aggressive drives of imperialism, and the desire to promote revolutionary change, and fundamental restructuring, in international affairs.

As Light has observed, however, the 'inescapable contradictions' integral to the overall theory were such that Soviet theorists were unable to achieve a satisfactory synthesis.[50] For example, the theory of peaceful coexistence failed to establish a clear and convincing reason why Western governments – presumed to be acting in the interests of their respective bourgeoisies – should engage in the kind of cooperation with the socialist states, through the UN and in other ways, that would in effect serve to accelerate their own demise. This theoretical framework continued nonetheless to lend legitimacy to the Soviet foreign-policy domain. The main currents persisted under Gorbachev. While resonating with his stress on the economic, security and ecological interdependence of states, however, the internal theoretical conflicts of the theory were also brought into still sharper relief. The characteristic Soviet arguments of the late 1980s about the deideologising of international relations, and the common interests of humanity in averting nuclear and ecological catastrophe, directly challenged crucial aspects of the class analysis on which traditional formulations of the theory of peaceful coexistence had been founded.

Secondly, IGOs were also viewed in the context of *theories of war*. This was especially the case with the UN itself. Perceived primarily as a security organisation, it was evaluated according to such criteria as its contribution to disarmament goals. Judgments about the UN generally were closely interwoven with contending arguments about whether war – whether between the capitalist and socialist worlds, or between combatants in local or regional conflicts – was avoidable or inevitable.

The latter answer was already being seriously eroded, especially on the part of the Soviet Foreign Ministry, in the Brezhnev period.[51] Conclusions suggesting the avoidability of particular wars could be indicative not of reappraisals of theory, however, but instead could be drawn empirically from conventional analyses of the correlation of forces in play in any given situation. If Soviet military strength, political and ideological will, and consolidation of the socialist project, were acting in effect to divert US ruling circles away from a path of war and on to the road of serious negotiation about arms control or the settlement of regional conflicts, then a pragmatic process of war prevention by the USSR required little or no adjustment of theory. But any venture into these areas raised ideological sensitivities. Gromyko, for example, had talked about the avoidability of local wars in 1962. Caution, however, grounded in awareness of Chinese ideological criticisms and other factors, checked the elevation of this contention into an ideological truth.[52] Gorbachev's emphasis on the politics of survival in an advanced nuclear age took the fundamental proposition several decisive stages further.

Thirdly, IGOs were an element in the increasingly complex Soviet analyses of the changing *world correlation of forces* in the 1970s and 1980s. The basic methodology aimed to weigh correctly all factors having a bearing on the central question of the relative fortunes of socialism and capitalism. The different historical phases of the prolonged and tortured crisis of capitalism – marked by such developments as the successive blows of the October Revolution, the Second World War, the collapse of the colonial system, contradictions among leading capitalist states, and deteriorating relations with developing countries – were major components of such assessments.[53]

Desperate Western attempts to recover lost ground by launching the Cold War – and then maintaining this through trade restrictions against socialist states, manipulation of the Third World and a costly arms race – were, of course, doomed to failure; but, as Lenin had warned, capitalism in such circumstances posed special dangers that required constant and alert monitoring. Hence the endlessly rehearsed case for the Soviet veto in the Security Council as a crucial mechanism for protecting the sovereignty and independence of small countries. To the extent that institutions in the UN system affected positively assessments of the world balance of forces – by helping in the perfecting of socialist society, for example, or strengthening progressive elements in developing countries – these could be viewed positively. On this criterion, the 1970s were a marked improvement over the 1950s.

Finally, the division of the world political economy into *two camps* had a dominating influence over Soviet thinking until well into the Gorbachev period. Articulated by both Lenin and Stalin in the early 1920s, the image of the two opposed worlds of capitalism and socialism permeated the 1924 constitution. The former was identified with 'national hatred and inequality, colonial slavery and chauvinism, national oppression and pogroms, imperialist bestiality and wars', and the latter with 'mutual trust and peace, national freedom and equality, peaceful coexistence and cooperation of nations'.[54] The two camps were not totally separate. Soviet strength gave progressive forces inside capitalist countries inspiration and a political ally. The concept of proletarian internationalism furnished analysts with a powerful auxiliary model of international relations, and a guide for political action in relation to emerging trends in the international system. While the basic image shone with renewed promise in the Cold War tensions of the late 1940s, later developments could not so easily be pounded into a shape that would allow them to be squeezed into these simple conceptual categories.

First, Soviet relations with many developing countries from the 1950s came to be marked in practice by a cautious mutual antipathy, even though there was a growing alignment between Soviet and G77 voting patterns in the UN General Assembly. The idea that these constituted a third zone of peace, a categorisation pressed by Khrushchev in 1956, was in many ways an unsatisfactory compromise, though it helped to provide a convenient rationale for Moscow's cultivation of relations with regimes that were often decidedly unsocialist. State capitalism in India, for example, could on this basis be legitimately viewed as progressive.[55] Third World countries increasingly, however, made use of the UN to criticise Soviet actions, particularly the invasion of Afghanistan in 1980. Calls for a new international economic order (NIEO), moreover, though championed too by the Soviet Union, were at the same time frustrating for Moscow to the extent that they often blamed socialist as well as capitalist countries for past misfortunes and present hardships. They thus denied what was in conventional Soviet analysis the central point: that socialism was fundamentally and qualitatively different from capitalism. As Brezhnev put it in 1981, world development questions could not be reduced 'simply to distinctions between "rich North" and "poor South"'.[56]

Secondly, relations among Western states themselves became increasingly complex. On the one hand exposing tensions between the US and Europe, or the US and Japan, was politically useful. It was also an analytical strategy that reflected, and underscored Soviet perceptions of the continuing utility of, the Marxist methodology of discerning layers and types of contradictions in any set of political relationships. On the other hand, in a nuclear and bipolar world, relations with the US had paramount strategic importance for the Soviet Union. Multipolarity, and US efforts to foster trilateralism, were for this and other reasons highly suspect. They threatened to marginalise the Soviet Union, reduce its voice in world affairs and annul the requirement of its participation in decision-making in the UN and in other forums.[57]

These various conceptual lenses go a long way towards helping us situate Soviet, and to some extent later Russian, perspectives on international institutions. Taken together they suggest that traditional attitudes towards the UN and the UN system were characterised by indifference, occasionally overt hostility, and at best an imperfectly resolved ambivalence.

The concept of peaceful coexistence, for example, failed to transform smoothly into an ideological framework of support for active multilateralism. Academic analyses of the 1970s and 1980s were sharply critical of Western pluralist notions of the potential of international institutions to grow into effective regimes or embryonic world governments. The costs to developing countries of submitting to the adjustments required by neoliberal IFIs likewise made these unacceptable as potential vehicles of East–West cooperation. Similarly, if war was avoidable, it did not follow, in Soviet logic, that UN peacekeeping forces were an appropriate avoidance instrument. UN institutions themselves were not as important, in other words, as the forces of class and state power represented within them. The Soviet instinct was accordingly to hunt for, and then denounce, evidence of US (or Chinese) manipulative tactics in international forums, and to commend evidence of receptivity to socialist state initiatives. Support for a UN mediatory role between the opposed sides in the Cold War was also invalidated by the persistence, if gradual weakening, of two-camp metaphors which took for granted the moral, economic and political superiority of socialism.

A more realistic picture, however, one more alive to the nuances of the political life of IGOs, sometimes emerged from more specialist Soviet analyses of the UN system. Morozov begins his 1982 analysis of international organisations by noting their two opposite tendencies: the struggle between peace, development, and protection of the sovereignty of states, on the one hand, and intervention in the internal affairs of states on the other.[58] Bodies such as the UN and the specialised agencies fit into a special category of 'intersystem [*mezhsistemnii*] international organisations', alongside international organisations of, respectively, the socialist world, developing countries and capitalist countries.[59]

In the literature of the 1970s and early 1980s, authors differed little in the significance they attached to the US presence in the UN. Echoing Khrushchev's 1962 denunciation of the UN as 'a branch of the US State Department', Baryshev traced a simple picture of domination by Washington. That this was not always evident to observers he attributed to the nature of the UN itself. The UN's mandate as an institution for promoting international peace and security compelled the US to mask its activities inside the organisation so that it could give the appearance of loyal membership while in reality pursuing its interests in all fields of UN activity.[60] Thus a lengthy record of US policies in the UN – undermining the UN charter by intervening in Korea in 1950, for example, using UN forces in the Congo in 1960 to protect the interests of Western monopoly capital, colluding with China in the Security Council in the 1970s, or using UN resolutions to justify intervention in the internal affairs of weaker countries[61] – was held to reflect dangerous manifestations of the deepening crisis of capitalism. This genre of attack intensifed in response to Washington's strategy of disengagement from the UN system in the early 1980s.

It followed from this trend of interpretation, as well as from more general theoretical assumptions, that Western analyses of the nature of the UN were defective. Bourgeois approaches based on an idealist hankering for stronger world institutions were either hostile instruments of US interests, or were fundamentally misguided because of their misunderstanding of the nature and importance of sovereignty. There was no prospect of the 'final liquidation of state sovereignty', Morozov argued, or even of the supposedly intermediate steps of 'supranationality' discussed in Western policy and academic circles.[62]

A similar fate befell Western analyses of global problems in the 1970s and early 1980s. It did not follow from assumptions made in the West about a global ecological crisis, Markushina argued in 1976, that states had to reduce their sovereignty. Just the reverse: without the attribute of sovereignty, states could not be expected to cooperate effectively with each other on the basis of equality.[63] The danger, another scholar wrote in 1988, was that many bourgeois authors used their identification of and emphasis on ecological and other global problems as a means of 'drawing in' socialist countries to such systems of international cooperation. These were therefore frameworks in which socialist states risked putting their interests under the control of the policies of the leading imperialist powers.[64] In the late 1980s, however, this view was being successfully challenged by *globalistiki* in the Soviet Union in the new synthesis taking shape under Gorbachev.

Yet even from the early years of the UN an alternative view was possible. The UN could not be wholly bad since it contained the socialist states. The act of participating, that is, required theoretically grounded rationales. These were logically obliged to draw for evidence on the good points of the UN. Such positive assessments were not difficult to craft. According to Soviet analysts, the long history of international organisations, dating from the international public unions of the nineteenth century, had already been influenced by positive developments such as the 1917 revolution and the influx of new states following decolonisation.[65] The latter change was not a matter of arithmetical additions, one author wrote in 1981, but represented an historic and qualitative change in the international forces represented in the UN.[66] This was despite the fact that some G77 elements displayed 'unrealism and extremism' in their failure to acknowledge both the differences between socialist and capitalist states, and the responsibility of the latter for economic conditions in developing countries.[67] Favourable commentary on the UN system was also evident in the 1970s and 1980s in Soviet evaluations of the work of UN technical agencies, particularly when this activity was viewed in the context of international scientific cooperation.

Ideological stress in the late 1980s on the imperatives of multilateral cooperation, and on the common interests of states, cast a different light on the UN. If, as the twenty-seventh Congress insisted in 1986, war was 'not a fatal inevitablity,' then active measures in a variety of international policy areas became justified to avert catastrophe. Signs of changes in Soviet thinking had been evident earlier. Western analyses of global problems, such as those of the Club of Rome, had in the previous decade been criticised for 'neo-Malthusianism'[68] and for their failure to understand the realities of sovereignty and class. Changing UN agendas, however, were among the factors producing shifts in Soviet outlooks. One writer noted that questions such as protection of the environment and the international use of natural resources were not significant in the UN before the second half of the 1970s.[69]

Appreciation of the importance of the negotiations in the Third UN Conference on the Law of the Sea was a decisive factor. Brezhnev gave cautious recognition to the significance of the new global problems agenda, particularly resources, energy, the environment, space and the use of the oceans.[70] In part this change also reflected the characteristic Soviet faith in the power of technology and science. However, much intellectual effort – compounded by political struggle – still had to be invested in the 1980s in attempts to effect theoretical reconciliation between these and traditional class analyses of international relations.

This process was still under way after 1985. There was mounting Soviet interest in Western concepts such as ecodevelopment (*ekorazvitiia*), and exploration of the use of social–ecological analytical frameworks grounded in ideas from the environmental sciences.[71] Indeed the growing dominance of environmental questions on theoretical as well as foreign policy agendas in the late 1980s was a powerful engine of change in late Soviet political thinking on world developments. Drawing on the cautious exploration of global problems of the early 1980s, this flourished under the new leadership's expanded conceptualisation of the international security problematique. Thus world environmental problems were held to indicate the 'objective necessity' of international cooperation.[72]

Such calls went a considerable way beyond the older focus on cooperation within CMEA frameworks, though the appeal of that model retained much of its former momentum in Soviet statements and initiatives in the UN system. Advocacy of enhanced international cooperation beyond the reach of the CMEA model, however, clashed with – and, given the domestic political climate of the late 1980s, began to weaken significantly – the theoretical structures underpinning the more constricted outlooks of even the recent past. It required explicit denial of the two-camp thesis. This was feasible within the theoretical constraints of historical materialism, for example by arguing, as Shevardnadze did in 1988, that the struggle between capitalism and socialism was not the 'dominant tendency of the current epoch'.[73] However this kind of reasoning, which implied in the view of conservative critics acceptance of the reality and long-term viability of capitalism, set up reverberating tensions of a kind that could not easily be contained by the tenets and practices of democratic centralism.

By the time of the collapse of the Soviet Union, then, much of the intellectual ground of theorising on international cooperation and the role of international institutions had already been reworked. Influenced by and converging with Western, particularly US, concepts, academic analyses routinely assumed states to be the primary actors of international politics and acknowledged the constraints imposed on states by the international system.[74] In policy debates on the UN system, the requirement of effective international cooperation on global problems through multilateral institutions was generally recognised. Traditional approaches, revitalised by association during the 1980s with neo-Marxist and other Western international political economy frameworks, also survived in the new theoretical pluralism of the early 1990s. A similar diversity marked the approaches of political actors to debates on the general foreign-policy course of the new Russia, as conservatives vied with pragmatists, Western-leaning intellectuals and officials, nationalists and others for control of an uncertain future.[75] The next three chapters examine changing Soviet and Russian Federation approaches to the work of UN bodies in the fields of economic policy, technical cooperation and international security.

3 Bretton Woods and After: Flirtations with Capitalism

PROWLING THE BASTION: FROM PRACTICE TO THEORY

International financial institutions impose costs on members and disburse benefits to them. The task of disentangling and weighing the factors in these equations, however, presents states with complex challenges – political and diplomatic as well as economic, domestic as well as external. The Soviet Union at first displayed serious interest in becoming a full participant in the Bretton Woods system. This option collapsed with the rise of Cold War tensions in the late 1940s. The probable shape of future military and economic blocs became discernible as Moscow refused to take part in the Marshall Plan, though whether a positive response would have given Washington second thoughts remains a moot point. The economic organisation of Eastern Europe became consolidated in the 1950s through bilateral arrangements, CMEA structures and a regional division of labour dominated by Soviet interests. Commercial and financial relations with Western countries were restricted partly by choice on the part of Moscow's economic planners, partly as a result of a lack of exploitable comparative advantages, and partly because of the Western countries' own imposition of strategic trade controls and other East–West trade regulations.

When this pattern began to set in the 1940s, the Soviet Union in practice had little interest, ideological or otherwise, in the world beyond Europe and the US. But as its attention to the Third World grew from the mid-1950s, a significant dimension was added to the Soviet outlook on the UN and on the specialised agencies. These proved to be increasingly useful arenas for competing with the US from an advantageous position. The entry of new member-states served to tilt the agendas of UN bodies, especially the General Assembly and ECOSOC, and of many of the specialised agencies, towards a focus on issues of international development. In the 1970s the Soviet Union became a strong advocate in the UN of a NIEO that would end the alleged discrimination of the existing order against socialist states, and at the same time promote the economic development of the Third World. Combined with its earlier critiques of the IBRD and IMF and of their manipulation by powerful Western states for their own ends, this rallying cry for international restructuring was embodied in theoretical analyses of the world economy that helped to shape, and provided a rationale for, Soviet policies in the UN system. Accompanying these pronouncements were confident, and increasingly indignant, denials of the ability of North–South imagery – especially when deployed by developing countries – to capture the reality of the deepening crisis of capitalism.

Soviet interest in IFIs revived in the following decade. A variety of secular trends beginning to be evident in the early 1980s, especially a marked slowdown in East–West trade and faltering domestic economic growth, drove the policy process. Membership of the World Bank and the IMF was eventually achieved by Russia and the other successor states after the collapse of the USSR. Yet economic conditions in Russia, and the issue of the appropriate Western responses, remained high on the agendas of G7 exchanges from the 1990 Houston summit to that in Tokyo in 1993. The pro-Western orientation of the Russian Federation, including the impact of its relationships with IFIs and the G7, likewise became issues on the agendas of its various domestic critics. Russia and the other ex-Soviet republics were, according to one commentator, on the way to becoming 'banana republics without the bananas'.[1]

This chapter examines the developments of the 1980s and early 1990s in the light of the experiences of two earlier periods: first, the short-lived and ill-fated investigation of the Bretton Woods option in the 1940s, and, secondly, the rise and fall in subsequent decades of the Soviet ideological critique of these institutions.

HESITANT ARCHITECT: 1942–6

Initial Soviet reactions in the early 1940s to the concepts that eventually took shape as the Bretton Woods system were ambivalent. Moscow appeared to support the creation of postwar international economic and financial institutions, particularly since these offered the prospect of significant flows of reconstruction assistance. Yet the plans for such organisations were also potentially threatening to crucial aspects of the Soviet central planning system. For example, the price-setting mechanism this entailed could not on the face of it be reconciled with the constraints of working within a tightly functioning set of international arrangements on exchange rates. This indecisiveness did not long survive the end of hostilities. As Cold War politics began to dominate relations among the wartime partners, so Moscow's earlier cooperative posture – and a measure of sympathetic support for Soviet membership of the institutions on the part of the main Western players – rapidly eroded.

Thus even if Moscow had proceeded in 1945–6 to full formal participation in the World Bank and the IMF, it is difficult to conceive of it having had the political will, or being allowed, to remain within these during the rapidly deteriorating political circumstances of the late 1940s and the consolidation of the Western and communist military and economic groupings in the 1950s. A brief exploration of these early Soviet–Western encounters nonetheless provides some intriguing insights into a period more characterised by serious East–West talks on international economic and financial questions than was the case at any time before the late 1980s. These constructive negotiations were a product of the momentum of wartime collaboration between the Allies. They were sustained, if only temporarily, by expectations about the postwar economic world on the part of both the USSR and the leading Western players.

The Soviet Union held to a foreign policy of economic cooperation with its Western allies so long as this did not substantially restrain its broad strategic goals in Eastern Europe. There seems also to have been some expectation on the part of Moscow that a serious approach to negotiations on postwar economic and financial issues could materially affect the shape and tasks of the future institutions to the benefit of the Soviet Union. The discussions of postwar reconstruction aid that were an integral feature of this multilateral planning process took place at a time of acute Soviet awareness of the extensive and long-term requirements of its chronically weakened economy. The possibility of future loans and other forms of reconstruction assistance, as well as reparations payments, thus gave Moscow a powerful incentive to take part actively in the building of the Bretton Woods system. At the Bretton Woods conference itself, the USSR was represented by a substantial delegation of six officials, three advisors and more than a dozen aides, under M. S. Stepanov, deputy people's commissar of foreign trade.

The Soviet outlook on the talks to some extent reflected pre-1939 habits. Russia had participated in the 1927 world economic conference, for example, even though it was not at that time a member of the League of Nations. It supported many of the sections of the final report of that conference, and chose to abstain rather than vote against others. After its entry into the League in 1934, Moscow similarly took an active role in the work of the Financial Committee and other economic bodies.[2] The exchanges of the early 1940s in a sense represented a wartime resumption of such practices. As in the 1930s, the Soviet Union did not in general leap to ideological objections as a means of sinking proposals. Plans and proposals were rather subjected to criticism on the basis of careful assessments of Soviet economic interests. For example, Soviet officials showed some evidence of being relatively more sympathetic to the White plan than to the Keynes plan, possibly because it dealt more explicitly with questions of loans for postwar reconstruction – consistently a high Soviet priority – and also because it tended to focus less than did British thinking on the construction of a working international monetary regime.[3]

The attitude of the US and Britain in the early 1940s was also marked by a belief that future Soviet membership of the proposed institutions was both desirable and, though clearly some difficult negotiations would precede this, practicable.[4] This was despite the fact that the USSR's state economy appeared to rule out the possibility of either its effective participation in institutional arrangements to regulate exchange rates or its adherence to the goal of a revitalised world economy driven in part by the gradual elimination of barriers to trade. In talks in the early 1940s the way was nonetheless paved for future institutions designed to prevent a return of the economic crises of the 1930s. For such an enterprise to be successful, it was generally assumed among the Western players, a universal membership was required. Further, however, the project also implied close interconnections between policy areas in the fields of trade and international payments, and also between domestic and international dimensions of government policies. On these points Western assumptions confronted impressive obstacles in the Soviet state economy. While Britain was probably more prepared than the US in the early 1940s to consider a postwar international economic regime which would adapt to participation by a nonmarket economy, at the same time London tended to be more intent than Washington on constructing a tighter set of financial rules than Moscow could accept.

On neither the Soviet nor the Western side were talks undermined by the temptation to resort to ideological recriminations. Wartime cooperation may have led to exaggerated impressions on the part of London and Washington of the degree to which collaboration could persist in the absence of a common enemy. Despite differences of approach between the two, the rigours of a socialist command economy were not generally seen as automatically precluding the possibility of Soviet participation in the postwar system. It is possible that in the background of Western approaches lay the thought that membership of the IMF and the World Bank might in itself be a catalyst of change in the Soviet Union. A more likely explanation is that universality of membership was regarded as such an important feature of the institutions in principle that the future policy implications of differences between the Soviet and the market economies were minimised. Keynes confronted squarely at an early date the contingent nature of Western planning for a financial institution: 'the position of

Russia, which might be a third founder, if she can be a party to so capitalist-looking an institution, would need special consideration'.[5] The desirability of framing approaches in such a way as to elicit the least unfavourable Soviet response was also a factor in Western discussions of the White plan in 1942.[6]

Soviet officials approached the negotiations of mid-1944 in a realistic mode. The requirement of protecting the socialist economic planning mechanism was not raised as an insuperable hurdle. Several issues had already emerged as central to Soviet interests. First, considerable weight was attached to the question of gold subscriptions to the IMF.[7] The Soviet Union identified itself as one of the group of states which had experienced occupation and economic devastation during the Second World War, and which were therefore entitled to concessions and exemptions. In addition, Moscow argued that Soviet gold supplies needed special protection because of the chronically weakened capacity of its economy to generate exports. It proposed, for example, that the IMF could formally be given the power to reduce the gold portion of subscriptions by as much as 25–50 per cent in certain circumstances. The Soviet view was also that stocks of newly mined gold should be excluded from the proposed rules governing member-states' obligations to use gold in obtaining their currencies from the IMF. Finally, officials objected to arrangements based on the storage of Soviet gold in the US.

A closely related matter was the non-convertible status of the rouble. It was clearly not compatible with the state economic-planning system to have the IMF treat the rouble like the currency of a Western country, or for the IMF to play a regulatory role in determining the international value of the rouble. The Soviet Union sought specific measures to safeguard its interests that would allow it in effect to alter the par value of the rouble. It also took steps to try to ensure that roubles would only be used for purchases directly from the USSR itself.[8]

Secondly, the Soviet Union was potentially one of the 'big three' members of the Bretton Woods institutions. In these, however, power was not simply to be an attribute of certain states, as in the League Council and the future UN Security Council. Under the proposed IMF rules, voting power was to be shared among members according to formulae based on their quotas, which were to be filled from national currencies supplemented by foreign-exchange reserves. The concept of weighted voting had wide political support among countries. A variant, of giving an automatic minimum of 10 per cent to the World Bank's largest contributors, was thought to depart too far from the principle, and was rejected at the Atlantic City meetings. During the course of the 1944 talks, the Soviet Union came round to the idea that enhanced voting power was worth the price of a sizeable subscription. The revised Soviet position on this question was warmly welcomed by others, particularly Treasury Secretary Morgenthau and the US delegation. The specific change envisaged would have given the USSR 13.64 per cent of the total IMF quota and 12.37 per cent of the voting power, making it the third most powerful country in the organisation after the US and Britain.[9] In addition, the Soviet Union would have had the power to appoint one of the executive directors of each institution.

Thirdly, Soviet officials continued during 1944 to pursue the goal of expanding the prospects for postwar reconstruction aid. Indeed in many ways the planned institutions were evaluated primarily according to assessments of the likelihood that the Soviet Union would be a direct and immediate beneficiary of their development assistance activities. This approach led to some distortion in the Soviet conception of the future system. Noting other states whose economies had suffered from wartime occupation, Soviet officials proposed that the criteria for World Bank lending should explicitly take into account 'the special position of these countries in establishing for them the most favourable rates of interest, terms and conditions of repayment of such loans'.[10] The proposed increase in the Soviet quota also put it closer to being able to influence such decisions on a day-to-day basis through the executive-director group.

Finally, questions of information and reporting posed particularly sensitive questions for Moscow. Delegates insisted, for example, that the Soviet Union should not be formally required to take into consideration the views of the IMF on monetary and economic policy matters when formulating its own domestic policies.[11] They also lobbied strongly for the principle that data on national economies in the possession of the IMF and the World Bank should be treated as strictly confidental, and be published only with the explicit consent of the member-state concerned. The Soviet Union drew up a specific list of headings under which data could in its view legitimately be requested by and supplied to the IMF. Data on gold production, holdings and transactions, for example, remained a matter of extreme delicacy for the Soviet Union throughout the exchanges of the 1940s. Indeed the data question alone would probably have jeopardised any hypothetical later Soviet role in the Bretton Woods system. The magnitude of loans and other forms of assistance required by the postwar Soviet economy would have imposed huge external demands for information and involved intrusive data-gathering procedures politically unacceptable to Moscow's economic planners.

Although the Soviet Union failed to get its way on a number of major points, including the plea for preferential treatment from the World Bank on the grounds of war damage, it nonetheless managed to obtain some significant modifications to the proposed workings of the Bretton Woods institutions. Had it joined, the negotiated arrangements would have made the Soviet Union a significant player in both the World Bank and the IMF in terms of subscriptions, voting power, and administration and management.

The decision in Moscow, however, was to reject – or, initially, to put on hold – the package negotiated by its officials at the US meetings. The Soviet Union signed the articles of agreement at Bretton Woods, but did not then become a member of either body. Even so some Western governments remained optimistic that the Soviet rebuff was not final. Other countries, including Australia and New Zealand, did not immediately take up membership. Partly with the USSR in mind, the deadline for states to join as formal original members was extended. Further, the Soviet announcement of its decision included the qualification that it was not deemed appropriate to join the institutions 'at this time'.[12] The Soviet Union was represented by an observer delegation of US-based officials, none sent direct from Moscow, at the new organisations' first meetings in Savannah in March 1946. It did not attend the meetings held in September in Washington. The state of East–West relations by the end of the year was such that the route to membership had in practice been closed.

The rapidly changing postwar political atmosphere also affected the international trade negotiations that led to the Geneva conference in 1947 establishing GATT. Talks on the creation of an international trade organisation (ITO) during 1945 met with a provisionally positive Soviet response. The Soviet Union supported these developments in principle in ECOSOC in early 1946. In the event, however, Moscow decided not to participate in the work of the preparatory committee in London that year, citing insufficient time to study the US proposals that were the main basis for discussion. The Soviet Union was not invited to the 1947 Geneva meetings.[13] Both sets of talks accordingly devoted less time to questions of the role of state-trading countries. The question was addressed in the GATT, but various draft provisions on these issues before the preparatory committee were dropped as a result of the Soviet absence.

The Soviet Union similarly did not participate – although it was formally invited – in the Havana Conference of 1947–8 on the proposed future trade organisation. This failed to materialise in light of growing US criticisms. Had it done so it would also, like the World Bank and the IMF, have been an important basis for Soviet participation in postwar international economic decision-making. The proposed structure of ITO, for example, included provision for an executive body with permanent seats for the USSR and the leading Western industrial economies.[14]

DEFIANT STRUGGLER: 1946–86

Soviet denunciations of the institutions of the Bretton Woods system as instruments of international monopoly capital form a second, and more familiar, context against which we can evaluate the changes that took place from the mid-1980s. Attacks on the IMF and the World Bank served a variety of political and propaganda purposes. They were important in terms of the USSR's relations with developing countries, and of the restrictions imposed on trade with socialist states by the US and its allies from the late 1940s. Thus in Soviet theoretical analyses in subsequent years a range of factors – Western protectionism, flows of capital out of developing countries, the growing problem of debt, and others – were seized on as external signs of the internal crisis of capitalism. Contradictions in this system mounted until the early 1980s, when the world was faced with 'the economic shocks resulting from the deepest crisis in the capitalist economy for fifty years'.[15]

The Bretton Woods arrangements, comprising the main intergovernmental financial instruments of Western states, occupied a place of special privilege in such monitoring. However it seems clear that in the rapidly altering economic, political and strategic circumstances of 1946–8 the Soviet Union did not fully appreciate the importance these institutions would eventually have in international economic relations. At the time, its own perspective on world affairs was almost exclusively concentrated on Europe and on its relations with the US. It took several years for emphasis to be placed also on developing countries, and for the dawning recognition of their growing significance in relation to East–West competition to be reflected in Soviet UN policies.

Continuing Soviet appraisals of the Bretton Woods system were increasingly accompanied by admonitions to the international community to create alternative structures. After discarding the 1940s outlook of disinterest in developments beyond the confines of the industrialised world, the Soviet Union began from the mid-1950s to define itself as the state whose model of economic planning gave it a unique affinity with Third World nations, and to urge the UN to pay more attention to problems of developing countries. This longer-term strategy, aimed at tilting the changing international correlation of forces by taking competition with the US into the South, could claim a series of successes in the 1960s and 1970s: for example, the convening of the first UNCTAD in 1964, the resolutions of various special sessions of the UN General Assembly on international development themes and the instruments of the NIEO.

As a result Soviet calls for a restructuring of international economic relations were able to draw for support on both Third World and UN pronouncements. Yet the Soviet record was at best one of qualified achievement. The shift in the substance and tenor of UN approaches to international affairs was far more a product of G77 than socialist-state pressures. UN resolutions and declarations often bore the characteristic marks of bargaining and diplomatic ambiguity that made them unreliable as tools of Soviet policies. Over the long haul, moreover, the Soviet Union failed to secure a stable East–South alignment of the kind that could have begun to translate Marxist–Leninist restructuring goals into economic realities.

These aspects of Soviet policies were two sides of the same coin. Advocacy of NIEO restructuring can be viewed historically against the political facts of Soviet and, for much of this period, socialist-state nonmembership of the Bretton Woods institutions. Criticisms of these, in turn, were indispensable elements in Soviet schemes for a fundamental reordering of international economic relations. In the process the Soviet Union repressed, but did not relinquish, the option of some form of future accommodation with Bretton Woods. We will look first at responses to this evolving system, and then at the Soviet pursuit of more radical alternatives.

The initial Soviet reaction to the early progress of the World Bank and the IMF was twofold: first, to call attention to the barriers Western powers were alleged to have erected to exclude the Soviet Union; secondly, to probe the possibility of exercising influence on them from outside through UN organs.

Thus in 1947 the Soviet Union criticised the basic rules and principles of the IMF, reiterating many of the issues raised in the earlier negotiations. In particular it singled out the formulae for determining voting power in the organisation, the question of a member-state's obligation to provide data, particularly in relation to gold and foreign-exchange reserves, the shipment of gold to the US and its storage there, the issue of the convertibility of the rouble, and IMF conditionalities contained in the rules governing member-state drawings on currencies.[16] This approach soon gave way to more straightforward fulminations against the IMF and the World Bank through UN bodies, especially ECOSOC. The domination of the IFIs by the US and the political representatives of international capital became the basis for a principled Soviet refusal to take any further steps towards membership.

Secondly, Soviet officials developed the case that the UN itself retained important economic and financial oversight responsibilities, particularly as a result of the institutions' agreements with the UN defining their specialised agency status. The Soviet Union was not alone in voicing these concerns. Among Western countries, Norway and New Zealand were also critical of the loose rules governing relations between the Bretton Woods organisations and the UN.[17] Soviet delegates tried to develop ECOSOC as the main institution under the UN charter with a mandate to review World Bank and IMF activities. This strategy was seriously hampered by the council's own decision as early as 1947, at the insistence of Western powers, that it was not part of its task to review in detail the substance of the two organisations' lending policies or budgets.[18] Though the Soviet Union persisted with these attempts, in practice the Bretton Woods institutions evolved as autonomous bodies operating beyond the reach of the UN.

The detailed and unrelenting theoretical critiques developed by the USSR from the late 1940s to the mid-1980s to sustain and rationalise these policies reveal significant elements in Moscow's thinking about IFIs. One important strand followed the conventional threefold route of presenting evidence of US manipulation of the policies of the institutions, identifying conflicts among Western countries on key issues and documenting the damaging consequences for developing countries.

First, since aid in general served imperialist interests, and since Bretton Woods activity in particular was 'one of the most characteristic manifestations of collective colonialism',[19] it followed that the leading Western states had a strong vested interest both in protecting the constitutional frameworks that legitimised their domination of these institutions and also in carefully shaping all decisions made by them. Working from such a precarious base, this was held to be a system that was bound to collapse. In a sense Soviet predictions – and, as in 1976, announcements[20] – of the death of the Bretton Woods system eventually proved correct, though not necessarily in the form and as a result of the causes identified in earlier analyses.

Secondly, the methodology as well as the substance of Marxist analysis serve to focus attention on evidence of policy disagreements, and divergent interests, among Western member-states. Thus splits in the IFIs were argued to be deepening in the late 1970s, partly as a result of decisions which in effect recognised the inevitability of the trend in the Western economic system towards polycentrism. Moscow maintained that Washington's reaction to the US recession of the early 1980s sharpened this tendency. The 1982 joint Bank–Fund meetings in Toronto, for example, 'demonstrated with utmost clarity the United States' desire to shift the burden of its economic problems onto the shoulders of its partners in Western Europe....'[21] Disputes between Europeans and the US in GATT meetings and in multilateral trade negotiations similarly provided a constant stream of data to support the proposition of chronic intraorganisational conflict. Thus the 'transatlantic duel' over agricultural subsidies between the US and the EC, and issues such as US opposition to European company dealings with the Soviet gas-pipeline project, became a focal point of this genre of commentary in the early 1980s. In such ways the capitalist system 'once more demonstrated its inability to restore peace and trust among its trade partners, who value their own pocket-books above their "common interests"'.[22]

Thirdly, the World Bank and the IMF were together a 'safe form'[23] for the imperialist export of capital to the Third World, both in terms of loans from the institutions and also through the links these had with private monopoly capital. However these were points on which the Soviet Union itself was vulnerable. Many developing countries in practice looked favourably, whether willingly or otherwise, on the arrangements created in the 1940s as sources of capital, technical assistance and trading opportunities. Nonetheless the Soviet Union objected to the ulterior motives it detected behind US proposals in the early 1970s to expand G77 representation in the IMF.[24] Specific changes, such as the development of the special-drawing-rights (SDR) system, or the discussions of the mid-1970s on the creation of a stabilisation fund in the IMF, were greeted with similar responses. Soviet officials pointed to them as evidence of the continued exploitation of developing countries and the perpetuation of their dependence on Western states.

In particular the resistance of Bretton Woods decision-makers, in league with the leading Western countries, to NIEO thinking was noted. At the 1976 Bank–Fund sessions in Manila, for example, developing countries' demands that 'all vestiges of colonial inequality and discrimination be removed from the sphere of international economic relations continued to receive no attention'.[25] This criticism arose particularly in the context of earlier IMF decisions to reduce reserves of gold, sales of which, argued the Soviet Union – which had its own stake in this market – would deleteriously affect the economic circumstances of developing countries. The general thesis gathered force in the 1980s as a result of the mounting debt burden of countries in the South, recession in Western economies and the introduction of more stringent conditionalities by multilateral donors and their insistence on the implementation of adjustment programmes by recipient governments.

The Soviet Union drew the same kinds of conclusions from developments in GATT. The use of GATT rules by Western states to legitimise free-trade areas, customs unions and a variety of other protectionist devices, was taken as evidence of their continued desire to preserve discriminatory practices in international trade. Such measures, it was argued in the 1970s, were 'extremely advantageous' for developed states.

The objective was the creation and maintenance of a favourable environment for exports, but they created 'new difficulties in respect to the national production and protection of the home market in economically less developed countries'.[26] The Tokyo Round similarly accentuated contradictions between the two sides of the trade policies of Western states – protectionism and liberalism – with still further costs to Third World economies.[27]

The Soviet Union made use of a variety of institutional opportunities presented by the UN system to press these attacks before larger international audiences. In ECOSOC in 1984, for example, delegates argued that the IMF and the World Bank, together with the ILO ('and even UNDP') – that is, the 'international organisations controlled by the West' – were being used 'to slow down and reverse the economic decolonisation of the liberated States and interfere in their internal affairs'.[28] A persistent theme in the critiques of the first half of the 1980s was the use of aid for political purposes. Western countries were condemned for adopting a strategy of forcing Third World countries to shelve their own economic development plans and to abandon significant parts of their public sectors. As Soviet delegates told the UN General Assembly's Second Committee in 1984, the IMF and the World Bank were 'really instruments of exploitation in the service of imperialist and neo-colonialist interests', and part of the larger design of the US to impose its will on others through economic warfare.[29]

These hallmarks of Soviet assaults on the Bretton Woods system retained their gloss throughout much of the Cold War period. From the late 1940s, criticisms increasingly ceased to point to specific deficiencies of the system that might be remedied through negotiations, and instead concentrated on exploiting evidence of these failings as part of Moscow's larger campaign for a fundamental restructuring of the world economy.

Even so some ambiguities persisted. For example the commonly cited principle, or slogan, of nondiscrimination could be interpreted in different ways. As a key principle of GATT, its use in Soviet statements could indicate a Soviet tilt towards Western neoliberalism and a spirit of cautious accommodation with IFIs. The formal Soviet commitment in 1955 in favour of multilateralism and nondiscrimination in international trade can be interpreted in this fashion.[30] On the other hand, Soviet appeals to the criterion of non-discrimination were also the base from which Western trade policies were condemned. From this perspective, the main Western targets were protectionism, the formation of trading blocs, strategic trade controls, credit restrictions and policies in general towards developing countries. The solutions, from this second perspective, were accordingly to be found not in reform of the Bretton Woods institutions, but in their eventual replacement by, or subordination within, new structures founded on NIEO philosophies.

Although the two perspectives were quite different in their assumptions and analyses, and in the policy conclusions drawn from them, Soviet approaches to UN debates often moved from one to the other in such a way that the distinctions were blurred. This ambiguity served some useful purposes, particularly in relation to changes sought by the USSR in trading relationships with Western countries. More often in UN bodies, extended critiques of the Bretton Woods system were used pragmatically as means of attempting to influence G77 delegations.

Landmarks in the evolution of this second framework included the first meetings of UNCTAD in 1964, the approval by the Sixth Special Session of the UN General Assembly in 1974 of the Declaration and Programme of Action on the Establishment of a NIEO, and the adoption by the General Assembly, also in 1974, of the Charter of Economic Rights and Duties of States. These became mainstays of Soviet pronouncements on international restructuring until the mid-1980s.

Supporting the charter in 1974, *Pravda* noted 'certain shortcomings', but saw it as the product of a changed international correlation of forces resulting from the strength of the socialist countries, the collapse of colonialism and other factors that together were creating 'a most favourable atmosphere for the establishment of a new international economic order'.[31] NIEO principles were defended in ECOSOC and other UN organs against Western criticisms said, in 1984, to be aimed at replacing them with 'such concepts as "interdependence" and "the free play of market forces" in order to legitimise the persistence of inequality and exploitation'.[32] Africa's economic and other problems could be resolved, for example, if all states implemented the charter.[33]

The diplomatic implications of this Soviet posture reverberated throughout the UN system. Two characteristic examples of the 1970s and early 1980s are the approaches adopted by Soviet delegations in UNESCO and UNCTAD.

UNESCO's importance in this context derived partly from its formal mandate in the fields of education, science and culture – all areas of profound ideological interest to Moscow – and partly from the large influx of new member-states from the early 1960s. The latter was a major factor in the transformation of the organisation into one increasingly oriented towards Third World economic development priorities. The 1960s and 1970s saw a series of Soviet initiatives directed towards sharpening UNESCO's weapons against colonialism and racism. In the process officials protested strongly against the mounting tide of Western criticism of ideological bias in the organisation, and firmly rejected calls for UNESCO's 'depoliticisation'.[34] UNESCO was thus a ready-made vehicle for Soviet attempts to bring UN bodies more into line with NIEO thinking.

Much of the form this took, of support for the creation of a new world information and communication order (NWICO), was already present in UNESCO. The institution's involvement with news-gathering issues dated back to the early 1950s. Its broad commitment to the principle of free flow of information, however, came increasingly under attack in the early 1970s from the USSR, which portrayed this as a cover for Western ideological penetration of developing countries.[35] From 1971, with growing support from Third World delegations, Soviet officials instituted a vigorous campaign to achieve a broad UNESCO declaration on the media that would reflect this more radical perspective. The strategy finally met with success at the 1978 and 1979 sessions of the UNESCO General Conference, and in a subsequent programme designed to channel development assistance to Third World news-media organisations. The crisis over the issue of 'information imperialism' was one of the chief factors, along with a broader array of complaints about programmes, administration and budgets, that precipitated US withdrawal from the organisation in 1982.

UNCTAD was even more central to the Soviet concept of the restructuring of the international economic system. The idea of holding such a conference, decided by the UN General Assembly in 1962 following the Cairo meeting of Third World countries, had been promoted by Soviet officials since the mid-1950s. UNCTAD meetings were for Moscow among the most closely monitored of all international forums. It was described in 1976 as 'one of the most important agencies of the UN'.[36] The Soviet Union followed a determined strategy of emphasising and attempting to elevate its stature. This was partly because of the conference's role, and that of constituent organs such as the Trade and Development Board, as a defender and articulator of Third World positions on international economic and financial questions. UNCTAD was also a more widely based negotiating forum that had as part of its mandate many of the long-standing Soviet concerns about East–West trade. Indeed in the 1970s officials resisted what they claimed were Western efforts to restrict the scope of UNCTAD to Asian, African and Latin American questions 'rather than with all the highly important problems of world trade and development'.[37]

Questions of East–West trade, in which the Soviet Union had a large and direct stake, were thus viewed as central to UNCTAD's mandate. This side of UNCTAD's continuing work, institutionalised in Group D, provided Soviet officials with a means to criticise a wide variety of Western trade and development assistance practices: strategic trade controls, protectionist devices, resistance to Third World demands for commodity trade stabilisation, lack of restraint over the activities of multinational corporations, and credit restrictions. On the last, for example, it was argued that the large expansion of Soviet trade with Western countries during the 1970s could not be sustained because of the continuing US policy of restricting the granting of credit to socialist countries.[38] At the UNCTAD 6 meetings in Belgrade in 1983, and following further measures instituted by Western countries following the Soviet invasion of Afghanistan in 1980, the socialist states drafted a declaration aimed at 'restoring confidence in international trade'. This focused on the 'expanding application by some developed market-economy countries for non-economic reasons of restrictive measures, trade blockades, embargoes and other economic sanctions incompatible with the provisions of the Charter of the UN', and raised particularly the problems resulting from the 'unilateral renunciation of contractual obligations' by Western countries.[39]

Yet questions of North–South relations were in practice the defining feature of UNCTAD. Soviet criticism of Western trade practices were thus crafted in terms of the general NIEO principles of equality, sovereignty and noninterference, as well as 'the basic principles, rules and norms of trade, such as the unconditional MFN and nondiscrimination'.[40] Indeed there was often a marked convergence between prevailing UNCTAD critiques of GATT and those developed by the Soviet Union. The UNCTAD secretariat, for example, like the Soviet Union, tended to be critical of GATT for its lack of an institutional base, inadequate treatment of issues of concern to Third World countries, its 'excessive preoccupation' with questions of intra-Western trade, and its 'virtual lack of consideration of the place of the socialist countries of Eastern Europe in the GATT system...'[41]

However, considerable Soviet diplomatic effort was sometimes needed to dissuade G77 delegations from adopting positions critical of the Soviet Union. This was a growing risk in UNCTAD and other international economic forums in the 1970s and 1980s, especially after the UNCTAD sessions in Manila in 1979. Attempts, as in the approaches of the Brandt Commission, to redefine international development issues in 'North–South' terms were strenuously resisted. Soviet commentary on UNCTAD 3 in Santiago in 1972, for example, made a point of criticising the 'false thesis' that the world was divided into rich and poor nations, as well as the 'venomous idea' that, for developing countries, there was no difference between capitalist and socialist states. The same 'strange, even false notes' were observed in the statements and voting behaviour of developing countries at UNCTAD 4 in Nairobi four years later.[42] The culprit responsible for spreading these lies was, not surprisingly, found to be China, at the time a scourge of superpower hegemonism, especially in its social–imperialist (or Soviet) form.

Thus at the 1983 meetings Soviet officials maintained there could be no ground for appeals to the 'common responsiblity' of developed states, East as well as West, for the Third World's economic crisis. Such ideas 'ignored the fundamental difference between the two social and economic systems and the essentially different nature of the relations of the countries concerned with developing countries'. Debates on compensatory financing were held to miss the point if they failed to recognise that trade problems affecting developing countries were caused by a 'malfunctioning of the mechanism of the market-economy system'. Such schemes were therefore 'not applicable to the economic relations of socialist countries and developing countries'.[43] The Soviet Union's own record of dealings with Third World countries on trade and development issues, however, as well as its repeated denial of 'responsiblity' for their problems, rendered it open to the charge of indifference to the South. Glowing recitals of evidence of expanded Soviet assistance to developing countries, and of increased East–South trade flows, were accordingly a vital tool of Soviet delegates in UNCTAD, ECOSOC and UN General Assembly Committee debates.[44]

These broad approaches to international economic and financial issues retained their momentum in Soviet approaches until the mid-1980s, and indeed into the Gorbachev period. Soviet officials called attention to 1984 as the tenth anniversary of the Charter of Economic Rights and Duties, confirmed at the end of 1985 its 'continuing validity', and urged the initiation of global economic negotiations to consider 'a radical restructuring of the international monetary and financial system and a democratisation of its institutions'.[45] The two latter concepts, restructuring and democratisation, were closely interconnected. Yet while the goal of 'democratisation' of the institutions of the Bretton Woods system could in a sense be accomplished through Soviet, and wider Third World, membership, participation in their work on the basis of existing rules remained politically and ideologically unacceptable to Moscow in the first half of the 1980s. It was also increasingly apparent by 1985 that differing Western agendas, especially that of the Republican Administration in Washington, and the refusal of Third World countries to share the Soviet distaste for North–South models of the world economy, set limits to what could be achieved through the means of the 1970s.

Further, actors other than states were increasingly pivotal in the economic policy areas dealt with by the UN. Multinational corporations were a predictably consistent focus of Soviet attention during the 1970s and 1980s in ECOSOC, UNCTAD and UN meetings aimed at the design of a regulatory code of conduct governing their activities. While it continued to criticise MNCs in UN forums as the main agents responsible for outflows of capital from developing countries, the Soviet Union acknowledged that work on a code had reached an impasse by the mid-1980s. The growing significance of NGOs in UN development work also posed problems. Few if any fitted definitions of the kinds of bodies active in the Soviet Union in organising and mobilising individuals. Soviet commentaries noted that many Western and international NGOs had a positive role in relation to such questions as apartheid, disarmament or women's rights. Most, however, were categorised as unrepresentative or 'unbalanced', and drawn from a restricted range of groups inside capitalist countries.[46]

CHASTENED SUPPLICANT: 1986–93

Alterations in the Soviet outlook on the Bretton Woods system in the late 1980s were a product of several factors. The requirement of the 'integration' of the Soviet economy into the world economy was a central feature of the reform goals articulated by Gorbachev in 1986. While conditioned largely by the persistence of chronic weaknesses in the economy, this new direction – which centred increasingly on the objective of membership of the IMF, the World Bank and GATT, especially when it became apparent that substantial and unanticipated obstacles lay in the way – also reflected a series of changes in the Soviet Union's international situation.

First, the shift was in a sense a logical corollary of the revised view of international institutions taken by Moscow in 1986–7. Soviet membership of the UN had not, of course, automatically meant membership of the World Bank and IMF, or indeed of any of the specialised agencies of the UN system. Further, as the events of 1946–7 had shown, the UN itself had negligible powers over the workings of the Bretton Woods institutions. Continued Soviet non-membership of the world's leading IFIs, then, was a conspicuous gap in the array of multilateral activities routinely undertaken by the Soviet Union, and one, moreover, that for Moscow had long underlined graphically their unrepresentative and discriminatory character. While denunciation of the latter trait had been the predominant Soviet response since the late 1940s, by the mid-1980s Moscow was moving rapidly toward the realisation that the condition of nonuniversality could be remedied, and other Soviet objectives pursued at the same time, by the simple expedient of taking out membership.

But it was the overwhelmingly Western personalities of the World Bank and the IMF that remained the central fact for Moscow. A deterrent to close contact for decades, this attribute now ironically became their most desirable feature. Almost until the end of the decade, Soviet commentary continued to refer to the IMF, the World Bank and GATT – often indiscriminately together with the OECD and other Western institutions – as 'organisations that function as part of the system the leading Western countries have created'. It was noted that the USSR was not a member of these 'even though the IMF formally operates under the aegis of the UN'.[47]

At first, economic calculations drove events. The Soviet Union approached GATT in 1986, and at the same time began talking of eventual membership of the IMF and the World Bank. The main evidence of fundamentally changing attitudes towards the UN itself did not come until the following year. As the larger process got under way, however, the two facets of this overall integration policy – the economic and the political – steadily reinforced each other.

Secondly, the growing attractiveness of the option of membership was in turn a product of other developments. There was unavoidable evidence by the mid-1980s that the strategy of fostering alternative, NIEO-based structures had led only to a succession of impasses in the UN system. More importantly, it was failing to address vital Soviet economic interests. This reevaluation was particularly compelling in light of the broader changes already under way in the early 1980s in Soviet–Third World relations, and the downgrading of formerly important links in Africa, central America and elsewhere.[48]

Significantly, these developments coincided with the Reagan administration's efforts in the first half of the 1980s to shift UN attention away from the kinds of North–South issues that had dominated agendas in the previous decade. The absence of a concerted and determined Soviet strategy to arrest this tendency – other than on a case-by-case basis as in UNESCO, or through the momentum of past policy declarations – is itself an indication of the degree to which confidence in earlier approaches was being eroded.

Thirdly, changes in the Soviet Union's international trading position contributed decisively to the new orientation towards IFIs. The USSR had already, by the mid-1980s, moved significantly away from the socialist-bloc model posited in the late 1940s as the core of an alternative international economic system. From the 1960s the Soviet Union gradually became a net importer of food, particularly through foreign grain purchases made as a result of the domestic requirements for fulfilling goals of expanded meat consumption. Exports continued to be dominated by raw materials, including a significant energy sector, a factor which made the economy vulnerable to shifts in external market conditions. Soviet analyses became increasingly concerned with the general slowdown of the country's foreign trade during the 1980s and the deterioration of its terms of trade.[49]

Beyond Eastern Europe, trade relations were neither balanced nor substantial. Soviet trade with Western countries doubled during the 1960s and surged dramatically, with a tenfold increase, in the 1970s. The 1980s were then marked by stagnation. Exports to Western countries in 1988 were marginally less than the 1980 level of $24.9 billion, with imports showing a small increase over this period.[50] These figures still represented only a small proportion of the world trade of either side. Although they remained pivotal in Soviet criticisms, the Western strategic trade controls in place since the late 1940s, together with other measures – the US grain embargo after the Soviet invasion of Afghanistan, for example, and the tightened restriction of oil and gas technology exports after the imposition of martial law in Poland – cannot adequately account for this slowdown. Similarly, difficulties in financing and credit probably had only a marginal impact on the volume and structure of East–West trade.[51] The underlying factors had to do with the general problems of the Soviet economy – including low and declining rates of economic growth in the first half of the 1980s and the uncompetitiveness of many manufactured goods on world markets – that the grand project of restructuring was designed to solve.

Fourthly, the Soviet Union's relations with regional CMEA member-states were changing. East European countries were interested in expanding trade and other ties with Western economies as a means of promoting their own economic growth, gaining access to technology, overcoming problems of external financing and escaping the constraints of non-complementarity inherent in the CMEA framework. Hungary, for example, adopted in 1978 a more openly determined export orientation in its reform programme, reversing the import-substitution approach that had been the earlier response to mounting trade deficits and hard-currency debts. This in turn prompted a series of internal economic and political reforms in the late 1970s and early 1980s.[52]

In this context, membership of Bretton Woods and other bodies was a natural focus of attention. The option had surfaced at various times since the 1940s. Poland joined the IFIs, but resigned in 1950; Czechoslovakia stayed in until 1955, but a combination of US pressures and Soviet criticism made continued membership impossible.[53] Later contacts indicated that Cold War tensions prevented a resumption of relations. Polish officials had discussions with IMF personnel in 1956, as did Hungary and also Romania, in the context of UNCTAD l meetings in 1964, but these talks led nowhere. The route to membership was finally taken by

Hungary, as part of its relaunched reform programme, in 1981; Romania, a special case, had joined in 1972; and both Poland (which finally joined in 1986) and Czechoslovakia retained their long-standing interests in moving in this direction as soon as circumstances allowed. GATT's membership in the mid-1980s included Hungary, Poland, Romania and Czechoslovakia; Bulgaria had observer status and requested formal accession in late 1986.[54]

The USSR itself explored the option of GATT membership in 1982, but the state of East–West relations at that time made this a non-starter. Thus as the 1980s progressed Soviet non-participation in these arrangements was increasingly looking like an oddity, and a condition that in the long term might turn into economic isolation. Significant too, in view of Soviet strategic sensitivities, were the growing links during the 1980s between China and the IFIs. Viktor Gerashchenko, head of Gosbank, wrote in 1990 that most CMEA countries were already members of GATT, the IMF and the World Bank, so 'full participation of the USSR in these institutions would be a logical step toward establishment of an integrated and universal international trade and monetary system'.[55]

Even so the Soviet Union proceeded cautiously in the mid-1980s in its approaches to the IMF and the World Bank. Partly as a result of UNCTAD encounters in the 1970s and at the 1983 meetings, officials had a keen sense of the main issues separating the Soviet Union from Western member-states. As in the 1940s, the question of convertibility was still potentially a significant obstacle. So too were issues of information, reporting and confidentiality, as well as the question of quotas and the distribution of voting power.

This caution also reflected the traditional style as well as the substance of domestic economic policies in 1985–7. These were marked by conventional party-led campaigns, for example against alcohol or for the modernisation of industry, rather than by serious measures aimed at structural change. In the UN, similarly, Soviet diplomacy tended to be framed still by the agendas of the first half of the 1980s and by older mental constructs. The arms race dominated attention, and Washington remained the prime adversary. For Shevardnadze at the UN General Assembly in 1985, the world was still the dichotomised one of 'continuing struggle between the forces of progress and the forces of reaction, between the forces of the future and those of the past...'[56] In this perspective economic questions tended to make an appearance more by way of revised definitions of the concept of international security than through far-reaching reassessments of Soviet economic interests. Economic security, the Soviet foreign minister stated at the 1986 General Assembly, was 'an integral part of a comprehensive system of international security'.[57] Similarly, much of the economic part of Gorbachev's foreign-policy thinking at the twenty-seventh Party Congress in early 1986 continued to be oriented around NIEO themes calling for 'the establishment of a new world economic order guaranteeing equal economic security for all states'.[58]

While there was more frequent Soviet discussion of Bretton Woods during 1986, in practice GATT appeared to be a more realistic and accessible starting point. It was more directly related to overall Soviet foreign trade objectives of expanding exports to hard-currency areas and devising ways to restrict imports, especially in view of falling oil prices. GATT also seemed to raise fewer problems in negotiations prior to signature, and held out fewer risks of external intrusions into domestic policy areas. In August 1986 Moscow requested participation in the Punta del Este talks. The purpose, explained a senior foreign ministry official, was 'to help develop international trade, including such trade between the USSR and GATT member-countries, and to strengthen cooperation and trust between them'. The Soviet Union 'could also acquire the experience it will need in the future to join GATT on agreed terms'.[59] The prospect that these multilateral negotiations would launch a new phase of closer economic integration among the world's economies was a key factor reinforcing Soviet fears of its own isolation.

Lack of early progress towards this goal – the Soviet Union did not gain even observer status in GATT until May 1990 – can be attributed to several factors. For their part, Soviet officials blamed Western attitudes, especially those of the Reagan and Bush administrations. Primakov wrote in *Pravda* in September 1987 that the internationalisation of the capitalist economy had produced two opposing trends: the socialist world's isolation, which was 'chiefly the current US administration's doing', and the 'development of world-wide economic cooperation'. Western countries were clearly trying to sabotage Soviet efforts to join GATT 'in order to keep our country from participating in a restructuring of international economic relations'.[60]

This analysis exaggerated what were undoubtedly significant Western concerns about Soviet membership. In 1986–7 these arose primarily from serious doubts about the political will lying behind, and the likely efficacy of, the reform programme in the USSR. Soviet participation in GATT also raised a number of specific issues. The balance of opinion on the part of Western contracting parties tended to be against taking the risk that early Soviet membership would be a factor likely to strengthen the viability of proposed economic reforms. Apart from other considerations this would have implied an interventionist stance that has historically not been part of 'the GATT ethic'.[61] There had also been problems in the past over anti-dumping and subsidy questions relating to exports from East European and other centrally planned economies, and this too prompted caution in Western responses to the idea of Soviet participation in GATT. A variety of Cold War-related questions, for example Poland's protest to the GATT Council in 1982 over the US suspension of its MFN status, were also part of the recent history of the treaty partners.[62] The structural protection of Soviet domestic prices from world trends added to this mixture of concerns. However the fact that other CPEs were GATT members indicated that these kinds of planning mechanisms as such, including the state direction of foreign trade, were not necesarily a barrier to membership.

Changes in the Soviet economic system during 1987 played an important role in accelerating the conditions required for GATT membership. These followed the general programme of measures set out at the twenty-seventh Congress. The reforms incorporated significant changes to the Soviet foreign-trade system. The new approach explicitly criticised the existing mechanism for marginalising export allocation, partly through the bureaucratic intervention of controlling bodies directed by the Ministry of Foreign Trade and the State Committee on External Economic Relations, and partly as a result of the implications of currency arrangements that were not geared to world market forces.[63] More emphasis was to be placed on joint ventures, bureaucratic decentralisation, the active involvement of a growing number of enterprises, within and outside the state sector, in foreign trade, and increased access for foreign companies in Soviet markets. Announcements of the changes were accompanied by statements confirming the Soviet commitment to stability in international trade and the international financial system and recognition of the facts of global economic interdependence.[64] With the expansion of industrial exports still a major goal, and in light of the continuing place of primary commodities in Soviet exports, some form of association with GATT became an even higher priority.

The early Gorbachev period was thus characterised by divergent tendencies in Soviet approaches to international institutions. The growing interest in GATT, the IMF and other 'Western' institutions was not necessarily inconsistent with the simultaneous pursuit in UN bodies of an NIEO. Both could comfortably be fitted within the broadly based theoretical framework of the restructuring of international economic relations to which Soviet officials had long declared themselves to be committed. The practical implications in terms of policy directions, however, were significantly different. Various groupings in Soviet governmental and party structures had different stakes in each. The 'Western' option, moreover, required profound modifications of earlier ideological formulations if it was to become the foundation of future external economic policies.

The diverse threads of international economic policies in the late 1980s were integrated under the rubric of the new thinking. The more specifically institutional aspects of these policies began to receive greater prominence in the period between the publication of Gorbachev's UN article of September 1987 and his General Assembly speech of December 1988. The route of serious multilateral negotiation was presented both as the only rational way forward in an interdependent world economy and also as a means of securing the removal of objectionable Western trade practices. The new thinking, according to the Soviet Union at UNCTAD 7 in 1987, 'should result in the complete replacement of confrontation in the international arena by a joint search for solutions to the most difficult problems presented by today's world economy.... All countries in today's world are linked by a community of vital interests, notwithstanding differences in their political systems, ideologies and views. In view of the increasing interdependence of states, it is not only difficult but quite out of the question for them to solve problems alone or in isolated groups'.[65] Unlike the old approach based on analysis of the correlation of forces, the Soviet delegate told ECOSOC in 1988, the need was to seek areas of convergence based on 'a balance of real, even if conflicting, interests...'[66]

This approach still incorporated the conventional demands for the abandonment of Western sanctions policies and other forms of discrimination against the socialist states, particularly the controls on trade in strategic items imposed through COCOM, as well as for the exploration of concepts such as 'disarmament for development'. G77 positions on commodity trade, debt, preferential access to developed country markets and the need for an effective North–South dialogue were also supported. The aims of the NIEO, particularly the Charter of Economic Rights and Duties of States, were in mid-1988 still 'as far as ever from being achieved', and in late 1989 were still being impeded by 'narrow egoistic approaches by a number of states'.[67]

Several difficulties continued to block the path to Soviet GATT membership. Western observers criticised the slow and piecemeal introduction of foreign trade reforms and their negligible impact on Soviet manufactured exports. The basic price system remained, as did state control of distribution and overall regulation of enterprises, including those in foreign-trade areas. Domestic economic growth, estimated at an average 1.9 per cent in the period 1981–5, slipped to 1.3 per cent in 1987 and to 1.5 per cent in 1988.[68] There was evidence of further deterioration in the terms of trade, particularly in light of accelerating decline in Soviet trade with other European CMEA members.[69]

GATT's accommodation to Soviet overtures thus came about more as a result of political decisions in Western countries than of evidence of effective domestic reforms. Soviet interest in closer relations with GATT and in participating in the Uruguay Round were confirmed by the Soviet Union in ECOSOC in mid-1988. Following Gorbachev's speech to the UN General Assembly in December, which outlined a course of closer Soviet cooperation with IFIs and continued informal talks with GATT and Western officials, Moscow stepped up its drive for GATT membership in autumn 1989.[70] From the spring of 1989 the Bush administration began to take more seriously the Soviet commitment to reform. GATT was discussed by Gorbachev and Bush at the Malta summit at the end of the year. Finally, at the December meetings of the GATT contracting parties, the US announced it would support the granting of observer status to the USSR.[71] This intermediate step was approved by the GATT Council in May 1990. The decision was greeted with enthusiasm from Moscow as one that would allow exchange of information between Soviet trade officials and the GATT secretariat, participation (though without voting rights) in GATT meetings and preparation for full membership.[72]

Though important as concrete evidence of a modest success of the integration goals of the Soviet restructuring project, the link with GATT was clearly not capable in itself of arresting the secular trend of decline in the economy and in foreign trade. Also during 1990, new restrictions were placed on both exporting and importing enterprises. Little progress was evident in the creation of the institutional underpinnings of a market economy. Setbacks in the reform programme, moreover, increasingly had to be viewed against the background of mounting tensions between the centre and the republics, some of which, for example, had adopted the tactic of withholding tax revenues from Moscow. The goal of Bretton Woods membership continued nonetheless to be central to Soviet thinking in the period 1988–91. This merged with the growing Western debate on larger frameworks of economic aid, including humanitarian and emergency assistance, to the USSR.

On both points – membership of the IMF and the World Bank, and other forms of assistance – the reactions of the leading Western states were clearly crucial. These were still governed in large measure by fundamental doubts about the pace and prospects of the Gorbachev reforms. The grounds of Western skepticism in the late 1980s have been summarised by Aslund: the ideological constraints imposed by Marxism–Leninism; political resistance to reforms at high party levels and a consequent lack of consensus on the desired direction of the Soviet economy; problems of nationalist unrest; the bureaucratisation of the Soviet economy and the dominant role of the state; various types of public unrest, for example among labour unions; inflationary pressures and other features of the economy; the difficulty of securing reliable statistics; and, finally, the problems inherent in the transition from a command economy to a market economy, especially if this was ambiguous or incomplete.[73]

These kinds of judgments were increasingly interwoven in 1990 with speculation about the political viability of the USSR, particularly as Shevardnadze's resignation fed speculation about a return to authoritarianism, and as Moscow adopted a tougher stance towards the Baltic republics. Appreciation of the problems of assisting the transition to some form of post-Union grouping while averting the violence, economic chaos and nuclear risks likely to be inherent in a series of disorderly fractures, also influenced Western approaches to issues of aid and IFI membership.

In addition structural change was under way in Eastern Europe. Trade among European CMEA member-states declined by 20–30 per cent in 1990. On balance the Soviet Union came out less worse than some others. It benefited, for example, from the oil and gold price increases that followed the Iraqi invasion of Kuwait. Further, from late 1990 currency reforms began to be implemented for Soviet oil exports, which in effect terminated the traditional subsidising of energy supplies from the USSR to Eastern Europe.[74] In practice CMEA ceased to function during 1990. A successor was heralded: the so-called Organization for International Economic Cooperation, described as part of the process of 'switch[ing] cooperation to market relations'.[75] However it was evident from the reluctance of East European governments, notably those of Hungary, Poland and Czechoslovakia, to work within such a framework that this could not function as a replacement for CMEA.

Thus by 1991 little had been achieved in relation to the goal of institutional integration of the Soviet into the world economy. Informal talks had not even progressed to the point where applications to join the IMF and the World Bank could be made. Deputy Foreign Minister Obminsky, commenting in early 1991 on this lack of progress, stated that many of the financial and economic problems facing the Soviet Union could be 'easily solved' by joining the IMF, the World Bank and GATT.[76] Observer status in the latter continued to facilitate access to information, contact with Western delegations and the preparation of domestic legislative and regulatory measures. The long-standing Soviet campaign against Western strategic trade controls, however, failed to produce changes. In early 1991 the Western allies adopted revisions regarding Poland, Hungary and Czechoslovakia. These countries, moreover, were drawn implicitly into the regulatory framework by agreeing to refrain from reselling certain Western items to the Soviet Union. The COCOM partners could agree only to defer decisions on the USSR itself.[77] The question of

Bretton Woods membership, then, was stuck in a logjam of larger East–West issues.

Crucial among these was the general question of the appropriate Western response to the Soviet, and to Gorbachev's, predicament. The Houston G7 meetings in July 1990 had confirmed Western reluctance to engage in a massive aid undertaking. Instead of variations on the 'grand-bargain' concept, specific options such as technical assistance, food aid and assistance in relation to specific sectors of the Soviet economy, particularly energy, were considered more likely to be productive. Similar broad conclusions were reached in later EC meetings.[78]

The multi-agency study (by the IMF, the World Bank, the OECD and the EBRD) set up after Houston reported that the old Soviet system was unworkable – 'there is no example of a successful modern centrally planned economy' – and that reform attempts were proving counterproductive. The former system was being marginally dismantled but was not being replaced by one based on market principles.[79] Price reforms had begun in mid-1990, for example, but after a year were producing price increases that fed growing fears of hyperinflation.[80] Other elements regarded in the IMF as desirable attributes of a candidate for membership remained stubbornly absent: for example, effective planning to achieve government deficit reduction, stringent credit restraint, a more energetic commitment to trade liberalisation, further steps towards currency convertibility, creation of a thriving and extensive private sector and the controlled diminution of the state sector. The post-Houston study can nonetheless be regarded as a tentative first step on the road to Russia's IMF membership.[81]

The process got more firmly under way in 1991. As the slowdown in the Soviet economy deepened, Moscow made clear its continued adherence to the goals of membership of the IMF and the World Bank, the phased elimination of COCOM trade controls and persistence with the reform programme.[82] The London G7 meetings in July 1991, to which Gorbachev had successfully lobbied for access, identified several key Soviet sectors for possible Western support, including transportation, energy, food distribution and consumer goods. It was also agreed that the USSR would become an associate member of IMF, with a decision on full membership to be made within six months or so. The formal Soviet application was submitted one week after the summit. Shortly afterwards the World Bank allocated funds for systematic research during 1992 on Soviet economic requirements and capacities. IMF staff initiated diagnostic studies which emphasised the need for Soviet institution-building and personnel training.[83] Both agencies established missions in Moscow.

These post-London developments were quickly overtaken by the pace of events inside the Soviet Union itself. Already in the spring, the question of the optimal balance of commitment to Gorbachev and to his Russian rivals in the 'other Moscow' was becoming the critical decision for Western governments. In the aftermath of the failed coup of August, the consolidation of power by the republics gained force. In the event it was not the USSR but Russia, and other ex-republics, which gained IMF membership the following year. The question was high on the agenda of Yeltsin's telephone conversation with Prime Minister Major, on behalf of the G7, in January 1992.[84] While we can speculate that the Soviet Union, had it continued to exist, would have taken this step, it is probably safe to conclude that Western states were more confident about a post-communist, and post-imperial, Russia doing so.

The Russian Federation's inherited relationship with the Bretton Woods institutions took shape amid fierce domestic controversy surrounding the government's pro-Western alignment. Both official and wider public criticism of the obligations and costs of IMF membership, including steps to control the budget deficit, mounted during 1992–3. The terms imposed by the IMF were condemned as 'too tough' by Vice-President Rutskoy, who publicly advocated abandoning the austerity measures agreed to with IMF officials.[85] Gerashchenko blamed the IMF-imposed tight credit policy for the sharp drops in Russia's industrial production.[86] The IMF's 'dogmatic' approach to Russia, its alleged failure to appreciate Russia's unique circumstances, neglect of the social costs of the removal of price subsidies and of other adjustment policies, and charges of its apparent readiness to treat Russia in the same way it would a developing country, also fuelled public protests and official concerns. The West generally was accused of using the aid instrument for anti-Russian propaganda purposes. Gorbachev's policies, as continued by Yeltsin, were criticised in *Pravda* in 1992 for their 'humiliating demands on us, the imposition on us of conditions for granting Western aid, and our passive acceptance of them.... From now on there's no escaping the IMF's grip, the interest and payments on loans, the demands and ultimatums'.[87]

From the IFIs' perspective, the central fact was the magnitude of the Russian economic crisis – though according to some estimates the food situation was on balance not as bad as in other ex-USSR republics – and the distance that would have to be travelled before the conditions for recovery could be secured. There was a decline of 15 per cent in GNP and of 9 per cent in industrial output in 1991, with exports declining by about 30 per cent and imports by 46 per cent in US-dollar terms. Industrial output in September 1992 was 29 per cent less than the figure of a year before.[88]

As a result of the earlier IMF studies, external attention focused among other things on institutional weaknesses in Moscow. There were major problems of overlap and duplication among the agencies responsible for various aspects of economic and financial policy, including external relations. These were reinforced by continuing disputes between the presidency and the congress, each of which retained overall responsibility for different bodies,[89] and by the political confrontation that flared between them in the spring of 1993.

In light of this combination of chronically weak economic conditions and intensifying domestic political debate, it was not surprising that tensions also surfaced between the government and the IFIs. IMF officials at various points expressed concerns about the pace and the efficacy of Moscow's actions with regard to the budget deficit, credit restrictions and currency reforms, let alone with the larger and more complex questions of private-sector creation. The question of the ex-USSR's foreign debt had arisen before the formal breakup of the country. After an initially strong stand of denial of responsibility, Russia and seven other republics in late 1991 signed an agreement with G7 representatives on the sharing of the debt (though a dispute persisted between Russia and Ukraine). The threat of hyperinflation led to the IMF's postponement of the planned establishment of a $6 billion currency stabilisation fund.[90] Talks on the question of debt-rescheduling between Russian and G7 finance officials continued in 1992, and a set of agreed relief measures formed a key part of the package announced at the G7 ministerial meetings in April 1993.

For their part Russian officials continued to protest conditionalities in multilateral discussions of aid. These talks, coordinated through the World Bank, took place in 1992–3 in a set of consultative working groups set up for each of the CIS states, in light of agreements at the donors' conference held in Tokyo.[91] Moscow criticised the IMF for failing to take steps to unfreeze the stabilisation fund, and Western countries for continuing to impose restrictions on high-technology exports to Russia. The government also extended the definition of the goal of integration with the world economy to include much closer association with, and eventual Russian membership of, G7 structures.

Throughout the period 1985–93 IFIs were thus crucial to the futures charted by Moscow. Early hesitations, prompted among other things by the accumulated weight of a variety of East–South commitments, had virtually disappeared by the early 1990s. Integration goals were pursued to an accompaniment of promises to the West of the rewards that would flow from association with a buoyant Soviet, or Russian, economy, and of warnings of the dire political consequences that would result from failure.

The links established were also inseparable from regime-maintenance objectives on the part of political leaders in Moscow. Renovation of the economy through such instruments was sought under Gorbachev partly as a way to revitalise the rapidly ailing Communist Party and to sustain the socialist vision into the next century, and under Yeltsin as one means to bolster a specific interpretation of the domestic institutional requirements of the reform process.

Even leaving aside the first of these, the strategy had mixed success. The main international institutional ties were secured. Western states recognised their stake in the country's future. This was periodically reaffirmed, in early 1989 for example, and in the Vancouver US–Russia summit and G7 assistance package of spring 1993. Moscow was not able, however, to achieve its long-term goal of the total elimination of Western restrictions on sensitive exports; the process of disbursement of aid was fraught with difficulties; and IMF and Western criticisms of the course and impact of reforms produced for Moscow a steady flow of obstacles to closer relations. Irritation with the prospect and the reality of conditionalities, and resentment at first the Soviet Union's and then Russia's mounting economic dependence on and growing foreign policy alignment with the West, meanwhile strengthened the hands of the government's domestic critics.

4 Interesting Diversions: The Politics of the Non-Political

Despite their seemingly innocuous appearance, the specialised agencies of the UN system have managed to provoke at times strenuous criticism from their members. In the 1980s unease on the part of both socialist and Western countries converged on complaints of waste and mismanaged resources. Yet states bring to these organisations diverse expectations and policy preferences. As Claude has commented, 'Postwar functional agencies have experienced difficulty in concentrating on important matters, rejecting trivial proposals, and abjuring interesting diversions'.[1] Criteria for distinguishing the trivial from the important, however, can sometimes be difficult to agree on. Western observers have frequently objected to the inclusion of 'political' items on agency agendas. The Soviet Union was often restless with definitions of 'technical' mandates that seemed to rule out debates and resolutions on the economic, political and security questions that it wanted to raise. Two specialised agencies, the WHO and the ILO, together with UNEP, are the focus of the present chapter.

SOCIALIST THEORY MEETS FUNCTIONALIST PRACTICE

From an ideological perspective, the Soviet Union tended to approach interstate functional cooperation from two different viewpoints. On the one hand, to the degree that cooperation on health, labour conditions, culture or other matters could be seen as strengthening progressive forces in the capitalist world, or as having some other positive bearing on the world correlation of forces, such practices were ideologically acceptable. On the other hand many institutions in practice bore such clear evidence of Western controls, according to Soviet analysts, that their utility as instruments for either revolutionary change, or for the containment of capitalism's aggressive impulses, appeared at best minimal. By concerning themselves with inherently domestic policy matters, moreover, these organisations constantly threatened to become the interfering tools of anti-Soviet forces. Functionalist thinking, and other rationales for technical cooperation through such agencies elaborated in Western countries since the days of the League of Nations, could accordingly be counterattacked by Soviet observers by exposing their failure to acknowledge the importance of class and sovereignty in international relations.

Each strand – the irrevocably suspicious, and the qualified and tactical readiness to participate – can be found in Lenin's views. Before the October revolution he had cautiously envisaged a possible Europe-wide scheme of international cooperation. Institutions, of a suitably non-monarchical character, would assist cooperative activity between governments in a variety of policy areas. Doubts about the reliability of capitalist states in such forums, however, came to predominate. Nonetheless this element of 'indecision in Lenin's early thinking'[2] about international institutions had a legitimising function. It ensured that Soviet participation in the work of international technical agencies, alongside the representatives of capitalist states, did not imply a rejection of the Marxist–Leninist canon.

This ambivalent response persisted. Inside the UN specialised agencies, the wider context of world struggle between capitalism and socialism remained their central defining trait in Soviet commentary.[3] Appeals to this context led to the characteristic Soviet approach. From this perspective Western states, pursuing the interests of their ruling circles, were accused of shortsightedly focusing on the so-called 'technical' nature of such organisations and of complaining of 'politicisation' whenever larger issues were addressed. This tendency was especially pronounced in the US in the early 1980s. The Soviet Union portrayed itself as more realistic. The two aspects – the technical and the political – were held to be integrally linked. Together with other factors, especially economic forces, they constituted the broader picture without which it was impossible to see these agencies in their true light. An organisation such as the WHO was thus for Soviet observers both a technical and a scientific body, and at the same time a major international forum for discussion of social, economic and political questions.[4]

In addition to shaping the Soviet outlook on the work of the UN specialised agencies, variants of this view also served useful foreign-policy ends. They justified attempts to restructure IGO agendas to compel attention to matters of broader Soviet concern, such as disarmament initiatives. They also vindicated the opposite Soviet tendency towards withdrawal, hostility or impassive stubbornness. Yet these are often counterproductive postures in UN agencies. Political costs could thus be minimised by drawing on, and putting into practice, those strands of Lenin's thinking that instead legitimised active participation in international institutions.

Expedient though it was, this Soviet contention nonetheless gave a distorted picture of the views of Western governments. These did not, as was frequently alleged by Moscow, consistently assume that technical issues could, or should, be hermetically sealed from the main currents of international politics or the world economy. In practice the difference between the two sides was a mixture of politics and procedure. The dispute was about the situations in which certain kinds of issues could appropriately be raised, and those from which they should be barred. This overlap between Soviet and Western views was one factor that helped agencies to continue to function during tense periods of Cold War confrontation, and which later facilitated the negotiation of East–West compromises on sensitive 'political' agenda items.

The Soviet Union had acquired a rich body of experiences in the handling by IGOs of social and technical questions before the UN itself was created. It had also acquired a core of hardened attitudes. The pre-1940s record did not augur well for a constructive postwar atmosphere. The ILO, the leading technical organ associated with the League of Nations, had included for Lenin many 'social traitors' whose presence necessitated an ideologically based mistrust of the organisation. Soviet assessments of the ILO continued in the 1970s and 1980s to hark back to its early years. Its basic character was held to reflect its origins as a bourgeois response to the rise of the world's labour movement in the wake of the 1917 revolution.[5] Citing the IL0's interest in the early 1920s in industrial conditions in Russia, one Soviet writer observed in 1984 that 'Today the successors of Albert Thomas never miss an opportunity to join or actively support the anti-socialist provocations of international capital'.[6]

Yet the Soviet Union could not simply shun even this organisation. It had automatically become an ILO member-state upon joining the League in 1934.[7] Politically, moreover, some kind of studied response was owed the ILO by the world's first socialist state. The ILO also provided Moscow with a convenient framework within which to meet labour-union representatives from Western countries, to expose to public view the shortcomings of capitalism, to defend the achievements of socialism and the role of Soviet unions (the subject of an ILO mission to the USSR in 1959), to strengthen the position of Soviet-supported international union groupings, and, not least, to lend support to those of the ILO's growing number of international conventions which might give added leverage to the socialist cause inside capitalist states.

Indeed the League of Nations period saw the beginnings of Soviet cooperation with a variety of functional institutions. At first Russia was not so much a participant as an object of attention from Geneva. It was marked by chronic economic weaknesses, continuing political unrest and widespread social problems. During the 1920s the League of Nations Assembly discussed famine in Russia, Western NGO relief efforts, the spread of disease, particularly typhus and cholera, and the refugee problem.[8] Soviet public health authorities formed links with the League's health committee as early as 1922, and Russia formally joined the International Bureau of Public Hygiene in 1926. Shortly after becoming a member of the League the Soviet Union invited the health committee to hold its 1936 meetings in Moscow. Soviet assessments of urgent needs in health and other policy areas were only one factor in this relationship. Strategic recalculations of the potential value of the League in the early 1930s, in terms of Soviet security interests, were crucial. These in practice guaranteed acceptance of the obligation to take part in Geneva's economic and social policy activities.

After 1945 the Soviet attitude was more positive. Moscow insisted that the international security objectives of the UN itself were paramount, but took a flexibly compartmentalised view of developments across the growing UN system. An enthusiastic supporter of its creation, the Soviet Union joined the WHO in 1948. Its participation ceased temporarily the following year. The WHO became a victim of Moscow's foreign-policy objective of resolving the issue of Chinese representation in the UN in the communists' favour. Expanding boycotts of UN bodies by the socialist states over this question proved unsuccessful and were later reversed. The Soviet Union rejoined the ILO in 1954 and the WHO in 1957. In the case of the ILO, membership was defended partly on the grounds that the organisation was no longer connected with the defunct League of Nations and had the status of an autonomous UN agency. Apart from the significant exceptions of the FAO and the Bretton Woods institutions, Moscow thus emerged from the late 1950s as an active member of a wide range of specialised bodies in the UN system.

Even so a skeptical wariness persisted. Participation had constantly to be justified. The cultivation of links with the growing number of developing countries in these institutions remained a powerful motivation, especially given the competitive presence of the US and, from the early 1970s, of China. The theme of the Soviet Union's role as the protector of small nations, developed in relation to the Security Council, was held to apply equally well in the technical agencies. Unlike capitalist states the Soviet Union understood the 'democratic principles of international cooperation' based on equality, reciprocity and noninterference in the internal affairs of states.[9] Participation by the socialist states, further, meant that it was possible for organisations such as the WHO to make decisions, despite the vacillations (*kolebaniia*) of the secretariat and Western member-states.[10]

Suspicion of the FAO lasted throughout the life of the Soviet Union. The roots of Soviet discontent with the organisation lay in the 1940s, when the US was accused of using the FAO to strengthen its position in the world and boost its exports. Despite occasional acknowledgement of its useful aid and technical-assistance programmes, the FAO was consistently criticised until the mid-1980s as little more than an instrument of powerful capitalist states.[11]

As the UN specialised agencies became increasingly oriented to the tasks of economic development in the Third World, the Soviet Union was forced to confront a tougher dilemma. It could deny the underlying assumptions behind such programmes projected by agency secretariats, and thus risk incurring the anger of G77 delegates; or it could take part in and help fund them, and so by implication concede that responsibility for the economic hardships of developing countries was shared by all of the North, socialist as well as capitalist. Since the noncomparability of socialist and Western countries on this matter was an article of faith,[12] Soviet delegates were often left with little choice but to move in several different directions, both critical and supportive, at the same time.

In each of these bodies, then, the Soviet Union jockeyed for position, in part through raising issues concerned with decision-making procedures or by criticising the alleged inadequacy of the recruitment of Soviet nationals in secretariats or of Soviet representation on executive organs or committees. Secondly, it pursued programme and agenda preferences derived from general foreign-policy orientations or ideological biases. Thirdly, there were selective and varying degrees of Soviet participation, and a mixture of proactive and passively responsive stances, in relation to the technical work carried out by the various organisations. The following sections of the chapter discuss each in turn, with a particular focus on Soviet and Russian Federation activity in the WHO, the ILO and UNEP during the 1980s and early 1990s.

CONFRONTING THE HEGEMON: THE POLITICS OF PARTICIPATION IN THE WHO, THE ILO AND UNEP

The Soviet Union's outlook on the WHO was remarkably stable. A generally supportive posture echoed the attitude towards international health cooperation taken by Moscow in the 1920s. Thus the organisation was valued for its work in combatting disease and promoting international cooperation on health issues. Premier Ryzhkov confirmed in 1988 that the Soviet Union held the work of the WHO 'in high regard' and that it favoured 'the active development of the broadest possible international collaboration in health and medical science'.[13] The WHO was also – and not inconsistently, in the Soviet view – seen as a convenient vehicle in the

UN system for raising foreign-policy questions such as the Arab–Israeli conflict, the situation in southern Africa and arms control.

As one of the organisation's dozen or so 'traditional donors',[14] the Soviet Union became a major voice in the WHO after resuming its seat in 1957. During the 1980s its assessed contribution to the regular budget, including the contributions from the Ukrainian and Byelorussian republics, was around 11 per cent. This amounted to US$28.1 million for 1984, rising to US$37.1 million for 1989.[15] Additional contributions were made, for example to the WHO Global Programme on AIDS in the late 1980s. In view of the nonconvertibility of the rouble, the figures give some indication of the extent of WHO activities – conferences, training workshops, collaborative research programmes – carried out inside the Soviet Union. The range and significance of this technical work will be discussed later.

Moscow's financial stake in the organisation led it to watch developments with a critical accountant's eye. In 1981 the Soviet delegation put itself on record as supporting 'stable budgets, in conjunction with improved efficiency, rational mobilization of resources and improved working methods, instead of increases in the budget'.[16] Despite significant differences among delegations over what these principles meant when translated into practice – for example over the identification of 'obsolete and unproductive' programmes, or over early 1980s plans for a new building at the WHO headquarters in Geneva – Soviet agitation over issues of financial discipline in the late 1970s and early 1980s converged with the increasing criticism being levelled at the WHO by Western delegations. Soviet delegates also made political capital out of the failure of some member-states to pay their budget assessments, and of others to meet payment deadlines. Measures were adopted by the WHO in the second half of the decade to regulate administrative expenditures, and programme budgets were trimmed by successive assemblies. These accomplishments were praised by Professor Denisov in the 1990 session. The WHO was 'applying measures long advocated' by the Soviet Union, including zero real-growth budget targets, selective programme cuts and a variety of in-house economy measures. Even so he still detected 'dissipation of resources on small, not always sufficiently effective, projects'.[17]

Like many other institutions in the UN system, the WHO was the object of Soviet criticism on another ground. The secretariat was held to be functioning ineffectively, and with built-in biases, because of inequitable recruitment practices. The Soviet Union repeatedly complained that only about one-half of its secretariat quota had been filled during the 1960s and 1970s. This amounted to 'political discrimination on the part of a non-political, technical organization'.[18] The strategy adopted by delegations to correct this situation, however, carefully avoided direct attacks on the organisation or its director-general. Instead officials followed the cautious route of initiating or supporting a succession of assembly resolutions calling for readjustments of the secretariat's geographical distribution. Formulae used in the UN were defended as more equitable than those used by the WHO. Attempts were made to rally diplomatic support from the more than 50 countries identified by Soviet delegations in the mid-1980s as being either un- or underrepresented. Continuing growth of the 'overrepresented' group was highlighted.[19]

Although small adjustments were made, the issue remained unresolved. Many staff members had long-term contracts. Historically and constitutionally, the WHO has laid considerable stress on technical expertise in making appointments. By the early 1990s Soviet and Russian Federation delegations were content to raise the question formally, note progress, but in practice to give priority to other matters.[20]

Despite the Soviet projection of its views as reform-minded, some kinds of changes in WHO procedures were politically threatening. Some countries expressed irritation in the 1980s at the lengthiness of assemblies. The issue was in part a veiled attack on 'political' agenda items, and therefore indirectly on the USSR. Yet many of these questions were a crucial part of the Soviet Union's overall approach to the WHO. Thus delegates insisted that health questions were broadly economic and political in character. Many problems arose from conditions inherent in capitalism, or from the residues of colonialism. The role of the state in the provision of health care was argued to be a central question for the WHO, as was the allegedly destructive impact on delivery systems of the activities of multinational pharmaceutical companies in developing countries. Further, it was regarded as incontestable that conflict in southern Africa, or a future nuclear war, had major implications for human health that put these kinds of questions firmly within the mandate of the WHO. Serious negotiations took place in the 1980s on the structure and organisation of assemblies and their committees, but the Soviet Union strenuously resisted proposals that would have had the effect of limiting its ability to focus on wider questions of the political economy of health.

The Soviet Union was also hesitant in the early 1980s about ideas for greater decentralisation of the WHO, which threatened to reduce its capacity to influence events at the centre. Decentralisation had appeal for many countries in light of the organisation's commitment to primary-health-care priorities, and of regional differences of approach to health policy. Regionalism was in any case already a working principle of the WHO. Formally recognised regional groupings had their own memberships, meetings, constitutions, secretariats and programmes. Taken too far, however, this could in the Soviet view seriously impair the unity and workings of the WHO, which was 'a world health army ... struggling against famine, disease and poverty and for social justice...'[21] This unease disappeared during the mid-1980s. In 1992–3 regionalism in the WHO was regarded positively by the Russian Federation as one further means of strengthening Moscow's diplomatic efforts to bridge gaps inside the faltering CIS.

In contrast, 'technical' matters in the ILO from the outset went to the heart of politically explosive questions about the place of organised labour and of private sectors in modern industrial societies. The more the ILO gave evidence of working well, the more its accomplishments raised for Soviet observers the ideological spectre of successful reformism. Failures and setbacks furnished additional proof of the extent of the domination of its structures by capitalist states. The organisation has historically been one of the most conflict-prone in the UN system. It was also one of the main beneficiaries of the Soviet policy shifts of the late 1980s and the subsequent transition to the Russian state.

Soviet suspicion of the ILO died hard. It was dismissed as the 'most conservative organisation in the UN system'.[22] In the context of the controversies over the fate of the Solidarity labour-union movement in Poland in the mid-1980s, which led to that country's withdrawal from the organisation, Soviet commentators claimed that the ILO had shown that it 'serves the interests of only one socio-political system, that of capitalism...'[23]

Central to Soviet objections was the distinctive tripartite structure of member-state representation in the ILO. In accordance with Article 3 of its constitution, each state sent representatives of its government, employers and unions to international labour conferences. After its resumption of membership in 1954 the Soviet Union, like other socialist states, fitted awkwardly into this formula. So, from Moscow's perspective, did Western states. This general constitutional picture thus opened the way for Soviet charges of the double representation of bourgeois interests on Western state delegations, and for Western refusals to recognise Soviet employers or unions as autonomous from state or party structures. The mutual recriminations that resulted had widespread repercussions because of the further division of labour in the ILO along functional lines.

Thus the question of the appropriate extent, and even the legitimacy, of socialist-state participation in the ILO employers' group rumbled ominously from the 1950s to the 1980s. Similar issues of representation permeated the ILO committees on metallurgy, chemistry, textiles and other industrial sectors.[24] Western states were accused of denying Soviet delegates the chairs of key conference committees by apportioning these on a 'political' basis. There were long-standing Soviet complaints, dating back to before its admission in 1934, of Western-state domination of the secretariat. When a Soviet national was appointed as one of the assistant directors-general in 1970, the uproar in the US Congress and its reach for the levers to halt funding were immediate.

On average once a decade or so (in 1964, 1974 and again in the early and mid-1980s), the Soviet Union reignited its campaign for the 'democratisation' of the ILO. The central questions revolved around Soviet representation (through the issue of recognition of the directors of state enterprises) in the employers group and, following the provisions of Article 7 of the ILO constitution, hence on the governing board itself. Structures, Soviet delegates maintained, had consequences. Those in the ILO allowed 'undemocratic methods' to be used 'by certain circles for unseemly political purposes and even in order to interfere in the internal affairs of individual countries'.[25] They allowed Western countries to continue to use the ILO as a base for 'political campaigns' against the socialist states.

These attacks, however, were not taken to the limit of threatened withdrawal. Rather the Soviet position was that 'radical improvements' in the ILO were practicable as well as necessary.[26] The changes were notoriously difficult to achieve. As Kostine noted in 1986, the issue constituted 'the most complex unresolved problem in the reform of the ILO's structures since it touches upon a matter of principle so far as the socialist countries are concerned, namely legal recognition of the legitimate right of representatives of directors of Socialist enterprises to be elected as members of the Employers' Group in the Governing Board'.[27] Efforts to reach a negotiated compromise in the early 1980s centred on a working party on structure. Progress was made on some issues, including the question of nonelected board seats, and the definitions of regions used in geographical distribution formulae. On the major issues, however, the Soviet Union found most Western countries unwilling to budge from their practice of 'flagrant discrimination against socialist industry'. The socialist states also had important reservations about prevailing ILO definitions of 'nongovernmental groups' generally, on the grounds that many in practice represented Western interests and that ILO structures did not therefore correspond to the 'objective realities' of the modern world.[28]

These were not issues that the USSR could credibly present as bearing on the main concerns of developing countries. In fact most of these in the 1980s tended to be in favour of one or other of a variety of compromise positions, in large part as a way to get the question off International Labour Conference agendas. To one (the so-called Briki formula) the Soviet Union was at first cautiously sympathetic, but then changed its view. The issue of recognition of the managers of socialist enterprises took on greater symbolic significance the more that Soviet delegates pressed the issue. A succession of mediation and negotiation efforts proved largely fruitless. Western states resisted suggestions that would undermine the principle of 'group autonomy' in the ILO; the Soviet Union and the socialist states continued to criticise the unrepresentative character of ILO organs vested with decision-making authority.

Change in the USSR led the way out of this impasse. At the 1987 conference the Soviet delegation said that their country now opposed 'stereotyped confrontation' in the UN generally and in the ILO in particular. Further, *perestroika* meant among other things that the managers of enterprises were now showing 'much greater entrepreneurial character'.[29] Signs of change had been evident in the employers' group the previous year, when the latest in a series of compromise packages became the basis for discussion. At the 1988 meetings Kostine declared the problems raised by the issue of directors of socialist enterprises 'solved'.[30]

Economic reform in the Soviet Union in the late 1980s thus cast traditional ILO structures in a much more favourable light. The ILO was increasingly portrayed as an organisation from whose experience Soviet reformers could learn: for example, in the task of creating and reorganising associations of employers through such bodies as the USSR Chamber of Trade and Commerce and the Union of Small State Enterprises, and in the restructuring of labour unions in a more pluralist direction.

In marked contrast to the line adopted for the previous seventy years, at the 1990 International Labour Conference Soviet officials began to talk openly and positively about the 'tripartite spirit of the ILO'.[31] The director-general of the ILO, Michel Hansenne, visited Moscow for high-level meetings in October 1990 amid a flurry of Soviet statements about the value of the ILO's experience to its current ambitious programme of law-drafting; and Gorbachev accepted an invitation to address the 1991 conference.[32] Shortly afterwards Gorbachev defended the changes in a more traditional vocabulary to the World Congress of Trade Unions meetings in Moscow. The Soviet Union was not giving up socialism; but 'We are departing from barrack-room socialism, from the command-bureaucratic system which restricted a person's freedom and restrained his creative abilities'. A now largely unsympathetic audience, the World Federation of Trade Unions continued nonetheless to attack ILO structures and aims in Geneva.[33]

Participation in UNEP during the 1970s and 1980s did not generate these kinds of institutionally debilitating issues. First, UNEP is a funding programme of the UN itself. Any larger questions that had a bearing on

Soviet interests could be raised by Moscow in ECOSOC or in the General Assembly itself. Secondly, the Soviet (and later the Russian Federation) role was institutionalised through its membership of the UNEP Governing Council.[34] Until the 1992 Governing Council meetings the USSR delegation was occasionally supplemented formally by either Byelorussian or Ukrainian delegations or both. Soviet views were also buttressed by other members of the East European group and by CMEA observers. Thirdly, the substantive issues handled by UNEP were for the most part not permeated, as were those of the ILO, by a network of ideological veins. Even during the 1970s and early 1980s, when Soviet perspectives on environmental questions differed sharply from the 'globalist' orientation of the UNEP secretariat and of many Western member-states, much of its detailed programme work was found either unobjectionable or valuable.

The representation issues for Moscow in UNEP, then, tended to be more low-key. Its system of short-term appointments came in for Soviet criticism in the 1980s on the grounds that environmental experts were being too heavily drawn from Western countries.[35] Soviet delegates also questioned the distribution of countries on the intersessional preparatory committee. This body, on which the East European group had three seats out of thirty, was taking an expanding role in the drafting of key Governing Council documentation in the early 1980s.[36] The question largely resolved itself later in the decade. As more states set up permanent missions to UNEP, intersessional exchanges grew. These were further institutionalised by the creation of the Committee of Permanent Representatives, which, through the leadership of its bureau, became the focal point of pre-council agenda-setting and decision-drafting.

THE MENACE OF DE-POLITICISATION

The Soviet strategy of linking the mandate of particular UN agencies with larger issues of political economy or international security was pursued in many institutions. In some cases in the 1980s Soviet delegates were content to make broad pronouncements on the dangers of nuclear war or of an arms race in space. In others, more intense diplomatic campaigns followed. Some organisations thus became testing-grounds for probing the demarcation and vulnerability of the respective boundaries of influence of socialist and Western states. Differing perspectives on international development issues provided the main sources of contention.

Conventional Soviet analyses of the WHO focused on its utility for developing countries. From 1961 the Soviet Union took a series of initiatives designed to commit the WHO to decolonisation and aid programmes. The influx of new states was in turn proclaimed as a direct cause, along with the role of the socialist countries, of the significant progress made by the organisation in the 1960s and 1970s. Similarly the question of the role of the state in health care, a standard theme of Soviet contributions to World Health Assembly debates, created opportunities for productive allusions to be made to the Soviet model.[37] This pattern of redefining the WHO as an instrument of Soviet defence of Third World interests, set early after Moscow's return in the late 1950s, continued in one form or another for the next three decades.

During the 1970s and 1980s the activities of multinational corporations (MNCs) offered prime targets. Not only did MNCs figure prominently in Soviet demonology and in the economic development dilemmas of G77 member-states, they were also central actors in many of the policy-areas addressed by the WHO. Thus Soviet defences of the virtues of African traditional medicine, for example at the 1976 assembly, formed part of a larger critique of the power of pharmaceutical companies.[38] These were major players, too, in the baby-milk-formula debates of the 1980s. It was 'difficult to determine where politics began in such issues', one Soviet delegate observed at the 1981 meetings.[39] The Soviet approach to such questions was to support concerted international action through such means as the International Code of Marketing of Breast-Milk Substitutes, the WHO Committee on Drug Policies, or revision of the codes governing advertising by the pharmaceutical industry. It was acknowledged that some MNCs were eager to collaborate with the WHO (in itself an important goal of many Western delegations), but Soviet delegates questioned their motives for seeking to operate with the organisation's blessing.

Any kind of WHO regulatory strategy was a potential source of concern for companies, especially, of course, if the hands of Soviet officials in Geneva were detectable in their formulation. This was particularly the case when Soviet advocacy went beyond conventional codes of conduct. Soviet delegates argued in 1988, for example, that the WHO should pay much more attention to the testing and licensing of pharmaceutical products, and work eventually towards the international harmonisation of such regulations.[40] On the face of it this could be seen as a basis for IGO–MNC negotiations, since many leading chemical companies and the industry associations were favourably disposed in principle to the goal of harmonisation. However there were marked, and in practice insuperable, differences of approach and substance between the Soviet and the companies' positions on this question. In the early and mid-1980s the Soviet critique extended too into the area of intellectual property. New discoveries in the field of medical technology and drugs should be made widely and quickly available, it was argued. The exclusive and exploitative nature of Western patent laws, however, made these goals unattainable.[41]

Many of these kinds of points were familiar territory for Western development NGOs in the 1980s. While these were not represented directly in the WHO, views critical of MNCs in the health area were occasionally articulated by Western delegations. As a result the gulf between Western and socialist-state positions on such questions was neither absolute nor divisive. The avoidance of intraorganisational conflict over such ideological differences was also reinforced by the constitutional rules and working culture of the WHO. For example, member-state delegations are represented primarily by officials with substantial medical or health science expertise. While this provision includes political appointees, notably ministers of health, it has meant in practice that defence of ideological or general foreign-policy postures has had to be elaborated cautiously within the governing technical framework of discourse.

There was nonetheless ample room in WHO committees and World Health Assemblies for promotion of the Soviet model of health care. Developing countries were the main target audiences. State planning in all sectors helped these countries, Soviet delegates insisted in World Health Assemblies of the early and mid-1980s. This was held to be particularly true of health, where technical questions were inseparable from the wider economic and political contexts in which health services were organised. In 1986 the Soviet Union successfully defended its strategy of airing these larger public health perspectives in the WHO executive board.[42] The direct value of Soviet experience to the Third World, and the importance of the restructuring goals of the NIEO and the CMEA's programme of health to the year 2000, were constant themes. For example, particularly following legislative changes in the USSR in the early 1980s, it was noted that all Soviet citizens were entitled to primary health care (a paramount WHO objective), with special attention being paid to annual check-ups.[43]

The efficacy of these tactics was limited in several ways. First, the Soviet approach to health care was not widely accepted, in either theory or practice, as a viable model by many developing countries. Secondly, Soviet officials were uneasy with the view that appropriate religious aspects of health care should be taken into account in the planning of projects and the delivery of services. This was both WHO conventional wisdom in the 1980s and an approach that found significant support among many G77 delegations. Thirdly, during the 1980s the WHO was increasingly resorting to 'global' phraseologies to characterise world health problems. This matched Third World intuitions, but it clashed sharply with the Soviet view that the important problems were capitalist, not global, in nature, and that the economic recession affecting health-care systems was a (predictable) feature of Western, not socialist, states. Soviet attempts to alter the terminology of documents and resolutions were generally unsuccessful.[44]

The Soviet Union made more progress with other questions that similarly mixed health concerns with foreign-policy goals. Thus Soviet delegates were active on the issues of a WHO role in relation to health problems in Israeli-occupied Arab territories, and the organisation's assistance to liberation forces in Namibia and the Front-Line States (FLS). The momentum of the issue of Palestinian membership of the WHO grew substantially from the mid-1980s. However it was the shifts of Soviet foreign-policy style under Gorbachev in the late 1980s that helped avert a confrontation. The USSR was ready to support any such application, Denisov told the 1989 meetings, but it 'advocates that a non-contentious solution be found... in the interests of maintaining normal international cooperation in the sphere of medicine and public health'. Following study of the question by the director-general, both the US and the Soviet Union came to the 1990 assembly with a view to supporting a compromise position. In addition to pointing out the legal and diplomatic difficulties surrounding the question, the US view was that the WHO should put the issue behind it and return to crucial questions of health care. 'Only through continued rejection of extraneous political issues can WHO continue to be a viable and relevant organisation to meet important global health needs'. The Soviet delegation concurred, putting on record its support of the Palestinian case but declaring itself in favour of a 'decision that avoids confrontation'.[45]

Much more vigorous was the Soviet pursuit earlier in the decade of the question of nuclear war and the risk of proliferation of weapons systems in outer space. The WHO became a major forum for the Soviet antinuclear campaign of the 1980s. Responding at the 1983 assembly to the charge that this was not part of the institution's mandate, one delegate said that it was difficult for him as a physician 'to see how WHO's strategy of health for all by the year 2000 could be implemented without investigating the possible effects of nuclear catastrophe'.[46] Or, as Minister of Health Dr Burenkov put it: '[P]eace and health are inseparable'.[47] Soviet success in securing a place for this issue on Assembly agendas and in resolutions was attributable in large measure to the activities outside the WHO of the Soviet- and US-led NGO, Physicians against Nuclear War. This process led in 1987 to a major report by a WHO committee on the effects of nuclear war on health and health services. After that the issue faded. By the beginning of the 1990s

Soviet references in the WHO to outer space were limited to the context of telecommunications facilities for linking medical centres.[48]

In general the ILO offered more profitable opportunities for pursuing foreign-policy hares. Prolonged attacks on the organisation's rules, goals and susceptibility to Western state control were an integral part of the larger Soviet critique of the ILO's place in a decaying world structure.

First, appeals to 'objective realities' were used as a means of opposing trends inside the ILO. Its wilful ignoring of these realities was a stock theme in Soviet rehearsals of the failings of the ILO: 'Wasting considerable efforts and money on secondary, often minor, programs and projects, the ILO has not in fact tackled the really important problems bound up with the task of ensuring real social progress and genuine social justice'.[49] This strategy involved deflecting Western attacks while countering with fresh charges. Defence of pro-Moscow international labour unions against Western 'insinuations' in the ILO was thus a key weapon, as was the Soviet defence of social and unemployment-insurance programmes against Western state questioning in the early 1980s of their 'allegedly excessive cost'. The ILO secretariat, held to be serving Western interests, was accused of hiding the 'real reason' for unemployment and lack of social services in Western countries, and of failing to acknowledge the fundamental differences between capitalist and socialist countries on these criteria.[50]

Secondly, Soviet delegates also made use of the ILO in the promotion of a variety of specific foreign-policy objectives. As with the WHO, the institution was hitched to the vehicle of disarmament, and in almost identical language (though usually with more simplistic reasoning). The 1986 conference became a base from which the Soviet Union criticised the US Strategic Defense Initiative programme. Earlier, implementation of the ILO's World Employment Programme, dating from 1969, was argued to be 'impossible without considerable progress being made in resolving the problem of disarmament'. In short, '[W]ork and peace are indivisible'.[51] There was a similarly active peace diplomacy in the ILO European regional conferences from the late 1970s.[52]

Soviet delegates continued to interpret their role as guarantors of Third World interests in the ILO. This had a long history. In the early 1960s the USSR had successfully campaigned to alter the constitution, which, in Article 35, had allowed colonial powers not to implement ILO conventions in their territories.[53] Officials devoted considerable energies in the 1970s to the questions of Namibian independence, apartheid (and its dependence on the support of Western countries), and Israel's post-1967 occupation of the West Bank and other Arab territories. In addition the linkage between disarmament and development was stressed during the 1980s. Soviet officials remained solidly in support of a tough sanctions line in the ILO Committee on Apartheid and of the ILO's role in the NIEO, and continued to remind representatives from developing countries of the 'rapacious activities of transnational corporations' on their territories.[54]

The new thinking in the Soviet Union had a profound impact on its position in the ILO. Some signs of change, at first more of style than substance, were evident at the 1987 conference. The fight against unemployment was declared the 'forefront' of ILO work, but the rationale was less ideologically crafted than before. Soviet delegates also claimed to detect progress in the secretariat's orientation to disarmament. By the late 1980s the effects of domestic change on Soviet policies in the organisation were more pronounced. The new thinking was 'fighting its way through the jungle of misunderstanding and prejudice'. The language of capitalist–socialist confrontation died, its place taken by talk of global interdependence, a single world economy, cooperation and mutual learning, and praise for the ILO's ethos and experience.[55] In this altered atmosphere the Soviet instinct to exploit the ILO as one of a range of foreign-policy instruments persisted, but the modalities changed as these were slowly brought into line with Moscow's policy shifts. Thus the 1990 International Labour Conference was used by Moscow to push forward the momentum of its wider diplomatic campaign for an international conference on the Middle East. Delegates were also successful in securing an earlier governing body resolution condemning Israeli actions in May that led to the deaths of Palestinians.[56]

As a relatively new body, UNEP, in contrast, never became a cauldron of Cold War politics. However, partly as a result of Soviet pressures, issues more distant than those conventionally defined by Western states as fitting its environmental mandate regularly intruded into its deliberations.

As in many other UN bodies, a frequent irritant for Soviet representatives in the 1970s was the Chinese presence. Traditional Chinese diatribes against 'social imperialism' were honed into sharp attacks on the Soviet Union over Afghanistan and in relation to the issue of Cambodian representation in the early 1980s. Friction between the two delegations over allegations of the use of chemical and biological weapons in Kampuchea likewise marked UNEP's 'special character' session in 1982.[57] For the most part, however, international forums like UNEP were not conducive to the formation of coalitions favourable to one side or the other in the protracted Sino–Soviet confrontation.

A succession of events during the 1980s ensured the vitality of Middle East issues on UNEP agendas. The Soviet and other delegations successfully secured the launch in 1980 of a programme of Palestinian assistance.

Arab indignation over a proposed Israeli canal linking the Mediterranean and Dead Seas rumbled through meetings of the early and mid-1980s. The project, contended Soviet delegates, was 'not only illegal and violated the legitimate rights of the people of Palestine and Jordan, but would also cause irreparable ecological and economic damage'.[58] Mexico and other developing countries negotiated a number of draft Governing Council decisions on the question. The mixture of environmental and larger political factors lying inextricably at the centre of the issue presented difficult problems for many Western delegations. These were resolved by abstention on key votes by the West Europeans, and by a negative vote in the case of the US, the latter on the grounds that resolutions contained 'political elements' that fell outside the competence of the Council.[59] The Palestinian *intifada* prompted a reinvigorated Soviet diplomatic campaign in UNEP in the late 1980s. This focused on allegations of environmental deterioration in the West Bank, including problems relating to settlements, deforestation, and pollution, as a result of actions by Israeli authorities.[60] The issue produced a broadly similar voting pattern in the UNEP Governing Council.

Iraq's invasion of Kuwait in August 1990 temporarily broke these habits. By coincidence the Governing Council was meeting (in its second special session) on the day of the attack. The Soviet Union joined Western countries in support of a Kuwaiti draft decision condemning Iraq. While the alignment itself was novel in UNEP, Soviet delegates were at least consistent in defending the appropriateness of 'political' issues on environmental agendas. Western delegations, worried that this might be the thin end of an ominous wedge, emphasised the uniqueness of the situation. The EC's position, expressed by Italy, was in general 'to avoid the politicization of UN technical bodies', but the Kuwait case was seen as clearly different and 'exceptionally serious'. This consensus was sustained into the 1991 session, though US–Soviet disagreement surfaced over the inclusion of a reference to arms control in one of the two decisions on the question.[61]

Other Middle East questions, however, revealed the persistence of the more traditional voting pattern of Soviet–Arab alignment, US opposition and European abstention. This occurred, for example, in votes in the early 1990s on Arab-sponsored resolutions on Israeli actions in occupied territories. Strenuous efforts were made to focus on environmental impacts, including the consequences of tree felling and interference with water resources, but the EC view was still that such drafts 'touched on political issues that came within the purview of other forums'.[62]

In the Soviet ranking of issues that could profitably be aired in UNEP, NIEO questions in practice often fell considerably outside its more conventionally defined foreign-policy interests. Similarly, while G77-sponsored draft decisions on the relations between apartheid and the environment were strongly supported, in practice Soviet diplomatic energies tended to be reserved in the 1980s for the Middle East and arms control.

As in the case of the WHO, the last question had a particularly resonant effect within UNEP. The Gulf War in 1991 served as a graphic reminder of the fact that all wars have environmental consequences. UNEP established an interagency task force to respond to the marine, atmospheric and other pollution costs of the war. At its third special session in 1992, the Governing Council called on governments to note 'the urgent need for the rehabilitation of the environmental destruction in the region'.[63]

Nuclear weapons had already put armed conflict firmly on UNEP Governing Council agendas. Western debates of the 1980s about the long-term atmospheric and ecological impacts of a nuclear war – the 'nuclear winter' – made UNEP a logical focus of Soviet disarmament diplomacy. As in the WHO and the ILO, the inseparability thesis was the key for prising open agendas: the environment and peace were indivisible. The fate of international environmental cooperation was held to be clearly contingent on the successful negotiation of an end to the arms race, especially the one that threatened in outer space. UNEP was fertile ground for such arguments, in part because of the diverse responses they elicited. China and the US lobbied to keep such questions out of UNEP and on the agendas of other UN bodies. Some Western countries, however, particularly Sweden, and many G77 delegations, tended to share the view that they did belong within UNEP's mandate, not least because of the likely environmental benefits of the reallocation of government expenditures that would follow in a partially disarmed world. One linkage convention – on the Prohibition of Military or Any Other Hostile Use of Environmental Modification Techniques (1976) – arguably set a precedent for deeper engagement on the part of UNEP in this area.

Soviet efforts were successful in securing a place for these questions in UNEP. For example, the major UNEP statement of 1987 on 'Environmental Perspectives to the Year 2000' bore many of the marks of earlier Soviet arguments about war and the environment, as well as the more recent formulations coming from Moscow about international environmental security. This stated, for example, that a 'comprehensive system of international security' was essential to ensure implementation of the World Charter for Nature. It called for 'progressive disarmament through detente, negotiation, and avoidance of the use of force as a means of resolving conflicts' in order to minimise the environmental impacts of wars.[64] Similarly the executive director's state-of-the-environment report, prepared for the UN Conference on Environment and Development (UNCED) in 1992, incorporated a major section dealing with war and the environment.

TECHNICAL PUZZLES: DIPLOMACY AS PROBLEM-SOLVING

Organisations such as the WHO, the ILO and UNEP were not only used as interchangeable instruments of foreign policy. Soviet, and later Russian, participation in them also exerted a variety of influences over behaviour. The rules of the game in the WHO, for example, put a high premium on technical expertise and rewarded players who made significant contributions to consensually defined technical goals. The Soviet Union was in this sense a loyal and conscientious club member. Even so its role at this level can also be seen in terms of a search for prestige. Soviet accomplishments in the organisation from the late 1950s, including sustained support for the WHO's smallpox and malaria programmes and promotion of primary health-care goals, were often highlighted in Soviet commentaries designed to extract propaganda advantage from these activities.

This duality characterised Soviet participation across a range of WHO programmes. The goal of primary health care, for example, formulated at a landmark conference held in Alma-Ata, set much of the framework of debate in the WHO in the late 1970s and 1980s. It was a goal that was open to differing interpretations. For Soviet delegates in World Health Assemblies it provided a benchmark for the elimination of allegedly wasteful activities and programmes. Among other things, this criterion was defined in terms of an emphasis on applied research designed explicitly with a view to implementing the WHO's health-care objectives. The goal of primary health care also implied 'the introduction of progressive social and economic changes in many countries, involving the establishment of state-run health systems'. Setbacks were attributed to the absence of such changes and to a reliance on 'dehumanising' Western medical approaches. In these, because of specialisation, the doctor tended to be 'remote from the patient, who was regarded merely as a collection of different organs, and not as a complete human being'.[65] Primary health-care goals also fitted conveniently into traditional Soviet preoccupations in the WHO, particularly workers' health issues.

A combination of its own and developing countries' interests served to define Soviet programme priorities. In most cases these were in line with slowly evolving WHO concerns, for example with malaria and diarrhoea. Soviet delegates supported activities related to these diseases, occasionally injecting suggestions for a differing emphasis: for more research on malaria in the WHO's tropical-disease research programme, health education in relation to diarrhoeal diseases or blindness-prevention programmes in developing countries.[66]

Other questions were of more immediate concern to Soviet health professionals. Cancer was consistently a high priority – reflected in Soviet participation in the International Agency for Research on Cancer (IARC) – as was attention to cardiovascular problems. From the early 1980s there was growing interest in the WHO's potential in relation to alcohol- and drug-dependency problems. This interest predated the leadership changes in Moscow in 1985, but was reinforced later by Gorbachev's own anti-alcohol campaign. These subjects were joined later by support for the WHO's mounting attention in the mid-1980s to problems of tobacco and health. Technical and educational materials from the WHO on smoking were used extensively by state agencies and news media in the Soviet Union in the late 1980s, particularly in connection with the WHO-sponsored world no-smoking days.[67] The efficacy of this campaign was limited. At the end of the decade tobacco in the Soviet Union was not so much a health issue as one of shortage of cigarette supply as a result of disruptions caused by the upheavals in Eastern Europe.

From 1987 officials were eager to show that the new thinking in Moscow was producing a readiness to acknowledge problems and a willingness to engage in multilateral cooperation to tackle them. At the 1987 assembly the Soviet delegation gave full support to the organisation's leadership role in relation to AIDS, reversing its earlier and more hesitant position that this question should be treated separately from other communicable diseases. Financial contributions were given to the WHO Global Programme on AIDS, and in the early 1990s delegates took a lead in raising the question of a possible international convention on its prevention and control.[68] The WHO was also closely involved with the work coordinated by the International Atomic Energy Agency from late 1989, with active Soviet cooperation, on continuing health effects related to the Chernobyl nuclear accident.[69] Similarly Soviet conversion to the cause of international environmentalism in the late 1980s strengthened interest in related areas of the WHO's work. Here, though, there is more evidence of continuity with concerns of the early 1980s. Officials at that time were likewise energetic in promoting activities such as the International Programme of Chemical Safety (run jointly by the WHO, the ILO and UNEP), and the investigation of problems of pesticide residues and other environmental contaminants in foods (a collaborative enterprise between the WHO and the FAO).

Finally, central to the Soviet role in the WHO was an extensive structure of multilateral collaboration on health problems, largely at the laboratory or research-institute level. Typical activities during the 1980s included the storage of stocks of particular viruses, as elements of world networks monitored through the WHO or the Centers for Disease Control in Atlanta; donations of smallpox vaccine for the emergency reserve maintained by the WHO; the organisation of training courses for public-health administrators in the WHO European region; and research projects, many in collaboration with foreign institutes, on questions such as occupational exposure to hazardous chemicals or breast cancer mortality.[70]

The ILO was less amenable to these kinds of cooperative endeavours. Institutionally it has tended to be more geared towards the production of international conventions. It was not until the late 1980s that political awareness of the weaknesses and changing requirements of the Soviet economy produced a marked shift in Moscow's outlook on the ILO. The setting of international standards by the ILO continued nonetheless before and after this change, and Soviet officials took an active part in the ILO committee and conference work upon which it was based.

Ideologically, however, the Soviet Union was resistant to the idea, attributed to capitalist circles, that the ILO should restrict itself to 'the purely technical aspects of social and labour issues'.[71] The convention-making role of the ILO was viewed as constructive, though, especially where agreements had some chance of fostering change in Western countries. The ideological objection that such tasks might thus feed a process of incremental reform and social conciliation, rather than dialectical change, in capitalism did not in practice constrain this activity. The Soviet Union's limited faith in the value of the ILO's convention work was diminished, however, when attention focused, as it did in the early and mid-1980s, on the downstream tasks of implementation and monitoring.

Soviet complaints about the ILO's monitoring machinery were closely tied to long-standing grievances about the organisation's structure. This machinery, little changed since its creation in the 1920s, had by 1983 become 'frozen with conservatism'.[72] At best the ILO bodies merely noted reports of violations by Western countries, officials charged, for example, in connection with the rights of labour unions. The organisation itself then did nothing in response. The way out of this 'standard-setting crisis', in the Soviet view, was through the 'democratisation' of the ILO supervisory bodies whose job it was to monitor observance of conventions by signatory-states. The USSR refused, however, to take part in the work of a committee set up by the ILO governing board to look into these and related questions, citing in justification its limited composition (the absence of directors of socialist enterprises) and its limited mandate.[73] Tension on this question was exacerbated by the ILO's handling of the Polish question in

1984–5, which was generating angry Soviet charges of interference in that country's internal affairs.

The 1987 International Labour Conference marked a turning-point. Kostine announced that the Soviet Union was ready to 'continue to make our contribution to improving multilateral cooperation within the ILO ... and we are ready if required to correct our attitude'.[74] Concerns were still voiced about the supervision of international standards, but the Soviet approach became steadily more conciliatory in the late 1980s as more pressing issues arose. Attempts to restructure a variety of Soviet enterprises, and to develop different kinds of tripartite consultative and other mechanisms linking government with unions and the slowly emerging employers' associations, led inexorably to greater Soviet enthusiasm to benefit from the ILO's experience, especially in view of union confrontations with the government in the strikes of 1989 and 1990.[75] Draft laws on employment, for example, and on the settlement of labour disputes, were designed following consultations between Soviet officials and ILO experts. In this changing context the role of the informal economy, the theme of the 1991 conference, was not only directly relevant to the Russian and Ukrainian situations, but was accepted as a legitimate topic for debate by the Soviet Union.

Despite the heated confrontations between Western and socialist-state delegations, then, the ILO continued during the 1980s with its main tasks of finalising conventions. Historically many had come out of the ILO process with regulatory provisions that made them unpalatable to some Western countries, particularly the US. In many cases the influence of the socialist states on the convention-making process was one factor making for US reluctance either to sign or to take steps that would serve to legitimise a collective ILO role in monitoring progress. While this in turn spurred indignant Soviet charges of US–ILO collusion in blocking implementation, Moscow had its own reasons for resisting or reinterpreting the provisions of some conventions, particularly where these touched on ideologically sensitive matters such as an individual's right not to join a labour union.

The Soviet Union nonetheless had a respectable record in the ratification of ILO conventions: 40 out of a total of 130 in the period from its resumption of membership in 1954 to 1970, for example, a number substantially lower than those for many West European countries but several times higher than that for the US.[76] Work was successfully completed during the 1980s on about 20 conventions, on matters as diverse as occupational safety and health, conditions relating to the termination of employment, vocational rehabilitation of disabled persons, asbestos, seafarers' welfare, indigenous and tribal peoples, night work, and working conditions in hotels and restaurants.[77]

Though absent from the Stockholm conference of 1972 that had led to its formation, the Soviet Union during the 1970s and 1980s was a strong supporter of the work of UNEP. This work included the data-collection tasks of Infoterra and specialist bodies such as the International Registry of Potentially Toxic Chemicals, the encouragement of international environmental conventions (for example, on migratory species, the ozone layer, global warming and biodiversity), the coordination of worldwide pollution-monitoring networks, the promotion of regional cooperation (particularly in relation to regional seas), and collaboration with other UN bodies (for example on chemical safety and the hazards of nuclear wastes). Such activities tended to raise few if any ideological problems. Many could also be viewed positively by the USSR as an offshoot of international scientific cooperation. When in the late 1980s the Soviet Union raised global environmental issues to the status of high-urgency politics, it was thus able to point to UNEP's backlog of fifteen years of experience as one of the cornerstones upon which a new order could be built.

Before those changes, however, some UNEP activities were judged more skeptically. The Soviet Union objected, for example, to some of the language used to describe issues at the special session held in Nairobi in 1982 on the tenth anniversary of the Stockholm conference. In line with the prevailing Soviet critique of Western globalist thought, the delegation denied that mankind was threatened with environmental catastrophe. It took a cautious view at that time of the emerging ozone-layer issue, arguing that firm evidence of deterioration had not been scientifically established. Soviet officials also registered concern that the globally ambitious thinking of the UNEP secretariat on issues of sustainable development and the mobilisation of the UN system for environmental protection could 'result in the unjustified broadening of the UNEP mandate'.[78]

As in other institutions, the USSR had its own programme preferences. To some extent the work of UNEP was viewed through the regional lens of European environmental cooperation. This took two forms. First, UNEP and the CMEA had a cooperation agreement which entered into force in 1979. Soviet cooperation with other socialist states on environmental questions was regularly highlighted by the official CMEA observer delegation in meetings of the UNEP Governing Council.[79] Secondly, the Soviet Union was an active supporter of wider East–West cooperation within the framework of the UN Economic Commission for Europe (ECE). While this took on new significance in the context of Gorbachev's promotion of the concept of international environmental security, the initiative dates back to

Brezhnev, who raised it in late 1975 in the wake of the Conference on Security and Cooperation in Europe.[80] The Soviet move was followed by vigorous diplomacy and the successful launch of the ECE's high-level meeting, which took the lead role in the development of the important ECE transboundary pollution convention of 1979.

Among other traditional UNEP concerns, the Soviet Union consistently put a heavy stress on environmental education. Indeed the key event in the area was a conference held in Tbilisi in 1978, largely on the basis of growing collaboration between UNEP and UNESCO. Following exchanges with other countries, particularly Egypt, Britain and the Philippines, the Soviet Union revived the flagging momentum of this work in 1985 in both institutions, calling environmental education and training 'one of the more important and successful areas of the environment programme'.[81] The organisation of environmental training workshops on Soviet territory was one element of a larger picture of scientific and technical meetings held there in part because of rouble nonconvertibility. A major instance was the Soviet hosting of the first World Congress on Biosphere Reserves, arising out of UNESCO's 'Man and the Biosphere' programme, in Minsk in 1985. Central to this continuing activity was Soviet interest in the administration and further expansion of UNEP's Infoterra network. In 1987 Ukraine (still then part of the USSR, but increasingly with its own tentative scientific and environmental links with European developments) called in UNEP for a strengthening of data-gathering and dissemination work in this area.

After 1987 Soviet interest in international environmental issues underwent a qualitative change. As in the mid-1980s, more effective cooperation was urged among relevant bodies, particularly UNEP, the WHO, the ILO and UNESCO. Now, however, the importance of environmental questions was endorsed at high political levels. These questions were redefined as central to the international security agenda. Further, many of the ideological barriers distancing the Soviet Union from Western and IGO concepts of globalism were broken down. Soviet initiatives – for example Gorbachev's proposal that the UN should establish a centre capable of responding to environmental crises, or that it try to negotiate a 'code of ecological conduct' binding on states – became the subject of formal and informal discussion at UNEP Governing Council sessions in Nairobi. The eventual openness of Soviet authorities about the Chernobyl nuclear accident, and active Soviet collaboration with international agencies in the International Chernobyl Project from 1989, were major indications of this change.

Soviet officials also worked more actively within the UNEP Governing Council's increasingly characteristic ad-hoc small-group framework, as well as in consultations through the committee of permanent representatives, on key issues: with Canada, Switzerland and Britain, for example, to prepare the 1989 draft decision on global climate change, and with Belgium, France, Malawi and Sweden on thc 1991 draft decision on regional activities of the International Geosphere–Biosphere Programme (IGBP).[82] Soviet and Russian Federation participation in the planning for UNCED in 1992 thus followed its by then firmly established pattern of engaging actively in multilateral environmental diplomacy. At the conference itself and in preparatory meetings, officials focused on questions of institutional change and development, especially the proposed establishment of a high-level intergovernmental commission on sustainable development.[83]

The Russian Federation from early 1992 thus turned its back on many aspects of the traditional Soviet style in technical IGOs. Gone was the combative element, the ever-present watchful readiness to engage in battle with the foes of socialism. Yet despite their protestations to the contrary, Russian officials were heirs of the upheavals of the Gorbachev years. The changes of the late 1980s, though, had been more often and more explicitly accompanied, because of their novelty and the postbipolar circumstances of the time, by clarifying rationales: that the relations of states should be deideologised, that the urgent common problems facing humankind necessitated active cooperation through UN agencies, that there had been errors in the Soviet manner of dealing with IGOs in the past. There was also a significant measure of continuity in responses to substantive questions on agency agendas between the two periods. Moreover, after 1992 Russia did not give up the right to raise 'political' issues in technical forums, or to support G77 delegations in their bids to restructure agendas. Indeed at one level a solid commitment to technical cooperation had been a feature of Soviet UN diplomacy since the late 1950s, though this was tempered for the next three decades by the overarching priority attached to the state of East–West bipolar relations.

5 Beyond Common Security: Russia, the UN and Conflict Resolution

Although Moscow's attitude towards global international institutions has lurched from time to time between hostility and a guarded welcome, at no time has it made a substantial investment in them as guarantors of Soviet or Russian security. Other mechanisms, national and regional, have performed that function. The UN has nonetheless been taken seriously on occasions as a constructive aid to great powers in the performance of their responsibilities, and the nuanced pursuit of their multiple interests, in relation to local and regional conflicts. This conception of IGOs as extensions of the nineteenth-century concert approach reemerged in Soviet responses to the UN in the 1960s, and was an important element in the new thinking of the late 1980s. The present chapter looks first at the Soviet Union's earlier views of the UN's role in light of its interpretations of the charter model of collective security, using the Middle East as an example, and then focuses on trends in Moscow's approaches to regional conflicts during the Gorbachev period and in the early 1990s.

INEVITABILITY OF THE STATE: THE COLLECTIVE SECURITY MODEL

The transition to the Russian Federation at the end of 1991 was characterised in the UN by significant continuities from the past. Both the Soviet Union and its 'continuer-state' had a commitment to deeper integration in the international economic system, including membership of the major economic and financial institutions. Both insisted, or just quietly assumed, that great-power status in the Security Council, with the full constitutional trappings of veto power, was their due. In the early 1990s, as in the early 1950s, Russian theory and practice in the UN rested on a core group of crucial beliefs about the role and responsibilities of great powers in relation to international conflict. Taking part in UN deliberations was one component in the larger project of securing the country's external environment in such a way that domestic goals could be more effectively pursued. Membership of the Security Council permanent elite was consistently viewed during the Soviet period as one of the pillars of the USSR's legitimacy in the international system and, especially in the 1960s and 1970s, as a concrete expression of the international community's recognition of the Soviet Union as a coequal with the US in high-level deliberations on war and peace.

In the late 1980s and early 1990s, however, continuities were far less evident than the drama of rapid change. From an earlier posture varying between studied caution and occasionally overt hostility, Moscow became one of the UN's most enthusiastic and vociferous supporters. This declaratory commitment was limited in practice in various ways: by the sometimes contradictory goals inherent in the larger project of renovating, and then rescuing, socialism in the case of Gorbachev, and, under Yeltsin, by a pluralist dynamic of domestic argument in which the government's pro-Western and pro-UN stance was itself a contentious and central feature. Although Russian officials in 1992 were quick to criticise the timidity of the old regime's approach to the UN system, in practice they inherited and made their own many of its chief characteristics.

These included support of peacekeeping operations by UN forces and a zest for debating multilaterally ideas for their future development. In its final few years the USSR ejected the suspicions of the past. It advocated the establishment of permanent standby forces under Security Council control, supported a proactive role by the UN secretary-general, talked of UN naval peacekeeping forces, and, in 1990, speculated about the use of UN monitoring teams to supervise independence referenda in the Union republics. Russian Federation support in 1992–3 for the idea of UN forces playing a more active role in the international protection of human rights, and receptiveness to the possible need for active UN intervention in intra-CIS conflicts (though in the context of a leading Russian role) was a natural extension of this reasoning.

Lying behind the transformation was a partially unresolved tension between two broad and differing orientations towards the UN's peace and security role. Corresponding roughly to the mandate definitions and underlying assumptions of Chapters VI and VII of the UN charter, the two are not mutually inconsistent. They tend to lead, however, to contrasting expectations on the part of states and other actors, different levels and types of commitments, and divergent views about the nature of conflict.

The formal *collective security model* dominated much of the bipolar Soviet period. Chapter VII defined for Moscow a set of guidelines for the appropriate collective responses of the international community to acts of aggression. In this statecentric model the security interests of the Soviet state, which included legitimisation of the requirement of idiosyncratic evaluations of the facts of aggression in particular cases, were further protected by the rules governing the distribution of power in the Security Council. The model also provided criteria for assessing the effectiveness of the UN and a basis for judging the actions of others.

From the mid-1980s this approach increasingly merged and overlapped with a *conflict resolution model* of the UN's role. The prevention, containment and mediation of conflicts were important elements. UN peacekeeping operations, a traditional target of Soviet criticism, were an integral part of this approach. The intellectual and policy struggle in the Soviet Union that led to broad acceptance of UN peacekeeping forces implied an investment of faith in their traditional rationales: that the positioning of a UN military presence between parties to a conflict could be a useful means of averting fresh outbreaks of local wars, assisting in the maintenance of cease-fire agreements and preventing the competitive political, and perhaps military, intrusion of great powers. The absence of the use of force, except in carefully defined and exceptional circumstances, distinguished conventional peacekeeping operations from Chapter VII actions. In the late 1980s Soviet analyses built on this conceptual foundation and explored and filled gaps in it, particularly in the areas of the UN's role in fact-finding, dispute settlement and mediation.

The UN's first Chapter VII military operation since Korea was launched while the Soviet Union was still engaged in this process. Soviet support for the Security Council's authorisation of the use of force against Iraq in 1990–1 was consistent with its earlier advocacy of a strengthened UN and a resuscitation of the defunct Military Staff Committee. The military success of coalition forces was viewed in Moscow as a vindication of this position. In addition, the lessons it drew from earlier situations in which a UN non-military presence was involved – the withdrawal of Soviet forces from Afghanistan, for example, and supervision of the Namibian independence process – tended to point towards the need for a more varied repertoire of response mechanisms on the part of states and IGOs.

In this more complex late and post-Cold-War environment, traditional Soviet thinking about the security roles of the UN had limited relevance. This reflected an intellectual heritage dating back to the early 1930s. The Soviet Union had eventually come to view the League of Nations in a cautiously positive light. Its premembership campaigns for world disarmament were replaced from late 1933 with a more realistic, if still inflated, assessment of the League's potential. There followed a pragmatic search for steps to revive the waning collective security aspirations of the organisation in the face of the succession of threats from Italy, Japan and Germany.

In view of the failure of the League of Nations, and even more of its decision in 1939 to expel the Soviet Union, the UN had a structure more acceptable to Moscow. This was underpinned by a strengthened version of the theory of collective security on which the League had been partially based. The combination of the provisions of Chapter VII of the UN Charter, the principle of great-power unanimity in the Security Council, and the binding character of council decisions on member-states, together held out for the Soviet Union the prospect of a marginally more secure external environment than was the case under the League of Nations – or than would have been true if the UN itself had failed to materialise. Further, this statecentric model, with its emphasis on the sovereign equality of states in IGOs, could with little difficulty be reconciled with conventional Soviet class analyses of the nature of the international system.

Much of the Soviet outlook on UN security structures remained largely unchanged into the early Gorbachev period. Defence of the charter model continued to be a stock feature of Soviet commentary. Digressions, particularly in the form of peacekeeping ventures, were routinely denounced. In the Security Council in early 1986, Ambassador Safronchuk attacked Western notions of the UN, particularly globalist variants, as little more than a justification for hegemonistic policies. Following positions confirmed at the twenty-seventh CPSU Congress shortly afterwards, Soviet officials in UN bodies continued to target imperialism as the chief threat to the security of nations and 'the fundamental reason for conflicts that have broken out in various parts of the world'.[1]

The alternative conceptions increasingly evident during the second half of 1986 were still carefully integrated with conventional Soviet wisdom, but began to point in significantly different directions. Elaborations of the idea of common security focused on the interdependence of the security concerns of states in a nuclear age. '[N]one of us can make provision for his own security without considering and weighting the security of others', Deputy Foreign Minister Adamichin told a UN symposium in Florence at the end of 1986.[2] The Soviet approach in the General Assembly at this time was to promote acceptance of the need for a 'global system' of peace and security. This incorporated proposals for the destruction of nuclear arsenals by 2000, the prevention of the spread of weapons to space, a complete ban on nuclear-weapons tests, a ban on the development of new weapons of mass destruction and the outlawing of chemical weapons, and a reduction of conventional weapons, all to be achieved through international controls.

This approach contained loud echoes from the past. The equation of peace-building with heroic initiatives was a traditional feature of Soviet UN diplomacy. So too was a heavy emphasis on issues of disarmament and arms control (and proposals in this area that carefully safeguarded Soviet interests), often at the expense of serious evaluation of other, arguably more realistic, instruments at the disposal of the UN. Gorbachev's 1987 article on the UN, his speech to the General Assembly the following year, and the succession of proposals for the reform and strengthening of the UN peace and security system, nonetheless indicated that more radical change was envisioned.

At the 1992 Security Council summit, Yeltsin was thus able to reiterate the main points of an approach already well charted by his predecessor. This centred on support for the UN's peackeeping role, mediation in intenational conflicts, a spirit of multilateralism and compromise, and cooperation on international peace and security issues in the UN with Russia's 'ally', the US.[3] Russian Federation commentaries seized on opportunities presented by the UN to explore a variety of possible uses of UN mediators, monitoring teams or peacekeeping forces. These included conflicts on the territories of the former USSR: 'Why not try to employ international mediation, in view of the fact that we are unable to extinguish the flames of enmity on our own?'[4] Russian officials raised the possibility of 'international police forces' protecting human rights at the UN Human Rights Commission in Geneva.[5]

Support for the UN was in a sense an obligatory part of the pro-Western package of foreign-policy ideas carried to the Kremlin by the new leadership. The zeal brought to this task, however, reminiscent in some respects of the early days of League of Nations membership, went beyond what was required for reassuring Western audiences about the depth of Moscow's commitment to domestic reform. Nor was the stance judicious in relation to Russian opinion. Allegations of a meek deference to international organisations, and of a failure to stand up for Russian interests, became prized weapons in the armouries of a variety of nationalist critics of the government in the early 1990s. In retaining and building on the core elements of the UN posture passed on by its predecessor, the new Russia was continuing to act in an old tradition: groping, in a changing world of uncertain futures, for the least implausible ways to improve the security environment beyond its borders.

To set these policy changes in historical context, this chapter looks first at evolving patterns of Soviet thinking on the UN, with particular reference to the record in the Middle East.[6] This record highlights recurrent themes of traditional Soviet responses to the UN's involvement in regional conflicts: first, an abiding suspicion of the concept and practice of peacekeeping by UN forces; and second, a spirited resistance to the idea of other UN organs, particularly the General Assembly and the secretary-general, sharing a significant role in international peace and security matters with the Security Council. Both stands were essentially defensive reactions to prevailing UN moods in the period from the mid-1950s to the mid-1980s. Each, however, was subject to modification when circumstances and interests dictated.

THE MODEL CHALLENGED: THE CASE OF PEACEKEEPING IN THE MIDDLE EAST

The Soviet Union's responses to the emergence of UN peacekeeping forces cannot, of course, be separated from consideration of its national interests, both in preserving existing UN structures and in relation to specific regional conflicts. Soviet interests in the Middle East varied between the 1940s and the early 1980s, but were defined in the context of underlying continuities. The Soviet Union was quick to recognise Israel, surrounded as it was alleged to be by the threatening presence of colonial powers, and combined this in the late 1940s with a measure of ideological antipathy to the Arab League. Identification with left-wing nationalist Arab regimes nonetheless became a longer-term feature of Soviet policy, as did ideologically grounded attacks on Israel and the support it enjoyed from the US.

This strategy, which entailed a search for partners to help secure a lasting Soviet presence in the region, had mixed results. Egypt, for example, grew restless with the relationship and rejected the Soviet link in the 1970s, and Iraq turned its back on its ally by invading Kuwait in 1990. Soviet arms transfers to the region often had hidden costs, including a tarnishing of the image of statesmanlike credibility required of a great-power facilitator of regional peace settlements. Similarly, declaratory and substantive support for the Palestine Liberation Organisation (PLO) repeatedly threatened to involve Moscow in interfactional Palestinian disputes that bore little relation to either ideological or strategic conceptions of Soviet interests in the region.

Yet underlying continuities were also apparent. From the early 1920s the Soviet Union had steadily expanded its range of diplomatic links and economic relations beyond a core area centring on Afghanistan, Iran and Turkey.[7] When the question of Palestine entered the agendas of the UN in the 1940s, the Soviet Union thus already had a strong basis from which to assert its claim, constantly reiterated in subsequent decades, to a right to participate in shaping the affairs of the region. As its ambassador told the UN Security Council shortly before the 1967 Arab–Israeli war, the Soviet Union 'proceeds from the fact that the maintenance of peace and security in the area directly adjacent to the Soviet borders touches upon the vital interests of the Soviet peoples.... [It] will continue to do everything in its power to prevent a violation of peace and security in the Near East'.[8]

This Soviet definition of its stake in the region was reinforced by events: the need for continued alertness to developments in its south-west border regions; the emergence of Islam as a political and ideological force that had significant transnational implications for central Asian regions of the USSR; the importance of Middle East oil;[9] strategic and political competition with the US; and, not least, the proven success of Israel as a regional military power, together with its capability to influence US security policies.

The UN eventually became an essential adjunct of Soviet approaches to the region's affairs. In turn the Soviet Union's participation in UN debates on Middle East questions also helped to shape its attitudes towards the organisation more generally. Moscow cast three main roles for itself: (a) as a powerful defender of Arab interests, (b) as an international guarantor whose role was indispensable for any lasting settlement of the Arab–Israeli conflict and (c) as a Middle East actor in its own right. However, its capacity to influence, let alone control, events was limited. In part it was the victim of a larger trend of the erosion of super-power influence in relation to regional conflicts.[10] But in addition to the constraints imposed on any external state, the Soviet Union had to battle against limitations of its own making. It was, as Chubin put it, 'unattractive as an economic model, limited as a technological partner, unacceptable as an atheistic state, and undependable as a military ally'.[11]

Soviet responses to the Arab–Israeli wars of 1948, 1956 and 1967 offer useful indications of its early outlook on the role of the UN. At the time of the 1948 war the UN was a newcomer to international politics. Although it was engaged on the ground in the region in a variety of ways, the innovative concept of UN peacekeeping – in the sense of the despatch of a UN force to a conflict that threatened to spark competitive great-power interventions – still lay some eight years in the future. Attempts to breathe life into Chapter VII of the UN charter, for example through the negotiations anticipated in Article 43 on the creation of a permanent UN force, had fallen prey to the Cold War. In these circumstances the Soviet response to the war was to support the call for a ceasefire, particularly since Israeli vulnerability was more apparent in the early stages of hostilities. Soviet officials also tried to move the locus of debate in the Security Council away from Chapter VI and more towards the enforcement measures set down in Chapter VII. However the Soviet Union then abstained on the key ceasefire resolution, possibly because by then the military situation had altered and the resolution was seen as too likely to benefit the Arab states.[12]

By the time of the Suez crisis in 1956 the blend of Soviet interests in the Middle East had shifted. The potential of Arab nationalism to act as a restraint on Western states in the region had become more evident. The UN had also changed. It had authorised the use of force in a major operation, Korea, and – through the 'Uniting for Peace' resolution of 1950 – had, illegally in the Soviet view, extended the competence of the General Assembly in areas of peace and security. Even so Soviet delegates found the objectionable 1950 resolution a useful procedural device in the circumstances created by French and British use of the veto in the Security Council in 1956.[13] The Soviet Union did not, however, oppose creation of the UN Emergency Force (UNEF). It pointed out that Egypt had consented to the presence of the force on its territory, and it argued that UNEF might be a device that could prevent further aggression. Soviet officials repeatedly charged, however, that the creation of the force was contrary to the UN charter. The charter set out clearly the procedures for the use of force by the UN, and these provisions, it was argued, gave the Security Council exclusive competence in such matters. Soviet officials rejected the idea that the UN secretary-general had any authority to make decisions on the composition of the force, and refused to make financial contributions to its upkeep. Since the situation had arisen as a result of the attacks by Britain, France and Israel against Egypt, it was 'reasonable and fair if the cost of maintaining the Force were borne by the States responsible for the aggression'.[14]

The Soviet approach in the UN to the 1967 war combined denunciation of Israel with a search for diplomatic accommodation. Both in public sessions and private exchanges, officials urged Security Council condemnation of Israel – initially on the grounds of aggression and later for its refusal to comply with Security Council calls for a ceasefire. Soviet commentary and academic analysis portrayed the Israeli attack as an instrument of Western schemes for dominance in the region.[15] Searching for consensus on key Security Council resolutions while simultaneously maintaining staunch support of Arab states taxed Soviet diplomatic resources. This multifaceted strategy was essential, nonetheless, for preserving the Soviet goal of being counted as a crucial player in all international developments concerning the Middle East.

It also implied a readiness to accept a role for the General Assembly. While the Security Council remained, for Moscow, the ultimate UN decision-maker in security affairs, the advantages of the General Assembly, as a court of world opinion, were appealing. The Soviet initiative skirted around the 1950 resolution, and simply noted Article 11 of the charter, which gives the General Assembly competence to discuss an issue of peace and security provided the Security Council itself is not doing so. The Soviet Union supported the crucial Security Council resolutions, particularly Resolutions 240 and 242 (on maintenance of the ceasefire and on Israeli withdrawal from occupied Arab territories). Delegates also incorporated within statements of the need for a political settlement of the Arab–Israeli conflict an endorsement of the 'inalienable right of all the States of the Middle East, including Israel, to an independent national existence'.[16] They remained sensitive to intra-UN jurisdictional issues. For example, officials insisted that the secretary-general's proposal to extend the UN observer group in the Suez Canal area was a matter for the Security Council itself to decide.

FROM NEW THINKING TO NEW STATES: CHANGING VIEWS OF REGIONAL CONFLICTS

As these early Soviet responses to the UN's evolving role indicate, defence of the charter model did not prevent the Soviet Union from making active use of the UN as an adjunct of great-power diplomacy, especially in an age of détente. A strategy of accommodation with Western states on the Security Council was one strand of larger diplomatic efforts, and one that was compatible with long-established Soviet views about the character of IGOs in a world of sovereign states. So long as the UN fitted into this context it could be viewed as playing a useful role, albeit in the final analysis still a relatively minor one. Even if not directly valuable, UN bodies could be useful forums for the patient construction of political atmospheres receptive to Soviet disarmament initiatives, or for lobbying that reminded developing countries of the dangers of consorting with Western states. When the UN strayed from this path, Soviet alarm bells rang. Its errors fell into two closely related categories: the habit of indulging in peacekeeping operations, which constituted unwelcome and illegal departures from charter principles; and the toleration of de facto shifts in the roles and relationships of UN organs.

The changes of outlook that became increasingly evident from mid-1986 produced policy reversals on both counts. Even so elements of the old core of beliefs remained. The Soviet Union, and later the Russian Federation, continued to see the UN primarily through the durable lens of a permanent member of the Security Council. Embracing the idea and the reality of UN peacekeeping and acknowledging the need for a measure of creative autonomy on the part of the UN secretary general did not in practice signify a major departure from Moscow's prevailing conservative definition of the limits of desirable institutional change. Both policy shifts and ingrained fears of change can be seen in Soviet and Russian Federation responses to the regional conflicts of the 1980s and early 1990s.

While the Middle East continued as a staple of Security Council agendas throughout this period, it was in relation to issues in southern Africa that the new thinking of the Gorbachev period first confronted real tests in the UN. The policy mix of the early 1980s continued. This combined denunciation of the US and other Western powers for support of the South African apartheid regime, advocacy of sanctions, UN assistance to liberation groups and the FLS, and a commitment to the independence of Namibia. However this package was increasingly grounded in the case for serious political negotiations in the region with UN help. Gorbachev drew broad strategic goals from the logic of conflict avoidance in a nuclear age. The Soviet Union 'opposes turning Africa into an arena for confrontation of any sort, not to mention military confrontation'.[17] Officials and academic analysts increasingly maintained that neither Moscow nor Washington had any vital interests to protect in the region, and that these circumstances should be exploited to bring about a lasting settlement of southern African issues.

The different threads were evident in Soviet approaches to southern African questions in the Security Council in 1986–7. Condemning Pretoria for its internal policies, occupation of Namibia and aggression against neighbouring states, Ambassador Safronchuk maintained that support for South Africa's actions in the region had 'but a single source, namely the same Western Powers that have been affording Pretoria direct protection and shielding that regime from the application of effective sanctions against it under Chapter VII of the Charter'.[18] The US policy of dialogue, or constructive engagement, with Pretoria was similarly criticised as an element of Western states' 'exhortation and persuasion and trifling with the racist regime'.[19]

The Soviet Union's own involvement in the region, including the indirect relationship through Cuban forces in Angola, was initially maintained by Gorbachev. Occasional incidents – as in June 1986, when two Soviet merchant ships in the port of Namibe in Angola were damaged as a result of South African incursions – were not portrayed as threatening to the Soviet–American relations.

The possibility of superpower confrontation in the region was further diminished in two ways. First, increasing Soviet emphasis was placed on the need to reduce tensions in southern Africa by 'political means'. This included, though clearly did not stop at, the renunciation by Pretoria of 'state terrorism' and interference in the internal affairs of other states. Secondly,

UN options were increasingly evaluated in the context of regional efforts. In another case, that of Chad in late 1986, Soviet deference to regional sensitivities, together with the older aim of fostering an anti-Western alignment, led Moscow to back the OAU position of opposing UN interference.[20] On southern Africa, Soviet delegates insisted that the UN did have various roles to play, but they were increasingly attentive to political efforts by regional organisations in southern Africa, such as the FLS, as well as to views expressed through the OAU and the Nonaligned Movement.

In a letter to UN Secretary-General Perez de Cuellar in January 1987, Gorbachev outlined a set of goals for the UN in southern Africa. These centred on the independence of Namibia, abolition of apartheid in South Africa, comprehensive mandatory sanctions by the Security Council and support for the FLS.[21] Soviet delegates called for more specific steps, such as the repeal of the state of emergency in South Africa and the release of political detainees. Significant areas of convergence thus emerged with the thinking of Western states, for example with the common positions developed by EC member-states in the General Assembly.[22] These became more apparent as the UN came to focus in the late 1980s on the independence process in Namibia.

The substance of Soviet support for this process grew easily out of its past support for the South-West African People's Organisation (SWAPO). Its style, however, owed more to the stress placed by the new thinking on negotiated settlements, the deideologising of disputes and the UN's role in conflict resolution. In Havana in April 1989 Gorbachev confirmed Soviet support for the Namibian independence agreements and the readiness of the Soviet Union to participate actively in implementing them. In line with traditional Soviet approaches, the Security Council was also used during 1989 to highlight the concerns of small countries, for example about incidents of harrassment of SWAPO supporters and the continuing activities of South African counterinsurgency personnel in Namibia. The success of the UN – 'the result of international joint action based on new political thinking'[23] – was thus held to vindicate Soviet participation in UNTAG, and also to send a clear message to UN member-states on other issues that even complex international problems were amenable to political and diplomatic resolution.

These kinds of lessons, when applied to the more unstable Middle East situation, reinforced the general trend of Soviet UN policy in the late 1980s. The differences between the two situations, however, and between the Soviet stake in each of them, created a need for a more diverse and more cautious approach. The air of proactive multilateralist detachment cultivated for use in southern Africa had limited viability in a volatile region close to the Soviet Union's own borders. In the Middle East as in southern Africa, nonetheless, a more 'balanced' approach – the favoured Soviet terminology of the late 1980s – was pursued.[24] This came to imply the requirement of Soviet diplomatic relations with Israel, in part as a means to the end of convening an international conference on the Arab–Israeli conflict. In May 1991 the new approach produced the first visit of a Soviet foreign minister to Israel. It also led in the same year to Soviet support for the General Assembly's formal abrogation of its earlier resolution condemning Zionism as a form of racism.

The bulk of the diplomatic work directed towards these goals took place outside the UN. The UN was nonetheless important for Soviet officials, not least for facilitating the display of pro-Arab credentials. Thus Washington was consistently blamed for the absence of a settlement in the region. It was 'crystal clear', Belongov stated at the end of 1986, 'that were it not for the military, political and financial support of the US, the Government of Israel would be acting in a completely different way, and the Security Council would have no need to consider the situation in the Middle East over and over again'.[25]

From the second half of 1987, however, attention shifted back to the Soviet call for an international conference on the Middle East. The idea had surfaced periodically in Soviet–American discussions in the 1970s. The campaign rapidly gathered momentum throughout the UN system in the late 1980s. Meetings of UN technical bodies and specialised agencies were harnessed to the task of building a broad international base of support for the idea. The Soviet objective was defined in December 1987 as a Middle East settlement 'on a just and lasting basis, taking into account the interests and rights of all States and peoples of that region'.[26]

The proposal, for a conference that would include the PLO and Israel and the five permanent members of the UN Security Council, received a significant push forward as a result of Shevardnadze's Middle East tour of February 1989, though it also became clear that Arab governments' interest was distinctly cool in some places and far from universal. Gorbachev's visit to Paris in July prompted renewed Soviet optimism that the question was now essentially one of timing.[27] The following May Vorontsov told the Security Council (at its session held in Geneva because of the impasse over the invitation to Yasser Arafat to come to a meeting in New York) that the 'political basis' for a Middle East settlement existed. He cited among other things the readiness of the PLO to talk with Israeli officials at an international conference, the 'broad support' for such a conference on the part of the international community, and the 'realistic position' adopted by the Palestinian National Council.[28]

While the Madrid conference thus represented the accomplishment of an important Soviet goal, the complex and occasionally disrupted process of Arab–Israeli–Palestinian talks that followed in the early 1990s indicated the elusiveness of significant mutual accommodation among the main parties to the conflict. A stream of issues was generated in the UN by Israel's occupation of Arab territories (including questions of Israeli settlements on the West Bank and responses to the Palestinian *intifada* from the late 1980s), actions arising from Israel's continuing preoccupation with its security interests in southern Lebanon, its adherence to traditional restrictions on discourse with Palestinian groups and its responses to domestic problems, such as the forced expulsion of a group of Palestinians in December 1992.

Except at the level of general principle, the Soviet search for a more 'balanced' approach to Middle East issues in the UN did not extend to giving equivalent weight to specific Israeli security concerns, for example about terrorism, Lebanese turbulence or the political risks of sustained encounters with PLO representatives prior to Palestinian de facto recognition of the state of Israel. Soviet delegates kept up pressure on the Security Council and other UN bodies to ensure continued attention to the issue of post-1967 Israeli-occupied territories and activities in the Israel–Lebanon border regions. In view of the obligations of the new thinking, however, and the simultaneous pursuit of a framework for a wider Middle East peace process, this was done in the late 1980s with greater restraint and tact than was the case earlier. For example, when the Security Council 'regrettably' had to meet in early 1988 to discuss the Israeli military presence in Lebanon, Belongov went to considerable lengths to emphasise that this was not because member-states wished to make Israel 'a scapegoat for the faults of others' or because they 'harbour[ed] a desire to express any prejudice regarding that country'.[29] In parallel with Arab delegates, Soviet officials resorted increasingly to international law – a succession of ignored Security Council resolutions, and arguments concerning the obligations in international law of occupying powers – to criticise both the Israeli presence and its activities in the occupied territories.

In relation to the Arab–Israeli conflict, the UN thus served a number of purposes for the Soviet Union in the second half of the 1980s. The political weight attached to moral condemnations of Israeli actions by IGOs might be minimal, but the alignments these efforts fostered had wider value for the USSR both inside and outside the UN. More important for the Soviet Union was the catalytic role played by the UN in relation to its overarching foreign-policy objectives of the period, particularly the convening of the Madrid conference and the subsequent peace process. Recognition of the utility of the UN as a respectful attendant of great-power deliberations thus marked a significant element of diplomatic continuity between the early Brezhnev and the Gorbachev periods. In the USSR's place on the Security Council in 1992, the Russian Federation set a course of continuity with the policies of the recent past: supporting the Madrid process, attaching a high priority to the Palestinian question at the UN, urging restraint on all parties and criticising specific Israeli actions held to have a deleterious impact on progress towards a lasting settlement.[30]

Iraq's invasion of Kuwait in August 1990, and the evolution of the UN's response from sanctions to the authorisation of the use of force, posed crucial tests for the altered Soviet perspective. While the situation could be accommodated comfortably within the framework of Soviet thinking about the UN in the late 1980s, the dusting off and actual use of provisions at the heart of Chapter VII of the charter created policy dilemmas for which Moscow was unprepared. Such steps as the resuscitation of the MSC had by this time become a standard feature of Soviet proposals on the future of the UN. In practice, however, regional conflicts facing the Security Council in the second half of the 1980s were often approached in a somewhat different manner by Soviet delegates. The characteristic reflex was to urge restraint, negotiation and compromise rather than a resort to coercive diplomacy. Contemplating the collective authorisation of the use of force settled uneasily within this evolving policy framework.

The Security Council's early condemnation of Iraq, and the legitimising of a naval blockade and economic embargo, were nonetheless viewed by Soviet analysts both as appropriate responses to aggression and also as evidence that the long-predicted renaissance of the UN was at last under way. However, these were interpreted as steps that would more likely avert than precede resort to force by the UN. As two authors observed later in 1990, the UN's 'prompt and determined action has largely cushioned the impact of the crisis, prevented it escalating uncontrolled in the opening stages and focussed all efforts on the search for a political solution to the critical situation'.[31] Soviet officials persisted at critical junctures with efforts to keep lines of communication open with Baghdad, and to argue the case in the UN for more time to be allowed for economic sanctions and diplomatic overtures to produce results. For example, in October Vorontsov delayed passage of the Security Council resolution demanding compensation from Iraq, and in November urged postponement of the deadline legitimising the use of force.[32] This general approach continued in early 1991,[33] and remained during and in the wake of military operations by coalition forces.

The fact of aggression and the elimination of a sovereign member-state of the UN could not be ignored. Soviet advocacy in the autumn of 1990 of a negotiated outcome was combined with a rejection of the Iraqi tactic of claiming a negotiating linkage between the Kuwait situation and that presented by Israeli occupation of Arab territories (though the need for a broader Middle East settlement was still defended by Moscow on other grounds). Yet condemnation of Iraqi actions and support for sanctions did not render the Chapter VII option of the collective use of force by the Soviet Union and its Cold War adversaries any more palatable. In these circumstances maintaining dialogue with Iraq was described as lying at one end of a spectrum; at the other end lay 'an invisible and ill-defined red line which we could not cross [just] because of our allegiance to our just-found new political philosophy'.[34] Internal Soviet debate about the validity of UN measures, and criticism from military personnel and others of the coalition forces' interpretation of Security Council resolutions, thus marked the early part of 1991.[35]

The military campaign against Iraqi forces fell considerably short of a full Chapter VII operation of the kind Soviet observers had earlier speculated about. Though the use of force was authorised by the Security Council, that body did not then, by means of the MSC, control the conduct of the war. Lack of use of the committee, and the delegation by the Security Council of its powers in practice to the US, formed an early complaint by Soviet critics of Gulf developments in September 1990. Nor did the UN already have at its disposal forces contributed by member-states as a result of agreements concluded through the committee. The composition of coalition forces, though broadly based, was not even loosely representative of the international community; two of the five permanent members of the Security Council did not participate (and one of them, China, had abstained on the use-of-force resolution). In practice, too, countries had disparate interests in responding to the disruption of oil supplies from the Gulf entailed by Iraq's actions.

Soviet commentary observed a similar pattern after the war. For example the Kurdish refugee aid effort in northern Iraq took shape more as a US-led multilateral effort than one coordinated through existing UN relief agencies; international proposals for postwar assistance to the region, while implying a supportive role for UN bodies, tended to focus on multilateral frameworks outside the UN;[36] and the UN-sanctioned air-exclusion zone over southern Iraq, designed later to protect Shi'ia communities from aerial bombardment, was enforced by Western states. In 1992–3 Russian officials became more open in their criticism of UN policies, particularly on sanctions. The government was also increasingly under fire at home from conservative snipers angered at Moscow's refusal to reverse its earlier betrayal of its friends in Baghdad.

The Soviet Union nonetheless followed up its support for the UN by continuing to urge Iraq to comply with Security Council resolutions. Russia did the same in 1992–3, adding a commitment to defend the United Arab Emirates against aggression and despatching two warships to the Gulf.[37] Further, the outcome of the Gulf War weakened, if only temporarily, the case of Soviet critics who had in late 1990 and early 1991 tried to rein in the growing force of the government's pro-Western inclinations in the UN. For Vorontsov at least, in the Security Council in March 1991, the experience warranted enthusiasm: 'For the first time the international community showed its united will in the face of the seizure of one State by another and was able to bring the aggressor to heel. Although this precedent may be imperfect, we should like to believe that it can prevent the emergence in the future of similar situations which are not in keeping with the new era of peaceful policy which, however difficult, is now emerging'.[38] The Soviet role in persisting with the search for a political settlement, a senior officer of the Central Committee's international department wrote at about the same time, had not led to failure; rather, awareness of Soviet views was one of the chief factors that had prevented the US from taking the war into Baghdad.[39]

Even in the spring of 1991, however, appreciation of the special features of the Kuwait situation tempered such assessments. The UN's response seemed to offer proof of the capacity of great-power unanimity on the Security Council to produce constructive results – a Soviet theme as old as the UN itself. In other ways, however, the nature of the problem the UN had faced constrained the fluent transfer of lessons to other contexts. This was a classic instance of aggression and territorial aggrandisement, a clear-cut violation of the principle of the sovereign equality of states. In the more murkily ambiguous situations in which the UN seemed increasingly likely to be involved in the post-Cold War era, there was no guarantee that such simple conditions would apply. Nor could there be any assurance that Soviet, or Russian, interests would necessarily be served in such situations by a comparable process of accommodation among the permanent members of the Security Council.

The Soviet Union's pro-UN posture arose naturally in a post-Afghanistan world of contracting Soviet interests and progressive disentanglement. It was reinforced both by the continuing logic of the US–Soviet nuclear and arms-control relationship and by the pro-Western alignment inherent in the pursuit of domestic economic restructuring goals. In some situations facing the UN, the growing detachment of Soviet concerns fostered reflex support for multilateral engagement, particularly where a possible alternative might have been an unregulated Western presence. In

1990, for example, the Soviet Union argued strongly for an extension of the UN force in Cyprus (UNFICYP). The work of the secretary-general in preparing a framework for progress towards a settlement was praised, and the grumbles of Western powers about the funding of a seemingly endless commitment were dismissed as distractions.[40] Moscow likewise endorsed UN activities in other regions, such as the observer group (ONUCA) in Nicaragua following agreements on the demobilisation of Contra forces in that country,[41] and the continuing UN role in El Salvador.

In the case of Yugoslavia, however, more immediate Russian interests were involved. The break-up of the country and escalating violence among its contending ethnic groups threatened the stability that had marked the political transformation of Eastern Europe. Russians also had historic Slav ethnic links with the area, particularly with Serbian communities. The problems of Yugoslavia showed 'how dangerous is the growth of separatism and national extremism, not only for each individual country, but also for entire regions', and that 'as the Cold War recedes into the past, problems and conflicts of a different kind crop up, even in Europe'.[42] Especially in late 1992 and early 1993, the prospect of spreading warfare in south-Eastern Europe gave this situation for Moscow a qualitatively different sense of urgency from others facing the UN.

Thus the Soviet Union and then Russia supported efforts through the UN secretary-general, as well as those of the EC and attempts through the CSCE process – adding its own bilateral 'friendly appeals' to the parties – to contain armed conflict and promote the chances of a set of politically negotiated settlements. The Russian Federation participated actively in the London conference of August 1992 and the foreign ministers' meeting in Geneva in December.[43] This larger diplomatic process incorporated support for, and close engagement in the task of making, the sequence of related Security Council resolutions of 1991–3 on an arms embargo, calls for a halt to the fighting in Bosnia-Hercegovina, economic sanctions, humanitarian aid, the declaration of an air exclusion zone over Bosnia (and the later decision to authorise its enforcement) and the investigation of violations of human rights in the former Yugoslavia.

Even so there was growing evidence of Russian unease during the second half of 1992 and early 1993 about the mounting anti-Serbian colouring of Western opinion, and concern that the UN might inexorably be forged at some point into a blunt instrument for propagating a one-sided view of the situation – especially in light of attacks on UNPROFOR personnel. Joint actions in the Security Council, Yeltsin observed, were 'not always easy'. It was 'psychologically difficult for us to adopt the decision [on sanctions] on Yugoslavia. It would be easier to abstain, but we voted together with other civilised states...'[44] In the swiftly deteriorating conditions of spring 1993, Russian delegates obtained the postponement of the Security Council vote on tighter sanctions by threatening use of the veto; they also blocked authorisation to bomb airfields in the no-fly-zone enforcement resolution. Throughout this period Russia argued the need for the Bosnian Serb viewpoint to be considered by Western delegations with an open mind. The foreign ministry criticised moves that could be seen as implying the isolation of Yugoslavia, or Serbia, from international organisations, especially the UN itself, as 'counterproductive'.[45]

CONSERVATISM IN PURSUIT OF CHANGE: THE POLITICS OF UN REFORM

The period from 1986–8 was marked by ceaseless Soviet meditation on the future of the UN. Later developments – the terminal stages of the Cold War, the success of the war in the Gulf, the dissolution of the Warsaw Pact, the need to respond doctrinally to US talk of a 'new world order', the continued institutionalisation of CSCE processes, the disintegration of the USSR itself with a clutch of ethnic conflicts and small wars in its wake, and the violent collapse of Yugoslavia amid a bundle of other threats from East- and South-East-European nationalisms – all in various ways conspired to keep the UN near the centre of Moscow's attention in the late 1980s and early 1990s. As these questions came closer to home, Russia sought ways to effect closer links between UN and regional processes, particularly through the CSCE framework. In UN debates delegates nonetheless avoided committing themselves to a radical overhaul of the system.

Even when the pace of change became more pronounced in mid-1987, much of the new Soviet approach to the UN continued to echo the style and rhetoric of the 1970s calls for a restructuring of international relations. Deputy Foreign Minister Petrovsky told the UN General Assembly's First Committee in October 1987 that the world was at a crossroads; 'new, bold approaches and unorthodox methods' were required. The UN had a role to play, but only if its members changed it: it could 'function effectively and meaningfully only when it breathes the oxygen of confidence'.[46] Much of the strenuous Soviet diplomatic effort to focus minds on the issue of change was channelled in two traditional directions: the use of the UN, first, to reinforce arms control negotiations being carried on beyond its auspices, and, second, to encourage conceptual innovation along lines more receptive to Soviet theorising about problems of war and peace.

The first of these was reflected in promotion of Gorbachev's proposals for the elimination of nuclear weapons by the end of the century. It also induced growing frustration with protracted UN processes, though the organisation's work of data-gathering through the Institute for Disarmament Research was generally praised. In 1990 the Conference on Disarmament was criticised as too slow, too prone to discussions of 'little relevance' to the real world and, in short, 'in need of intensive therapy'.[47] The second approach called for elaborations of the common security elements of the new thinking. This centred on proposals (for example by Shevardnadze at the 1987 UN General Assembly) for the building of a comprehensive system of international security and the development of distinctively Soviet interpretations of the concept of a new world order.

Such responses tended to imply only limited scope for acceptable institutional change, particularly in the central security structures of the UN. In Japan in June 1991 Petrovsky reacted coolly to suggestions for changes to the composition of the Security Council and deletion of the charter's outdated 'enemy' provisions (in Articles 53 and 107): 'It would be very dangerous to start changing the UN Charter because the world has entered a period of changes, and these changes are very deep'.[48] Proceeding from this conservative posture – that in normal times there was no need to consider change, and in turbulent times it was too risky to do so – the Soviet argument about revitalisation of the UN tended to be cast in terms of the renovation of existing, but nonfunctioning or ineffectual, structures, such as the Military Staff Committee, and the refinement of proven techniques, such as peacekeeping or data-gathering.

Other than in the details, this strategy was on the face of it little different from the periodic attention to questions of UN reform characteristic of the Brezhnev years. Then, too, the Soviet Union had been attracted to a conception of the UN as a launching pad for grand pronouncements on international security, progress towards a peaceful world and the peaceful settlement of international disputes. A desire to make use of the UN to protect the Soviet Union's position as a great power was also common to both periods. As Kozyrev argued in a 1990 article, the Security Council could make a contribution to the stabilisation of areas of regional tension; and, at the same time, 'an opportunity is being created for the Soviet Union to preserve and strengthen its status and influence as a great power in the world community through political means at less expense'. As before, defence of the charter model remained key to Soviet approaches. The strengthening of global and regional security structures required a central role for the Security Council, Petrovsky wrote in 1990. Moreover, 'Under the new conditions the right of veto is acquiring a positive character and serving as a telling argument in favour of the achievement of unity among the members of the Council'.[49]

The new approaches differed nonetheless in several ways. First, the theoretical assumptions about the international system and the nature of war from which they were derived were undergoing radical change. A second difference lay in the political will not only to invest substantial diplomatic energy in the pursuit of proposals, but also to make accommodations as a result of exchanges with other states. In this regard the consensus-seeking informal discussions surrounding Security Council sessions were taking on much greater importance in the late 1980s. Thirdly, a reluctance to give serious consideration to structural change did not deter Soviet officials from engaging in innovative thinking about the instruments already available to the UN for dealing with armed conflicts: for example, the good offices of the secretary-general, observation groups or peacekeeping forces. Finally, the new thinking appreciated the need for an active role for other organs of the UN, and particularly for the General Assembly to become a more effective partner of the Security Council on matters of international peace and security. The last theme, however, was not taken to a point of convergence with G77 views; the proviso of final Security Council authority was built into Russian as it was into earlier Soviet pronouncements.

Of these issues, it was the Soviet focus on peacekeeping that was most characteristic of the transformed atmospherics of UN meetings in the late 1980s. The predominantly noncoercive peacekeeping role devised from the creation of UNEF in 1956 had its origins in a variety of intermediary practices inherited from the UN's first decade and from the more limited repertoire of the League of Nations. The Soviet Union quickly shed its former hostility to these mechanisms. Some ideas appear to have been put forward not so much as realistic initiatives, but more as devices to implant discussion of peacekeeping options more firmly on UN and other multilateral agendas. An example is Shevardnadze's proposal in 1988 for the permanent members of the Security Council to establish a UN naval peacekeeping force.

Various proposals were put foward by the Soviet Union in the UN Special Committee on Peacekeeping Operations, for example in discussions of Secretary General Perez de Cuellar's 1989 report on the UN's peacekeeping role. Some flowed from a catholic interpretation of Article 39, which gives authority to the Security Council to determine 'the existence of any threat to the peace, breach of the peace, or act of aggression'. This charter provision was used by the Soviet Union as a broad constitutional canvas on which to speculate on the deployment by the UN of policing units or other forces in relation to a wide variety of issues: drug trafficking, terrorism, nuclear piracy and shipping safety, as well as the stationing of observation posts in areas of regional tension.[50] Officials responded positively to ideas to enhance the capability of the UN to respond to conflicts, including the proposal for the establishment of an international training centre for peacekeeping personnel. Other Soviet proposals were patterned on the thinking underlying Chapter VII, particularly the concept of permanent UN standby forces and a pivotal role in peacetime as well as in the conduct of military operations for the MSC.

The Russian Federation stayed close to this line. First, the post-Cold-War requirement of a strengthened UN, particularly one with an effective peacekeeping arm, was declared an important objective of Russian foreign policy. Yeltsin told the January 1992 Security Council summit that Russia was 'prepared to continue partnership between the permanent members of the Security Council'. Russian diplomacy would aim to contribute to the 'final settlement of conflicts' in various regions. Moreover, 'We are prepared to play a practical role in UN peacekeeping operations and contribute to their logistical support'. He echoed other delegations' support for the idea of a 'special rapid-response mechanism' at the disposal of the Security Council, and referred to the international protection of human rights as 'our top priority'.[51] The last point was becoming an increasingly important focus of Russian analyses of international security questions, particularly in view of the issue of ethnic Russian minority rights in the Baltic states and other parts of the former USSR.

And secondly, the new government maintained much of the skeptical outlook of its predecessor on questions of institutional reform. Yeltsin conceded at the Security Council summit that some parts of the UN were no longer relevant, and that 'We should do away with those structures which yield no practical benefit to Member States'.[52] In practice this view was less a plea for dismantling and reconstruction and more the product of earlier Soviet criticisms of duplication among UN bodies, lack of effective coordination among them and inadequate concern on the part of the secretariat for the budgetary implications of programmes. More radical institutional reform issues were aired by several states in the charter committee in 1992–3. These included elimination of the charter's 'enemy state' references, expansion of the Security Council (for example with a view to the inclusion of Japan, Germany and India as permanent members), and a revision of the rules governing use of the veto power.[53] When such questions were raised Russia usually responded cautiously, as Soviet officials had done earlier, with a defence of the newfound effectiveness of the UN under its existing charter – its role in the Gulf War, for example, and its potential value in relation to problems of terrorism, ecological emergencies and the drug trade.

In 1988 the General Assembly's committee on the UN charter completed work on a draft declaration, adopted shortly afterwards by the General Assembly, on the 'prevention and removal of disputes and situations which may threaten international peace and security'. Supporting this development, the Soviet Union later used it as part of its case for a general international convention on the peaceful settlement of disputes. These developments were partly a response to the preparation by the secretary-general, as a result of resolutions of the 1984 General Assembly, of a *Handbook on the Peaceful Settlement of Disputes between States*. This major document was completed in 1991. In 1989 and in subsequent committee sessions Soviet delegates focused on ways to improve the UN's fact-finding role in relation to international conflicts, following a set of proposals submitted by Czechoslovakia and the German Democratic Republic. This work culminated in the adoption by the 1991 General Assembly of a Declaration on Fact-Finding by the United Nations. Soviet delegates also took an active interest in the charter committee in the issue of 'rationalisation' of the UN's procedures in relation to international disputes, particularly with regard to the effectiveness of the General Assembly and the question of monitoring compliance with UN declarations and resolutions.[54]

The Soviet Union also attempted to reorient the long-term agenda of the charter committee around its own interpretations of the security requirements of a post-Cold-War world. This was done through a working paper, based in part on informal consultations with the US and other delegations, introduced at the 1990 meetings and discussed by the committee the following year.[55] In it the Soviet Union called, among other things, for a broadening of the secretary-general's role through such devices as the 'more frequent exercise' of Article 99 (which defines the secretary-general's right to bring matters to the attention of the Security Council), and the more regular submission of information to the Security Council on conflicts. It also raised the question of enforcement actions vis-à-vis a state 'that has breached the peace or failed to comply with Security Council decisions'.

Two broad areas received increasing attention from Moscow: the anticipation and prevention of armed conflicts, and the strengthening of the connections between regional and UN response mechanisms. On the first, the delegation highlighted 'potentially explosive situations ... caused by internal socio-economic and other factors', the mediatory functions of the secretary-general, and the possible formation under UN auspices of 'an extensive network for monitoring, collecting and processing information on the situation in areas of conflict'.

Secondly, in a renewed emphasis on Chapter VIII of the charter, the Soviet Union identified a need for expanding cooperation between the UN and regional organisations, and enhanced recognition of regionalism as an approach to conflict resolution.[56] The Soviet notion of the Security Council, or just its permanent members, acting as 'guarantors' of regional security settlements was part of this approach. As officials elaborated the proposal at the 1991 session, member-states of regional organisations should 'make every effort to achieve pacific settlement of local disputes' through these before referring issues to the Security Council. For its part the Security Council should 'where appropriate, utilise regional organisations for enforcement action under its authority,' and no such actions should be undertaken without its authorisation.[57] As armed conflicts spread in the former Soviet Union, the Russian government turned increasingly to the concept of UN recognition of its 'special responsibility' in the area. Yeltsin called in early 1993 for 'special powers' to be granted to Russia by the UN to permit it to act as a guarantor of regional stability.

These various charter themes were also taken up, with little substantive change, by the Russian Federation. It submitted revised versions of the Soviet Union's 'New Issues' paper to the 1992 and 1993 committee sessions. Delegates argued that the changes that had occurred since its original drafting in 1990 made all the more urgent the need to enhance the effectiveness of the UN. Russia also prepared a draft declaration on improving cooperation between the UN and regional organisations. Like earlier Soviet efforts, this attempted to link the key objectives of promoting enhanced regionalism, particularly with an eye to CSCE processes, with a global framework in which an essentially unaltered Security Council still held centre stage. A variety of regional instruments were put forward for consideration: regional peacekeeping forces, police units, and military and civilian observers. Their potential functions were as diverse: for example, fact-finding, separating combatants, monitoring cease-fires, and even 'maintaining law and order in the event of the outbreak of disorder and confrontations on ethnic, national or religious grounds...'[58] A similar range of ideas was aired in discussions at the Helsinki summit in July 1992.

Advocacy of these roles was a natural corollary of the Russian Federation's campaign in a number of UN bodies, springing from the problems of ethnic minorities in ex-Soviet republics, to legitimise the principle of international intervention under the banner of the protection of human rights. Qualified as they were by ambiguous criteria, for example that intervention in such cases be undertaken by invitation of 'the Government recognized as legitimate by the regional organization',[59] the Russian proposals provoked sharp criticism from other delegates. Some developing countries, already uneasy with the apparent readiness of permanent members of the Security Council to use that body's charter powers to the full in the regional conflicts of the 1990s, were concerned that such developments would weaken still further the legal barriers to great-power intervention in the internal affairs of states.

These debates of the early 1990s are significant as indications of the transformation of Moscow's thinking on the UN in the period since 1986. Traditionally a tireless defender of the principle of the sovereignty of states in the UN, it now sometimes seemed more attracted to a latter-day version of the Brezhnev concept of limited sovereignty as a basis for legitimising intervention in its neighbours' affairs. Old-style opposition to peace-keeping and other forms of UN meddling had already been swept away by Gorbachev. The UN itself was embraced as a crucially important institution for steering a post-Cold-War international system through the treacherous waters of sub-national strife.

Even in its reduced economic circumstances, however, and despite the constricted range of its foreign-policy concerns, Russia in the 1990s was clearly not set on a course of disinterested peacemaking. It had vital interests in both Europe and the Middle East. In the final analysis, its Security Council veto still guaranteed protection from UN interference in sensitive areas of its external relations.

Part II
China

RUSSIA
MONGOLIA
HEILONGJIANG
Harbin
JILIN
Changcun
LIAONING
Shenyang
NORTH KOREA
SOUTH KOREA
Urumqi
XINJIANG UYGUR AUTONOMOUS REGION
GANGSU
NEI MONGGOL AUTONOMOUS REGION
NINGXIA HUI A.R.
Huhhot
Beijing
Tianjin
HEBEI
Yinchuan
Taiyuan
SHANXI
SHAANXI
Xining
QINGHAI
Lanzhou
Jinan
SHANDUNG
Zhengzhou
HENAN
Xian
JIANGSU
Hefei
Nanjing
ANHUI
Shanghai
Hangzhou
ZHEJIANG
XIZANG AUTONOMOUS REGION
NEPAL
SIKKIM
Lhasa
BHUTAN
SICHUAN
Chengdu
Chongqing
HUBEI
Wuhan
Nanchang
JIANGXI
Changsa
HUNAN
GUIZHOU
Guiyang
INDIA
Dacca
Kunming
YUNNAN
GUANGXI ZHUANG A.R.
Nanning
Canton
GUANGDONG
FUJIAN
Fuzhou
Taipei
TAIWAN (Republic of China)
BANGLADESH
BURMA
Hanoi
Hong Kong (Br)
Chankiang
Hainan Island
LAOS
Vientiane
Rangoon
BAY OF BENGAL
THAILAND
Bangkok
VIETNAM
CAMBODIA (Kampuchea)
Phnom Penh
SOUTH CHINA SEA
Manila
PHILIPPINES
INDIAN OCEAN
Kuala Lumpur
MALAYSIA
INDONESIA
Djakarta
CHINA AND SOUTHEAST ASIA

6 From Periphery to Pole: China and Multilateralism

China's early experiences with twentieth-century international institutions elicited little enthusiasm for multilateral ventures. The League of Nations' failure to check Japanese aggression in the early 1930s and from 1937 could not be said to have undermined Chinese expectations about collective security, since there had been little faith in the reliability of that body in the first place. The Treaty of Versailles had, in Chinese eyes, legitimised violations of Chinese sovereignty in the case of the former German area of Shantung. China nonetheless became a member of the League. The unexpected absence of the United States, however, then further restricted any hopes that may have been pinned onto the organisation by the Chinese authorities.

While in contrast, both nationalists and communists emerged from the Second World War with a measure of guarded optimism about the future United Nations, the People's Republic that was created four years later was in effect barred from participation in the UN by the United States until this policy finally crumbled in 1971. That decade gave Beijing a practical base of experience of UN affairs. China's stake in the UN system was consolidated and grew steadily during the 1980s and early 1990s. The historical, economic and foreign policy contexts of this course of events are the focus of the present chapter.

LEAGUES OF ROBBERS: HISTORICAL PERSPECTIVES ON INTERNATIONAL ORGANISATION

Though occasionally elected to terms on the League of Nations council, China remained a marginal voice in Geneva. China was a problem for the League, a troublesome item on several of its agendas. It was neither a source of constructive institution-building nor a recognised player in the balance-of-power games of the interwar years. Lacking an effective national government, scarred by continuing internal turbulence and the impacts of a lengthy period of foreign intervention, and weighed down by a chronically weak economy and a vast population, China was clearly not a great power. Indeed only with difficulty could it be fitted into conventional

European definitions of a state. Although its government was sometimes able to exploit the weakened postwar position of the countries that retained a stake in Chinese affairs, in the final analysis China did not have the attributes that would have made it acceptable to the European powers as a member of the international community.[1]

The weakness of Qing officials in the face of the foreign encroachments that had gathered force from the mid-nineteenth century was the most salient political and psychological fact for both nationalist and communist Chinese. The remnants of China's 'semi-colonial' past, including the extraterritorial authority exercised by foreign governments in defined jurisdictions in China, were still present in the 1920s and 1930s. The Chinese government used the opportunities presented by membership of the League of Nations to raise the issue of the 'unequal treaties' by which other countries had exploited China's weaknesses to gain territorial and other concessions. The European powers were naturally reluctant to consider change. In 1929, for example, discussion of this question revealed a strong and widespread resistance to any alteration of the status quo, particularly on the part of France, and fears that compromise in relation to the Chinese situation could jeopardise the position of the colonial powers in other parts of the world.[2] China's territorial integrity and independence had been recognised in the Washington agreements of 1921–2. However this formal step was qualified in practice by the political and economic reality of the Western powers' 'open door' policy in dealings with China, and also by the growing US and European acknowledgment of the legitimacy of Japan's naval presence in the Pacific. The opium trade was similarly for many years a source of heated debate in League forums, but in practice international agreements and attempts at controls had little effect.

China presented the League of Nations with both development and security problems that lay far beyond the capacity of the organisation to handle. Much effort, particularly on the part of the secretariat, was invested in plans for technical assistance, especially in public health. The Chinese government also sought extensive aid in many areas, including transportation, flood control, education, agriculture, rural cooperatives and administrative reform.[3] Activities were hampered, however, by the limited authority of the Guomindang authorities, the de facto political and military autonomy of many areas of China, and also by the traditional Western view of China as a geographical area for the competitive exercise of influence and altruism rather than as a sovereign equal. China's economic and political problems were in any case too monumental to be tackled effectively by a distant and weak international institution.

The rapid Japanese advances in China in 1931, and the formation of a puppet Manchurian state nominally under Chinese administration, only belatedly gripped the attention of other states' delegations to the League of Nations. The alleged ambiguities of the situation – resting on Japanese claims to the right to protect its nationals and property in an area regarded as not formally a part of China – reinforced the temptations of inertia and passivity, especially in light of the de facto division of large areas of China into spheres of influence for foreign powers. Sanctions against Japan were not in practice thought an appropriate option. As the Western consensus edged during 1932 towards a less equivocal stance, Japan announced its decision to withdraw from membership of the League. By the time of the renewed Japanese advances of 1937, the League of Nations was still less a credible source of potential international support for China. The Guomindang government nonetheless tried to arouse Western opinion in the League of Nations by identifying Japanese attacks as threats not only to China but also to the interests of other foreign countries with interests in Shanghai and elsewhere on its territory.[4] These appeals reinforced bilateral assistance from some states, particularly the US and Britain, but the League itself remained a bystander.

The League's responses to a variety of Chinese issues during the 1930s thus served to confirm Chinese indifference towards or disenchantment with the organisation. For their part the Chinese Communists displayed little interest. It was for Mao Zedong in 1932 'a League of Robbers by which the various imperialisms are dismembering China'.[5] Given China's internal political situation, moreover, it is not clear that a more active League of Nations strategy, even if it had been possible, could have contributed much to the resolution of China's long-term problems. The nationalist government was not committed to domestic economic and political reform, preferring to direct what resources it had into inflated military budgets and, particularly before the Japanese attacks of the late 1930s, into campaigns against Chinese communist strongholds rather than Japanese forces.

The Chinese experience with the League of Nations was nonetheless important in shaping approaches to postwar order on the part of both the communists and the Guomindang. First, for Chinese officials the record of the League of Nations showed conclusively that collective security organisations had to have teeth. China had been one of the few League of Nations members to take a strong stand against Italy's actions in Ethiopia in the mid-1930s. Respect for the territorial integrity and the principle of the sovereign equality of states was accordingly viewed as a keystone of the future United Nations. Chinese thinking also revealed a lingering measure of distrust of great powers, and a preference for building structures that would allow smaller countries to have more influence over multilateral decision-making.

Secondly, Chinese officials drew from the conditions of the 1930s the lesson that a collective security organisation that failed to emphasise the economic underpinnings of world order would likely prove as ineffectual as its predecessor. Security concerns, that is, had to be balanced with serious attention to economic development and a commitment to programmes of assistance for poorer member-states.

Thirdly, China brought to the deliberations of the 1940s a Confucian sense of the moral order underlying any stable and enduring set of political arrangements. This prompted greater faith in the potential of international law, the elaboration of codes and sets of principles governing the relations of states, and the design of detailed procedures for the peaceful settlement of international disputes than was to be found among Western delegations to the wartime conferences.

There are some intriguing points of comparison between these views and those articulated later by the People's Republic of China in the UN. For example, having finally taken China's seat in 1971, Beijing likewise emphasised the importance of codified principles – in this case the five principles of peaceful coexistence – as a basis for world order; it turned skepticism about the great powers into a protracted campaign against the hegemonial pretensions of the superpowers; and it became an ardent advocate of UN leadership in restructuring international economic relations. Such similarities and continuities, however, have to be viewed against the context of the fundamental changes that took place both in China and in the international system in the late 1940s.

Yet China was in practice involved only peripherally in the wartime negotiations on the United Nations. Its participation – and its securing of a permanent seat on the Security Council – was less a product of its international stature than of Washington's need for a pliantly reliable ally in its own dealings with Britain, France and the Soviet Union. The US also hoped to bolster through such international means the precarious domestic position of the nationalist government. The Chinese were thus present at Dumbarton Oaks 'to be blessed, not to reform the Church'.[6] Even so the UN charter contained sufficient to make it broadly acceptable to China. On the one hand the commitments to economic cooperation and the provisions governing the role of the International Court of Justice, for example, did not meet Chinese aspirations; but on the other hand China's seat on the Security Council, and the sanctions machinery set out in Chapter VII of the charter, clearly differentiated the UN from its discredited predecessor.

More significant in the mid-1940s was the position of the Chinese Communist Party. Mao confirmed in April 1945 that the party 'fully agree[d]' with the proposals for the United Nations.[7]

SOCIALIST ARCHAEOLOGY: CONCEPTIONS OF WORLD ORDER

In a sense this pro-UN stance on the part of the communists represented a tactical response to the situation faced by the party and the People's Liberation Army. In the mid-1940s it was a realistic calculation to view some form of temporary political accommodation with nationalist forces, in part as a result of encouragement by US officials in China, as a transitional prelude to full communist victory. A more sympathetic perspective on international institutions also reflected the more moderate diplomatic position on China's future in world affairs to be found in some sections of the party, one that was characteristic of the internationalist orientations of those attracted to the views of Zhou Enlai. From this viewpoint realism meant acceptance of the argument that China's interests could best be pursued through the normal instruments of statecraft, participation in IGOs and working relations of mutual benefit with Western countries.

The rapidity and scale of PLA victories in 1947–9, however, could not have been foreseen even a short time before. When the People's Republic was formally established in October 1949, Mao's leadership group brought to its task variants of a world view forged from several components. It was an amalgam of traditional Chinese conceptions of world order; nationalist views created in part by decades of foreign activities in China and a history of foreign seizures of territory; Marxism–Leninism; the experiences of over two decades of internal armed struggle against the nationalist authorities; war against Japan; and a variety of pragmatic responses to the turbulent international system of the 1930s and 1940s. Attitudes towards the UN were an integral, if mostly peripheral, part of this wider picture. Socialism in its European, and especially its Soviet, form was thus a key ingredient shaping this complex mixture of orientations towards the world beyond China's borders, but it was not the only one. Marxism–Leninism, moreover, was adapted to Chinese conditions and given a distinctly Sinified character, especially after the rupture with the Soviet Union in the late 1950s cast the Russian approach to socialism in an increasingly disreputable light.

Chinese views of world order in the period 1949–71 bore the imprint of older Sinocentric conceptions of the Middle Kingdom's role in the international system, then, just as the socialist world-view that characterised the

1950s and 1960s formed a foundation for later neomercantilist adaptations. This multi-layered approach to thinking about world order often resonated too with appeals to Confucian ideas, particularly the assumption that a stable and harmonious political order could only be established on the basis of an underlying moral order. These views were important not only because of the way they moulded responses to international institutions. They were also useful policy instruments. The Chinese interpretation of the concept of peaceful coexistence, for example, helped legitimise the struggle against Soviet and US hegemonism, reinforced the historical and legal rationales for Chinese territorial claims against other states, provided a philosophical counter to the rival world-order conceptions of other states and in general underscored the rhetorical assumption of the peaceful character of Chinese foreign policy.

The socialist framework of the 1950s and 1960s contained various strands that, if taken to their logical conclusions, could have implied divergent policy responses to the UN. Such diverse tendencies were rarely explicit, however, because of the unifying effects on Chinese opinion of exclusion from the UN, the practice of democratic centralism and its stress on the containment of factionalism, and the integrating force of Maoist precepts.

First, peaceful coexistence principles could be interpreted to mean an openness to the development of relations with Western countries, a readiness to negotiate and reach compromises with adversaries (and regional neighbours) and an acceptance of the conventional methods of diplomacy. At the Geneva conference of 1954, for example, Zhou made a point of including in the Chinese delegation two master cooks to assist him in the task of 'making friends'.[8] Viewed from this perspective the UN could be seen, once China had recovered its seat there, as a normal and constructive feature of international relations. A second perspective took more diligently the duties incumbent on a socialist state, particularly following the signs of a Soviet lapse into revisionism and rightism after 1956. The appropriate view of the UN from this angle was derived, with the aid of Marxist–Leninist theory, from the formative experiences of China's civil war and the rise and consolidation of the communist movement. Dominated by the US and other great powers, the UN was both an enemy to be resisted and an arena within which revolutionary states could help push the world correlation of forces in progressive directions. This image was also consistent with the Chinese notion of peaceful coexistence, but stemmed more from the imperative of resisting neocolonialist interventionism that formed one of its bases.

In practice a variety of ideological as well as political constraints contained the possible emergence of conflicting views about the UN system during the 1950s and 1960s. First, Mao's 'three-worlds' conception of international relations facilitated the simultaneous pursuit of potentially divergent policies. It initially made a conventional differentiation between the capitalist, socialist and Third Worlds, and later refined the first category to accommodate distinctions among various Western countries. The latter step thus built on traditional ideas of contradictions within and between capitalist states, and at the same time offered a theoretical rationale for Chinese diplomatic overtures to West European countries.

Secondly, while China maintained a long-standing identification with Third World countries, often the predominant emphasis of both policy and theoretically grounded analyses was on the main centres of power in the capitalist world. China's Third World links were developed sporadically and selectively in the 1960s and 1970s, and not on a scale suggested by Beijing's declaratory commitments to NIEO principles.

Thirdly, theoretical conceptions of world order were frequently grounded in interstate rather than class analyses. The principles of peaceful coexistence articulated initially by Zhou at the end of 1953 in the context of Sino–Indian relations, and later defined as a framework for the management of international relations generally, were essentially a set of guidelines for the conduct of relations between the governments of states. Similarly, though ostensibly based on a class analysis of the 'social–imperialist' character of the Soviet Union, even theoretical attacks on Moscow relied heavily on realist analyses of the nature of power in international relations, and of the dangers to international society posed by ambitious states. In short the constraints of manoeuvring within an international society of states in practice made statecentric guidelines for action unavoidable for the Chinese.

China's view of the UN in the 1950s and 1960s thus compounded displays of angry indignation at being excluded from the organisation by Washington, with obstinate denials that the UN fulfilled any useful purpose. The issue was closely connected with internal Chinese politics. Apart from the symbolic and instrumental value of participation, securing China's seat in the UN was a means of preventing the nationalists' Taiwan base from permanently dividing the country through a spread of international recognition of its claim to represent China. For a few months before the outbreak of the Korean War in June 1950 there were signs that the impasse at the UN over Chinese representation, which had occasioned a Soviet and East European boycott of UN organs and specialised agencies, might be ended. The war, however, combined with the rise of the China issue in domestic US politics, forced the possibility back into an indefinite future. It led to combat between UN forces and the PLA, the formal condemnation by the UN of China as an aggressor – a symbolic step which assumed considerable practical significance in later years in General Assembly debates on the Chinese representation issue – and a consolidation of defence ties between the US and the authorities on Taiwan.

As Sino–Soviet tensions mounted later in the 1950s, the UN thus became increasingly irrelevant or even dangerous to China. Its leading body, the Security Council, was dominated by four states each in different ways an adversary of China – including one, Britain, which retained a colony on Chinese territory – in collusion with the defeated forces of the former nationalist regime. Alternative structures outside the UN, and new directions inside the organisation based on the large influx of newly independent states from the late 1950s, better fitted Chinese conceptions of international organisation. Beijing emerged as an enthusiastic supporter of UNCTAD developments from 1964.

UN peacekeeping activity was in general condemned by China as a form of great-power intervention not sanctioned by the UN charter. The 1950 'Uniting for Peace' resolution was particularly criticised as an illegal deviation from the charter's rules governing the responsibilities of the Security Council. But there were exceptions. In 1956 China supported the creation of UNEF. In the Suez crisis two colonial powers – Britain and France – had been checked by the UN, albeit primarily as a result of US interests in the Middle East; and the non-aligned states, particularly India, were emerging in the mid-1950s as supporters of a more proactive UN role in relation to regional conflicts. The Chinese position on Suez did not, however, set a precedent for its response to later UN peacekeeping operations. Apart from other considerations, the rationale for these – providing the means to insulate local conflicts from competitive intervention by the superpowers – was at odds in the late 1950s and early 1960s with the Chinese view that it was the Soviet failure to resist US imperialism more vigorously that was an underlying cause of war.

For much of the period from 1949–71, however, China was of marginal concern to the UN. The UN likewise rarely occupied more than Beijing's peripheral vision. Domestic and regional preoccupations all but obliterated attention to UN developments. China had no substantial security stake in membership. Nor were any economic interests likely to be served by recovery of its seat in UN bodies. Membership of the Bretton Woods institutions was not at that time viewed as an option either by the IFIs or by the Chinese. The prospect of UN participation assumed particular importance, though, in the context of the unfinished business of the civil war and the continuing Guomindang hold on Taiwan. This situation in turn represented a long-term constraint on China's strategic flexibility in that it obstructed the path to serious consideration of any eventual move towards some form of accommodation with the US. Some provisions of the UN charter, such as the prohibition of interference in areas of domestic jurisdiction and encouragement of the pacific settlement of disputes, were singled out as especially compatible with Chinese concepts of peaceful coexistence. These also gave the Chinese useful political ammunition with which to attack US, and later Soviet, policies.

The goal of acquiring China's seat in the UN and routine praise for the principles of the UN charter thus never fully disappeared.[9] The UN was nonetheless a temporary casualty of China's domestic turbulence of the 1960s. After the onset of the Cultural Revolution – and in light of external developments such as Indonesia's temporary withdrawal from the UN – the Chinese set their sights on the UN with renewed ferocity. Old resentments were revived; the UN was merely an instrument of US imperialism; the Western powers' exclusion of China meant that the UN could not be regarded as a representative body; it employed double standards in its handling of international conflicts; and manipulation of the UN by powerful Western states and the USSR was thwarting the just demands of developing countries. By the late 1960s Beijing appeared to have lost all interest in the UN and even in the task of replacing the nationalists there.[10] This posture proved temporary. During 1969 Beijing began to institute a return to normality in its diplomatic relations, and in the interval until the successful General Assembly vote of October 1971 campaigned actively and effectively for its right to take its seat in the UN as the sole representative of China.

ACTORS IN A *HUAJU*: THE CAUTIOUS DIPLOMACY OF UN MEMBERSHIP

Having secured both China's seat and rejection by the UN of a 'two-China' compromise that would have allowed the nationalists to remain in the organisation, Beijing put into practice a diplomacy of gradualism and caution. The ideological denunciation of the UN that characterised the late 1960s was shown to be an aberration. The UN became for China a normal part of international relations. In place of the excesses of the previous decade, normalisation and quiet diplomacy became guidelines for Chinese foreign policy in the 1970s. Imperialism, of both the classic and the Soviet kind, was denounced. More important, however, were the steps Chinese officials took in UN forums and in informal encounters to defend the interests of developing countries, occasionally playing the role of intermediaries between Third World and Western positions. China in effect defined itself as the sole permanent member of the Security Council with no aspirations to great-power status, and the only one with a commitment to a new international economic order. In practice officials showed a distinct lack of readiness to try to use the UN as the instrument of a revolutionary foreign policy.

These themes were signalled in China's first responses in 1971 to the resolution of the representation issue. The change was portrayed as an indication both of the resumption by China of its proper role in world affairs and of the inevitability of the decline of great-power pretensions. China was 'one of the founding members of the UN', so it was 'both natural and right for the government of the PRC, the sole legal representative of China, to have its legitimate seat in the UN'.[11] Manipulation of the UN by the superpowers was giving way in the face of the 'irresistible trend of history' towards greater democratisation and the equality of countries: 'the affairs of a country must be handled by its own people; the affairs of the world must be handled by all countries of the world; the affairs of the United Nations must be handled jointly by all its member-states....'.[12]

China's new role as an actor on the stage of this Western-style *huaju* during the 1970s was shaped by a combination of external and domestic circumstances. On some of the most important international questions of concern to China the UN was a marginal player. The situation in Indochina, for example, both before and after the withdrawal of US forces and the unification of Vietnam, continued to influence developments in China's relations with Washington and Moscow. For the most part Beijing made use of UN membership on this cluster of issues, as on the Soviet invasion of Afghanistan at the end of the decade, to publicise its views of the dangers to international and regional security posed by the USSR and its accomplices. The UN could realistically be viewed as a more central actor in relation to North–South issues. From the outset, in preparations for UNCTAD 3 in 1972, Chinese officials made clear their intention of supporting G77 goals and promoting change in international economic relations.

Further, and in contrast to the 1960s, China's domestic political battles of the 1970s did not spill over into UN policies. While the changing fortunes of leftist traditionalists and Dengist reformers affected the style and rhetoric of Chinese diplomacy in New York, these did not fundamentally divert the lines of continuity established in 1971–2. In the longer term, however, as the economic modernisation programme gathered force from the late 1970s and as Beijing began in the 1980s to draw out the policy implications of its growing conviction of the interdependent character of the world economy, underlying continuities in China's approach to the UN system were increasingly intermingled with signs of change.

These questions will be examined in more depth in the next chapter. As a prelude to that discussion it is useful to sketch in some of the main features of Chinese thinking on the UN that were evident during this first formative decade of membership.

First, in relation to the peace-and-security mandate of the UN, China tended to apply in practice the cautiously positive outlook adopted by Mao in 1945. The basic constitutional set-up of the UN was not questioned. The permanent membership core of the Security Council, now in the Chinese view made representative for the first time since 1949, was accepted as having the leadership role in carrying out the council's responsibilities in these areas. The principle of great power unanimity had been endorsed in Chinese commentary on the UN from the 1940s. This was interpreted in practice to mean that occasional use of the veto was appropriate. China employed this only twice – on the issue of membership for Bangladesh and on a Middle East resolution – in its first five years of Security Council participation. More significant was Chinese entry into the spirit of multilateralism that lay behind Security Council decision-making. Thus Chinese officials developed a flexible stance of not participating in some questions in order not to frustrate the possibility of a consensual outcome. They took part in the informal behind-the-scenes exchanges of council meetings but, in line with the Chinese principle of defending the interests of small states, insisted that such discussions should not cross the line that would distort them into the shabby practices of secret great-power collusion.

The UN's peacekeeping role, however, remained for Beijing a regrettable consequence of a long history of superpower manipulation of the UN, and an activity that threatened the fundamental principle of noninterference in the internal affairs of member-states enshrined in Article 2(7) of the charter. Indeed US–Soviet interest in UN peacekeeping had been condemned by Beijing in the mid-1960s as a device by which Moscow and Washington aimed jointly to create an international police force serving the cause of imperialism. The special circumstances of 1956 had prompted Chinese support of UNEF – a pragmatic decision in which Beijing suppressed its opposition to attempts to enhance the international security role of the General Assembly – but the UN's later creation of forces in relation to the Congo, Cyprus and other conflicts met with Beijing's disapproval and, once it was inside the UN, a principled refusal to contribute financially to their costs. Even so, as in the case of the Security Council's renewal of the mandate for UNFICYP in 1971 and the creation of a force following the 1973 Arab–Israeli war, the Chinese preference was to stand back and allow other council members to take the crucial decisions rather than to employ the powers at its disposal, including the veto, to block action.[13]

Secondly, a similarly cautious and unhurried tone characterised Chinese approaches to other areas of UN activity during the 1970s. Chinese conceptions of the economic bases of power and world order fitted comfortably with the philosophical outlook of the delegations from Third World countries to the UNCTAD sessions of the 1970s, and to the General Assembly's deliberations on international development issues and the creation of an NIEO. China had more tangible interests to promote in such arenas. It aimed to counter the Soviet strategy in Group D of using UNCTAD as a basis for assailing Western positions on key issues while at the same time underlining its own low-profile support for G77 aims. In UNCTAD bodies as in other UN forums, the Chinese tended to adopt a more compartmentalised view of the functions of committees and organisations. They resisted, for example, the characteristic Soviet aggregation of development issues with questions of disarmament and its peace strategies. China also had a specific interest in political discussions in UNCTAD likely to affect some primary commodities, particularly tungsten.[14]

Thirdly, China's participation in the agencies of the wider UN system in the 1970s marked a decisive shift from the situation in the previous decade. In the 1960s China had been almost completely absent from the world of IGOs. Its entry into the various UN specialised agencies was accompanied by the same blend of cautious professionalism and wariness about great-power motives that it displayed in the UN itself. Some significant differences from the Soviet approach were evident from the beginning. As a member-state of UNESCO, for example, China did not appear to put a high priority on expanding the number of Chinese nationals employed in the secretariat.[15] Finally, Beijing combined this extensive activity in the UN system with a growing interest in participation in international NGOs.[16]

TOWARDS NEOMERCANTILIST GEOPOLITICS

During the 1980s various domestic and external factors combined to give IGOs greater salience for China. The course of economic modernisation adopted from 1978–9 entailed among other things a determined expansion of trade and investment links with Western countries. It was recognised in Beijing that achievement of these objectives rested in part on the efficacy with which China could manage its relations with existing international institutional arrangements, particularly GATT and the Bretton Woods system. Obstacles encountered in bilateral trade relations, especially with the US, reinforced this lesson.

The late 1970s and early 1980s saw the entrenchment of a more moderate, Western-tilted foreign policy following the political defeat of the radical leftist faction which had sought dominance after Mao's death in 1976. The posture was defined as an independent one. China, that is, would build on the relationship with the US while avoiding the pitfalls of dependence, and also edge cautiously towards a negotiated accommodation with the USSR. Both aspects would be anchored in its identification with the Third World. The Soviet Union's invasion of Afghanistan and its continued involvement in that country's affairs, and the situations in Cambodia and the Middle East, in varying ways reinforced this shift of direction. Further, as in the border fighting with Vietnam, China did not rule out the use of force in defence of its interests. The events of the late 1970s and early 1980s also encouraged more serious Chinese attention to the peace-and-security role of the UN. This led, in a policy reversal, to the beginnings of a stance of solid Chinese support for the concept of UN peacekeeping.

The option of pursuing party- and state-led economic modernisation has a long history in Chinese communist politics. For much of the PRC's history before the late 1970s this competed unsuccessfully with more ideologically respectable versions of socialist planning. The project of the 1980s went considerably beyond earlier experiments with export promotion and the encouragment of foreign investment, as in the mid-1950s, early 1960s and again in the mid-1970s. This did not mean, however, that during the 1980s Beijing became committed to Western-style notions of economic interdependence and the liberalisation of international movements of goods and capital. Neoliberal ideas of the interdependence of the global economy did assume greater significance in Chinese theoretical formulations. In policy terms, however, it was evident that the economy was to remain as far as possible the exclusive preserve of the state, just as the state was the incontestable arena for party activity.

These principles permeated the formation and running of the Special Economic Zones (SEZs), which were set up as a primary and rapid means of export promotion by attracting foreign investment on the basis of China's comparative advantage in labour costs. Other reforms centred on foreign-trade mechanisms and directions. Though a series of subsequent changes modified the initial framework,[17] the guideline of state control led to strong initial resistance to developments that would hand over a significant measure of autonomy to enterprises or that might threaten the state's capacity to engage in import substitution as a twin path to growth.[18]

The viability of the assumptions underlying the modernisation programme became crucial issues in the 1980s and early 1990s. First, the course taken by China implied an essential role for IFIs. In the longer term this raised the question of the extent to which progress was feasible without growing structural interdependence, perhaps with significant foreign-policy overtones, between China and Western states. The possibility of economic and political dependence had traditionally been viewed in Chinese debates as a threat to the values of self-reliance and socialist planning. The external implications of the modernisation programme were thus vulnerable to, and risked generating, a revival of the domestic political battles of the 1960s and 1970s.

Secondly, the form taken by the modernisation goals rested on the simultaneous cultivation and control of entrepreneurial activity, especially on the part of foreign-trade enterprises. For many Western critics this appeared an awkward combination that seemed likely to collapse eventually in the direction of either greater statism or an enhanced private-sector decentralisation. As far as Chinese rationales were concerned, there was no inconsistency among the approaches to economic development. All were integrally related to the task of 'building socialism with Chinese characteristics'. Further, the existence of factional struggles of the kind identified by outside observers, particularly between conservatives and reformers, was strenuously denied.

Thirdly, the economic goals of the 1980s were designed to be pursued without costs to China's political system. The political restructuring plan set out at the Thirteenth Party Congress in 1987 remained conventionally defined in terms of socialist democracy and the need to renovate the governmental system to accomplish modernisation goals. This was accompanied by a renewal of ideological criticism of 'bourgeois liberalisation', characterised by Deng Xiaoping as based on false Western notions of democracy and denounced as inherently antisocialist. Ironically, the late 1980s conjuncture of the party's economic and political reforms, as well as Deng's own political heritage as a Maoist era reformer, became bases for the domestic political attacks on Chinese political structures that culminated in the repression of the prodemocracy movement in 1989.

The record of the 1980s and early 1990s nonetheless demonstrated a high degree of success of modernisation goals, particularly in terms of China's foreign trade. Exports almost doubled between 1978 and 1980, from US$9.7 billion to US$18.3 billion. These figures climbed to US$51.7 billion in 1990 and to US$60.9 billion in 1991. Imports over the same period rose at a less rapid rate (from US$10.9 billion to US$38.5 billion). This record reversed the pattern of the late 1970s and the first half of the

1980s of significantly higher levels of imports than exports. Further, the foreign-trade sector grew at a higher rate than the domestic economy.[19] According to Lardy's analysis, the sources of this foreign-trade boom were varied. Centralised planning through the state authorities provided the major impetus to expansion in the initial stages, during the late 1970s and early 1980s, but other factors became important in the later phases.[20]

The second defining characteristic of China's external links during this period was the continued adaptation of policies and theoretical world-views to change in the international system. Geopolitical logic tended to point Chinese leaders towards broad policy conclusions consistent with those arising from the neomercantilist route to economic growth. Both pointed, for example, towards the centrality of China's relationship with the US. Not only was the US a source of capital and a potentially huge market for Chinese goods – factors which required constant Chinese attention in the late 1980s and early 1990s to congressional and other domestic US assaults on China's MFN status – in strategic terms it represented a counter to both the Soviet and the Japanese poles and, as the process of Soviet collapse accelerated in the late 1980s, a partial guarantee of China's ability to remain immune to disintegrative pressures.

Yet the relationship had inbuilt costs. It could be an instrument of bourgeois liberalisation. This was not so much as a result of Washington's policies, since the republican administrations from 1981–93 defined US security interests in terms of careful maintenance of the link with Beijing, but rather through the import of consumerist values or threatening political ideas as a result of trade promotion, cultural and media contacts, or the return of US-educated students. China's stake in the relationship, then, did not fundamentally alter its views of the nature of US society. The media and research institutes remained receptive during the 1980s primarily to evidence, including domestic economic and racial unrest and contradictions in US relations with the EC and Japan, that suggested support for the traditional hypothesis of eventual, or imminent, structural collapse.[21]

Yet Chinese observers were also acutely aware of changes in the international system. Older verities, such as superpower competition and collusion and the dangers of social imperialism, were eroding. New power centres were emerging, regionally and globally. A variety of unanticipated issues, such as the environment, were taking on new prominence on international agendas. China was being compelled, especially as a result of participation in the UN, to make assessments of its interests in relation to a widening range of complex questions, from IMF policies in the Third World, to the Gulf War, to ozone-layer protection. In part such requirements were met by globalist adaptations of traditional Chinese world-order conceptions, for example by means of the growing scholarly interest in world history frameworks[22] or by the expanded use of specialists in research institutes and in agencies more directly connected to the foreign-policy community.[23] The kinds of intellectual and policy challenges posed by the changes in international politics of the late 1980s and early 1990s, however, were unprecedented in the history of the PRC. Perhaps it is not surprising that, in a time of rapid and turbulent external change, China's political leaders sought, and found, reassurance in foreign-policy principles defined over three decades earlier.

This cluster of ideas centred on the five principles of peaceful coexistence. To these were welded the concept of an NIEO from UN debates of the mid-1970s, together with the earlier reflex commitment to the principles of the UN charter and the rhetorical opposition to hegemonism.[24] This amalgam provided guidelines for interpreting, and steering a course through, the changing world of the 1980s and 1990s, and for portraying China's own actions in a favourable light. The principles of peaceful coexistence were held to have influenced the UN directly, particularly General Assembly resolutions on the peaceful settlement of disputes between states and encouragement to the development of international law. These ideas also assisted the Chinese more practically in the task of criticising, and offering an alternative to, the 'new-world-order' thinking emanating from the Bush administration in the early 1990s.

The need for such an alternative was underscored by China's participation in the Security Council's deliberations on the Gulf crisis in 1990–1. As the foreign minister put the general question underlying this specific context: 'What kind of order should be established in the world so that peace can be preserved?'[25] Abstract formulations of the optimal future world order from Washington were regarded as flawed. These appeared to the Chinese to rest on questionable assumptions about both the desirability and the feasibility of US leadership of a post-Gulf-War, and post-Cold-War, world.[26] Commentary in Chinese publications continued, as in the late 1980s, to develop the theme that the world situation was improving. Evidence of a general easing of international tension, however, could not in the Chinese view be taken to imply an absence of local wars or a smooth path to the peaceful resolution of regional conflicts. Seen from this perspective the Gulf War was significant because of the continuing effects it would likely have on the UN and on the evolution of international mechanisms for maintaining security.[27] As these mechanisms took shape it was important for Beijing in the early 1990s that they did so on the basis of world-order conceptions more compatible with its own than with US approaches.

Many of the kinds of lessons drawn from the Gulf War, however, were already present in Chinese analyses of the 1980s. Support for the UN's peacekeeping role was increasingly viewed as consistent both with Chinese principles of peaceful coexistence and with those of the UN charter. In 1978 China had supported Security Council resolutions on the Middle East and accepted the utility of the UN sending forces to areas of international conflict.[28] The pursuit of multilateralism through the UN, and the gradual adoption of a posture cautiously sympathetic to a more proactive and interventionist UN role, was reinforced by China's foreign-policy shifts of the late 1970s and early 1980s and, more specifically, by the Soviet invasion of Afghanistan.

Thus in 1984 the Chinese delegate to the UN special committee on peacekeeping said that 'In this most turbulent and volatile world, there is a universal demand for strengthening the peacekeeping capability of the UN'.[29] While these operations were now regarded as consistent with the UN charter, China's support was still qualified in some respects. It insisted, for example, that forces should only be sent at the request of the country concerned; that their operations should be governed by clear mandates; that the Security Council retained overall responsibility; and that the costs be borne by states 'on the merits of each case'.

During the first half of the 1980s this emerging posture of support for the UN was tempered by criticism of the organisation on a number of counts. Chinese officials continued, as in the 1970s, to act as fiscally conservative critics of waste and duplication of UN activities. While the UN was generally praised for its work in the cause of decolonisation, the ending of apartheid and the promotion of international development, China often drew attention to the slow pace of change. That is, because of the policies adopted by certain states the results of the General Assembly's declaration on an NIEO were, by the time of that document's tenth anniversary in 1984, still 'far from satisfactory'.[30] In the peace-and-security field the UN was described by Foreign Minister Wu Xueqian in 1983 as 'rather flabby in the settlement of many important issues'.[31] Two years later the UN's role in relation to international security was seen to be eroding, largely because of a lack of political will in 'some quarters'.[32] The key to the UN's success in this area was argued to be the principled adherence by states to the UN Charter:

> Whenever the Security Council strictly observes the purposes and principles of the UN Charter, reflects the just demands of the great majority of UN members, particularly the Third World and small and medium-sized countries, and pools collective wisdom through full consultations,

> it achieves successes in its work. Whenever the purposes and principles of the Charter are contravened and the will of the big powers is imposed on the Security Council, it suffers setbacks.[33]

This broadly conservative approach to charter interpretation was in part a response to China's Soviet problem. From the mid-1980s the tone of defensive indignation in some of Beijing's rhetoric gradually receded. Several factors contributed to this move. First, a more positive attitude towards the UN was partly a delayed consequence of the modernisation programme. As this deepened, and as the booming activity in the SEZs gave the Chinese economy an increasingly dual character, so China's relations with GATT, the IMF and the World Bank became more crucial to the task of economic planning. The world economy was as a result being described by Chinese more and more in the language of Western neoliberalism – as interdependent, interrelated and an 'integral whole'. Indeed, according to some Chinese analysts, the growing integration of the post-Cold-War global economy was seen as a foretaste of a new phase of prosperity, in which China would be an active participant, beginning in the late 1990s.[34]

At the same time, however, Beijing retained a strong declaratory commitment to NIEO values. The 'irrationality' of the existing world economic order could not be ignored by a socialist developing country. The UN was thus essential as a forum in which the tensions between these potentially conflicting roles of China – as a developing country whose economy had a rapidly Westernising sector and as a socialist instrument of radical change in international economic relations – could be resolved.

Secondly, the UN itself was judged to be tackling international disputes and regional conflicts more effectively, for example in southern Africa, Cambodia and the Middle East. The changing Chinese outlook was evident in 1985 during the fortieth anniversary meeting of the Security Council at foreign-minister level, and in Zhao Ziyang's speech that year to the General Assembly. China began to gain more direct experience of the UN through observer participation in several operations, including an election-monitoring role in Western Sahara and Namibia. This experience led officials to identify fact-finding as one of the most important ways in which the UN could contribute to international conflict resolution. Although the UN continued to be viewed primarily in terms of its potential utility for enhancing security or for catalysing fundamental change in the world economy, Beijing also took more seriously the rise of other global issues on UN agendas. In the General Assembly in 1988, for example, Qian focused on the potentially major role of the UN in dealing with such questions as environmental protection, the control of population growth, public health and the utilisation of scientific and technological developments.

Thirdly, the initiation of the reform programme in the Soviet Union in CPSU meetings in 1985–6 was also a source of much Chinese analysis that indirectly influenced attitudes towards the UN. Chinese attention was directed both to the foreign-policy elements of Gorbachev's restructuring goals, which were seen as the means to secure the external environment while internal reforms took hold, and to the implications of the domestic economic changes directed towards the renewal of socialism. If the latter succeeded there appeared to be a possibility, from Beijing's perspective, that the negative external consequences of the years of Soviet stagnation could be eliminated as the USSR moved towards a more vigorous and genuine socialist path. Further, signs of Soviet foreign-policy change in the Asia–Pacific region, particularly Gorbachev's Vladivostok speech of July 1986, suggested that Moscow would be moving during the late 1980s away from interventionism and towards a comprehensive search for politically negotiated settlements of regional conflicts.[35]

These changes clearly had profound implications for China's own relations with the USSR, particularly in view of the Soviet withdrawal from Afghanistan. The more unsettling aspects of Soviet instability only became evident later in the decade. Change in the Soviet Union thus highlighted the attractions of multilateralism for the Chinese. IGOs occupied a major place in the Soviet Union's new thinking; and within the UN, Soviet officials appeared to be approaching regional conflicts and international problems in a manner more consistent with Chinese principles of peaceful coexistence. Further, China could not afford to be isolated from a tendency that might generate a fresh spirit of close collaboration in Soviet–American relations.

Finally, the changing structures and tendencies of international politics in the late 1980s and early 1990s pointed the way towards a role for international institutions that fitted Chinese peaceful coexistence theory. The collapse of bipolarity and the rise of competing economic and military centres of power was taken as evidence to support the general proposition that the great powers were no longer able to dominate world politics, the international economy and the UN in the ways they had in previous decades. None of the rival centres, in Europe or Japan, were of sufficient stature – or engaged in the kind of behaviour – to provoke a Chinese charge of hegemonism. In these circumstances the UN's role in fostering a world order that was neither anarchic nor hegemonistic was appealing. As one analyst wrote in 1991, it had become

> a universal demand to set up a new international political order in defence of world peace and stablity. A new international political order should not be the replacement of the old bipolarity by any new bipolar or tripolar domination of the world. Instead, the role of the United Nations should be brought into full play in light of the world trend of multipolarity. The international behaviour of all countries should be subject to the generally recognised norms governing international relations.[36]

The UN, moreover, was founded on the basis of the joint principles of the sovereign equality of states (in the General Assembly) and the special responsibilities of certain larger countries (in the Security Council). Chinese opposition to great-power privileges did not necessarily imply an objection to the second of these principles. What was important, according to Chinese explorations of the theme of future institutional order, was that the permanent members of the Security Council did not approach their task with a view to their own aggrandisement.[37]

Thus in the late 1980s China became a seasoned advocate of UN peacekeeping operations. These were described in 1991 as 'the symbol of the active role of the UN in international affairs'.[38] Attention to the political and security aspects of world order, moreover, often appeared to have displaced the traditional Chinese focus on world economic structures. Yet this support was tempered by caution. First, China appreciated that its interests in specific cases were unlikely to be served by the routine application of abstract sets of dispute-settlement guidelines. Beijing took a generally supportive line in the Security Council in relation to the Gulf resolutions of 1990–1, but reverted to the earlier device of non-participation in the vote on the use-of-force resolution.

Secondly, a favourable Chinese view of the UN's newfound activism of the 1990s was contingent on recognition by other member-states, especially the other permanent members of the Security Council, of the importance China attached to certain key principles of international relations. In the frequently repeated Chinese view, peacekeeping forces had to respect the sovereign integrity of states; the UN was not, and should not try to become, a world government that replaced decision-making by states; and it should not develop a penchant for interfering in all disputes. While Western discussions in 1991–3 on the revitalisation of the UN were thus generally welcomed in Beijing, Chinese commentary harboured doubts about the capacity of the Russian and Western governments to understand and to practise in the UN the principles of peaceful coexistence.

This background of Chinese reappraisals of the UN shaped policies in a number of areas. The next chapter examines in more detail Beijing's approaches to its relations with IFIs, the work of technical agencies and the international peace-and-security role of the UN.

7 Understanding the Times: The UN System in a Complex World

China's ties to the diverse activities of the UN and its related agencies in economic, technical and security areas became far more intricate and complex in the 1980s. China brought on board officers of IFIs to help it plot a track of modernisation through the exacting terrain of ideological compromise, economic transformation and domestic political turbulence. As a permanent member of the UN Security Council, China had a crucial role to play in relation not only to continuing issues in Southern Africa and the Middle East, but also in the 1990s to mounting post-Cold-War ethnic and subnational conflicts. China would continue to support UN goals, Premier Li Peng said in May 1991, even though as a developing country it faced 'arduous [tasks of] domestic construction'.

The developments of this period ushered in a greater Chinese willingness to suspend disbelief about the potential of the UN system. They also inaugurated an intense period of analysis of the rapidly changing international system and of China's place in it. In the 1990s it was becoming still more vital for decision-makers in Beijing to 'understand the times', one of the skills traditionally ascribed to great men. China's status as a developing country, together with the voting alignments and consultative reflexes that stemmed from this self-definition, represented one of several lines of continuity linking this with the late Maoist period. This chapter looks first at the course of the structural relationship between China and the World Bank and the IMF; secondly, at Chinese policies in the WHO, the ILO and UNEP; and, thirdly, at China's responses to selected questions on the agenda of the Security Council.

DEFINING THE WORLD ECONOMY: FROM IRRATIONALITY TO INTERDEPENDENCE

China approached IFIs in the 1980s from different directions. As a developing country it was committed to support the struggle for a restructured world economic order. Like many Third World nations – but unlike

China itself before the beginning of the modernisation programme in the late 1970s – Beijing became keen to use multilateral instruments as one of the foundations of its own economic-development planning. China accepted the practice of receiving aid. In the 1980s it no longer interpreted the donor–recipient relationship, at least in its own case, as necessarily one of dependence and economic power. It meanwhile continued to extend modest amounts of aid to Third World countries (and even a substantial commodity loan to the USSR in 1991). China's growing involvement with the IMF and the World Bank, and also with GATT, constituted a defining feature of the decade that saw a deepening commitment to the goal of integration with the world economy. The simultaneous retention of socialist principles of development became an increasingly troublesome burden.

This longer-term strategy did not deflect China from its pursuit of NIEO goals. In the early 1980s Chinese analysts saw the deadlock in North–South relations as further evidence of the structural crisis of the world economy. Ways to break the impasse were investigated. A 'new type of international economic relations' might emerge, for example, on the basis of expanded South–South cooperation. Zhao Ziyang outlined the principles that would nourish such a programme: 'equality and mutual benefit, stress on practical results, diversity in form, and attainment of common progress'.[1] The Charter of Economic Rights and Duties of States and other basic NIEO instruments of the mid-1970s were for China the key architectural plans for the new order. The conditions faced by developing countries – declines in commodity prices, worsening terms of trade, protectionism in capitalist countries, fluctuations in exchange rates, high interest rates, debt and restructuring problems, a decline of development assistance measured in real terms and outflows of financial resources to donor countries – were repeatedly cited in Chinese commentaries. All were held to be vital to effective North–South dialogue. More particularly, officials maintained in the mid-1980s that the UN was 'an appropriate forum for engaging in North–South dialogue and promoting multilateral economic cooperation' and that 'consideration should be given to ways of strengthening the role of the UN in this respect'.[2]

These conditions persisted into the 1990s. Chinese observers found substantial evidence of the growing 'solidarity and cooperation' of the countries of the South.[3] Turbulence in Eastern Europe and the upheavals in East–West relations posed major challenges of interpretation for China. In ECOSOC meetings on this question in 1991, Vice-Foreign-Minister Liu Huaqin detected long-term benefits in the end of the Cold War, but a continuation of problems for developing countries in the short and medium terms. These problems were much the same as those Chinese officials had been emphasising in UNCTAD, ECOSOC and other forums since the 1970s: reverse capital flows out of developing countries, for example, and difficulties of access for their products in the North. By the 1990s these were joined by a 'growing tendency to bar the developing countries from the international economic decision-making process' and by 'ever more stringent political conditions attached to foreign aid'. In sum, according to Liu, the North–South gap was widening, and this was due to the 'unfair and irrational international economic order'.[4]

In the aftermath of Tiananmen in June 1989 the Chinese government had a deeper stake in some aspects of these issues. China rejected Western criticisms of its human rights record, particularly in the UN Human Rights Commission, and condemned its opponents for failing to acknowledge the collective right of development.[5] This point was central to Chinese elaborations on NIEO themes. Just as the theory of peaceful coexistence underscored key principles of interstate relations such as sovereign equality and noninterference, so the theory of development emphasised the importance of national choice in the determination of economic planning frameworks. Taken together these produced the characteristic Chinese stress on both the unacceptability of conditionalities in the provision of development assistance, and the need for the full participation of the South in the management of the international economy.

China's style in the UN system, however, was to maintain a low profile. This often stood out in sharp contrast to the impatient Soviet zeal for highly visible campaigns. The approach was partly due to China's traditional diplomatic culture. In addition China lacked the automatic bloc presence guaranteed to the Soviet Union for most of the UN's history. Its status as a large developing country led to reflex support for G77 goals, while its unique character distanced it somewhat from the political organisation of Southern interests: for example its permanent place on the UN Security Council, its sheer size, its importance in South and East Asian regional politics, its nuclear weapons status, its retention of a communist-led governmental and economic system, and its complex networks of special relationships with the US, Russia and Japan. China did not fit easily into the formal group structure established in UNCTAD in the 1960s. At UNCTAD 3, for example, it was elected to the Trade and Development Board from Group A.[6] For China to throw its weight around in such circumstances would have been counterproductive.

In some parts of the UN system, however, China did occasionally behave more unequivocally as a Southern coalition partner. Beijing's policies in UNESCO combined a search for points of leverage that could tip the organisation towards NIEO objectives, with a practical interest in administrative efficiency and in projects that would directly benefit China. China continued to be an active supporter of the concept of a new world information and communication order (NWICO) during the 1980s. In the UN Committee on Information in 1989 the Chinese delegate argued that 'imbalances' in the structures of news-gathering and dissemination had a deleterious effect on international development. An NWICO would 'enhance a wider and better balanced dissemination of information' in all nations, and 'ensure the diversity of sources of information'.[7] Yet in practice much of China's orientation to UNESCO was pragmatic and project-oriented. It participated in a wide range of activities: the 'UNESCO Club' programme linking schools in member-state countries, preparation of a textbook on vocational education for the Asia–Pacific region, and designation of protected natural areas for inclusion in UNESCO's official listing of the world's biosphere reserves. Beijing also made use of the institution as a means of hosting conferences in China that could enhance its regional and wider international prestige.

Thus the Chinese commitment to NIEO objectives was tempered by a variety of more immediate policy concerns. Specific modernisation goals entailed acknowledgment of China's need for development assistance from external sources. Between 1978 and 1990 assistance to China from the FAO, for example, totalled approximately US$20 million for 86 development projects. Over the same period China provided about $1 million in assistance to Third World countries through the FAO, for example by supplying pesticides to African countries to combat locusts in the late 1980s. Similarly, by the second half of the 1980s China had become one of the UNDP's highest priorities. The programme's assistance to China reached $165 million in the period 1986–90; about one-half of this went to industrial projects and about 20 per cent to projects in the agriculture and forestry sectors.[8] Significant though such programmes were, they were overshadowed by the development-assistance implications of China's engagement with the Bretton Woods system.

During the 1980s China's growing entanglement with IFIs and the protracted negotatiations for access to GATT nudged it towards a more neoliberal adjustment-oriented posture. Chinese interest in the Bretton Woods system predated the Dengist period. A group of senior Chinese officials was convened as early as 1972 to explore China's future relations with the World Bank and the IMF.[9] Beijing demanded China's seat in the IMF. While the timing was propitious – officials from Beijing were then moving into China's seats in the UN and the specialised agencies – in practice the domestic political situation in China, as well as reluctance on the part of the US, made consideration of such a step unrealistic. The

Chinese economy was also not compatible with the route to IMF membership. After Mao's death, the reemergence of Deng and the defeat of leftist factions, the Chinese government proceeded with a more serious examination of the Bretton Woods option in 1979. The formal establishment of diplomatic relations between Washington and Beijing at the beginning of the year, and the first signals of a market- and Western-tilted economic modernisation programme, facilitated such developments. Yet access to loans and drawing privileges appears to have been only one factor in the Chinese decision. Beijing was initially probably more attracted to the political and diplomatic advantages of IFI memberships, the access to information on the world economy this would afford, and the strengthening of bilateral relations with leading Western countries that would likely follow.[10]

Several issues predominated in subsequent talks. These included the status of Taiwan, the size of the Chinese quota and the related question of China's representation on the executive board of the IMF. In effect the IMF had implicitly decided on recognition of Beijing as the rightful possessor of China's seat before the negotiations themselves were concluded. The quota set for China (SDR 1.8 billion in 1980, rising to SDR 2.39 billion in 1983) ranked it ninth in the IMF. China thus regained (what Taiwan had lost in 1960 in disputes over the Chinese quota) the automatic right to appoint an executive director of the IMF, and so became the first communist country in this situation.[11]

China's use of the newly available sources of external funding began with a World Bank project to improve facilities and training in higher education, an urgent priority in both Washington and Beijing in view of the lingering costs of the Cultural Revolution. While relations were subject to periodic obstacles – as in the Chinese imposition of limits to investment in the retrenchment of the early 1980s – a succession of Chinese decisions confirmed Beijing's long-term commitment to reform strategies. The reform programme was taken a significant step further in 1987, for example, with changes to the investment system, and increasing Chinese interest in areas such as software development and applications and personnel training.[12] The relationship was marked by growing interaction and convergence between Chinese and World Bank views on such matters as price systems and market forces, the autonomy of enterprises and the need to control inflation. In 1981–9 the World Bank and the IDA approved a total of US$7.4 billion for projects in China, and more than US$3.2 billion was actually disbursed during this period. Particular emphasis was placed on agriculture and rural development, energy, and transportation. IBRD and IDA priorities in agriculture focused on reform of the Chinese grain-subsidy system, the development of rural enterprises, encouragement of high-value crop cultivation and the import of cheaper grains, and rationalisation of financial institutions in rural areas.[13]

This degree of dependence threatened to collide with the cherished Chinese notion of self-reliant development. Bank-defined projects were also drawing on Chinese funds that might otherwise have been directed elsewhere. Yet China avoided the external imposition of politically costly adjustment strategies. World Bank officials acknowledged that the course of Chinese reform during the 1980s was such that conditionalities were not necessary, and this understanding formed the basis of the structural adjustment loan of 1988.[14] The process of deepening integration with Western economies through the Bretton Woods institutions nonetheless had major implications for China's orientation towards NIEO issues in UN forums and for domestic Chinese policies.

First, as a matter of principle China was an active and consistent supporter of positions taken by developing countries in the IMF (the Group of 24). China consistently put debt questions high on its own agenda for IMF meetings.[15] Chinese views strayed occasionally, however, into criticism of Third World views. For example China argued against the call of Latin American countries for a moratorium on debt repayments. Officials did support the rescheduling scheme negotiated in the mid-1980s, however, and appeared to see this as a possible basis for a more far-reaching solution of debtor countries' problems. In IFI meetings China tended to be more inclined to view itself as mediating between Northern and Southern viewpoints. It frequently steered a middle course between Southern criticisms of structural adjustment on the one hand and IMF advocacy of market-oriented discipline in developing countries on the other. As Li Guixian expressed this general, if still ambiguous, approach in the 1991 IMF meetings, developing countries 'should steadfastly continue with adjustment policies that are commensurate with domestic situations and conducive to economic growth'.[16] Chinese views incorporated criticism too of Western countries. These were repeatedly chided in the IMF for failing to reverse protectionism and for lacking the political will to coordinate their economic policies more effectively in the G7 and other forums. Chinese officials also joined in the chorus of European criticism of the external implications of the US budget deficit in the 1980s.

Secondly, a number of direct and indirect consequences for China's internal politics and policies flowed from the course of integration. Though confined formally within a socialist planning framework, China's modernisation plans rested on assumptions that matched in several important respects those of its newfound friends in the IMF and the World Bank.

Especially, though not exclusively, in the SEZs, Chinese economic policy-makers were increasingly oriented to policy criteria corresponding to those of Western analyses of markets, price reform, the decentralisation and deregulation of the foreign trade sector, progress towards the greater autonomy of enterprises, and the integral role of external development assistance and credit in the overall economic planning process. Jacobson and Oksenberg conclude that convergence rather than external influence better characterises the relationship: 'Had the World Bank and IMF not happened upon the scene, Deng and company probably would have launched many of the changes in any case'.[17]

Yet while it was China that initiated the process of domestic change and external linkage, the existence outside China of a powerful and politically sympathetic constituency for reform was an important variable sustaining its general course and influencing specific developments. In line with conventional IBRD practices, there was close association between Chinese and World Bank officials in the process of project selection. The path on which China was embarked also pointed to the wisdom of its actively seeking out IFI advice on macroeconomic policy questions, especially in the context of the the 1988 structural-adjustment agreement. Specific recommendations for sectoral change were accepted, for example in relation to coal-price reforms in the early 1980s. The requirement of dealing on a regular basis with officials from the Washington institutions, moreover, had a significant impact on public administration in China as agencies were continually created and modified with a view to enhancing China's capacity to handle these relations.[18] China's increasingly decentralised system of economic decision-making, and the assumption of greater power at provincial and local levels, constrained the ability of agencies in Beijing to direct its course and control undesirable effects. Efforts to check this process by administrative changes in 1989–90, particularly as regards the foreign-trade sector, had only minimal effects.

World Bank and IMF staff were particularly insistent on emphasising the problems stemming from inflation and from the continuation of China's double exchange-rate system.[19] Inflation dropped temporarily in the two years after the 1988 agreement, though at the cost of rising unemployment and growth in the budget deficit. Both sides were aware of the impediments obstructing progress on such questions. Beyond an undefinable point, however, their removal would have made the overseers of the reform programme in Beijing and in provincial governments vulnerable to the charge of irrevocably abandoning socialism.

The Chinese party leadership failed to stem the spreading political turmoil of 1988–9, which culminated in the rise and subsequent repression of the prodemocracy movement. Both aspects represented a failure of Deng's earlier campaign against bourgeois liberalisation, and of the party's reaffirmation of socialist conceptions of democracy and economic development. Ironically Dengist economic reformism, including the external ties central to the modernisation drive, was one of the factors precipitating societal demands for corresponding political and constitutional change. The possible social and political costs of the reform programme had been discussed earlier between IBRD and Chinese officials, although the magnitude of the 1989 political crisis in China could not have been anticipated. It was evident nonetheless that IFIs did not see these events as a cause for fundamentally disrupting relationships patiently constructed during the 1980s. Nor did Beijing view them as a reason for terminating, or even modifying, its long-established denial of the legitimacy of external criticism of its political system. Realistic expectations of the resumption of multilateral assistance came as early as January 1990 with the lifting of martial law.[20] The process accelerated in the early 1990s. China extended the scope of reforms, particularly – under renewed US pressure – in the area of intellectual property rights in 1991–3; and Japan, followed by other G7 countries, unfroze loans and resumed the path to normalisation.

The course of China's relations with GATT was less sure, in part because of the more decentralised character of these arrangements. The congressional politics of Sino–American trade, and particularly of China's MFN status, also had an important bearing on developments. Beijing had signalled interest in participation in GATT in 1980 (China had been a signatory before the communist takeover of 1949) and successfully applied for membership of the Multifibre Agreement at the end of 1983. While the latter move was specifically designed to protect China's interests in the international textile trade, especially in light of protectionist pressures in Western Europe and North America, the Chinese made it clear that MFA participation was also seen as a stepping-stone to GATT accession. The expansion of China's foreign trade and the sequence of reforms to its foreign-trade regulatory mechanisms in the 1980s reinforced GATT's attractions. So did the hope that participation would bring with it an end of the US practice of subjecting China's MFN status to annual reappraisal.

Indeed these reforms were also made in part with a view to expediting the GATT process. Chinese trade officials had earlier outlined steps being taken to decentralise the economy as part of the case for accession. China had also sought developing-country status under GATT rules as a means to protect the role it still accorded the state in economic development, and in order to gain preferential access to Northern markets through the generalised system of preferences. Formal negotiations commenced in 1987. In line with GATT procedures China first submitted a report on its foreign trade, and affected GATT contracting parties addressed questions in turn to Beijing. A specially created GATT working party served as the central liaising and negotiating mechanism. In its report, and in later talks, China stressed the strength of its commitment to reform and the extent of its trade with GATT countries – amounting to about 85 per cent of China's total foreign trade, the bulk of it with the US, the EC, Japan and Hong Kong.[21] Further, deficits incurred in the late 1980s were turned into trade surpluses in the early 1990s.

Both developed and developing countries expressed concern about a Chinese presence in, or, more strictly, reentry to, GATT. The latter group included some of China's leading competitors for access to industrialised nations' markets. Washington complained about the lack of transparency in China's foreign-trade system and called for more easily available data. US trade officials were concerned too about the still considerable role of state planning in the Chinese economy, arguing that this constituted grounds for suspecting significant subsidisation of China's exports. European concerns about the vulnerability of key sectors to threats from cheap Chinese imports had been prominent in EC–China relations since the 1970s.[22] These issues, and the formal GATT requirement of bilateral negotiations between applicants and contracting parties, prolonged the negotiations much longer than was anticipated on the Chinese side. The experience contrasted unfavourably for Beijing with the expeditious settlement of issues surrounding IFI memberships. In 1988–9 Chinese officials became increasingly restless with the process and accused Western countries of seeing China not as a trade partner but as an economic threat.[23]

While agreement in principle on the main issues had been reached by the end of 1988, political events in China the following year delivered a heavy blow to the prospects of early success. Negotiations in the working-party framework were postponed until September (though GATT officials insisted the delay was not related to Western post-Tiananmen sanctions). The progress of the talks was helped by the anticipated resumption of multilateral lending to China, and also by the now general acceptance of Beijing's case by G77 contracting parties. For its part China continued to stress its desire for full participation in GATT. In further documentation submitted in October 1991, Beijing maintained that the reforms of the previous decade had brought China into conformity with the requirements of GATT accession. In response to continuing US criticisms in the early 1990s, for example, officials defended their interpretation that Chinese export subsidies had been eliminated and that significant progress was being made on the convergence of official renminbi exchange rates with market rates.

Political and diplomatic factors, however, were crucial. First, the question of Taiwan's relations with GATT complicated matters; Taipei submitted its own application early in 1990. Secondly, in the aftermath of the Tiananmen events US congressional opinion made Beijing's human-rights record in effect the main criterion for its evaluations of China's MFN status. Thirdly, the wider political context served to refocus US attention on long-standing specific complaints. These included China's retention of a variety of import quotas, a diversity of foreign-trade rules and practices among the provinces, lack of transparency and allegations of Chinese foot-dragging on the question of safeguards for sectors of Western economies that might be threatened by future dumping or export surges.[24] The first formal post-Tiananmen negotiations with the US on GATT did not take place until early 1993, following the conclusion of a bilateral trade agreement the previous October.

THE USES OF SECTORAL COOPERATION

Technical cooperation through the UN specialised agencies had traditionally fitted in well with Chinese conceptions of multilateralism. To the extent that these conducted their lives on the basis of peaceful-coexistence principles and served the interests of international development, they were to be applauded. China was quick to point out agencies' failings – for example, alleged budgetary extravagances, a lack of commitment to North–South dialogue, intrusion into members' private affairs (such as human rights), or weakness in the face of Soviet aggrandising pretensions. After its reentry in the early 1970s Beijing also aimed to profit indirectly from IGO meetings held on Chinese territory. One of the early opportunities for China to claim evidence of its continued international respectability after the 1989 crackdown came with the Asia–Pacific regional meetings of the FAO, which were held in China for the first time in March 1990. As for the case study of the Soviet Union, I will look in turn at Chinese policies in the WHO and the ILO, and in relation to UNEP.

In the 1920s and 1930s health represented one of the main policy areas in which there were constructive links between China and international agencies. This priority was a feature of the 1980s and 1990s. Indeed the WHO became increasingly relevant to Chinese requirements during this period. Public-health reform occupied a central place in the modernisation programme. In contrast with the ideological excesses of earlier decades, moreover, the Chinese now placed considerable emphasis on technical training and the traditional professional virtues. In the early 1980s cadres working in health care, as in other fields, were to be 'socialist-minded, younger in age, better educated and professionally competent'.[25] The WHO experience was seen as directly useful in connection with China's ambitious legislative and administrative plans for health policy in the 1980s and 1990s. These focused on the provision of primary health care (PHC) in rural areas and the integration of these concepts into health-policy planning at all levels. Several important laws and sets of regulations on health care emerged in the 1980s, including a major law on infectious diseases, regulations on AIDS and planning for a framework Primary Health Care Act as the basis for further administrative development during the 1990s.

Chinese delegates to World Health Assemblies defined China as one of the organisation's developing-country member-states. As a developing country, officials told the 1991 assembly, China 'shouldered an extremely heavy task in disease prevention and treatment'.[26] China's basic orientation towards the WHO, then, was that of a country in urgent need of long-term external assistance. China's own emphasis on PHC goals blended productively with the orientation of WHO secretariat staff towards international health problems, especially with regard to the relationship between health and development. In sum, as China informed the 1989 World Health Assembly, 'we particularly hope for the attention and sympathy of WHO and other Member States in such fields as primary health care, planned immunisation, health manpower development [and] health legislation and management'. Active cooperation was also sought in the areas of scientific and technological information, professional exchanges, and equipment.[27]

The role of demandant was new for China in the UN system. Although it was ideologically legitimate in the 1980s 'not only to make contributions but also to accept aid',[28] Chinese health officials took active steps inside the WHO to ensure that the first part of this formula was not neglected. For example, China stressed the value to other developing countries of its own distinctive approaches to rural health care, and particularly its approaches to training local medical personnel to serve the needs of communities dispersed across a vast country hampered by inadequate communications, transportation and access to hospitals, specialists and technical equipment.

Similarly in traditional medicine China had a distinctive reservoir of expertise to make available to the international health-policy community. Development of this 'rich store of theoretical and practical experience' was explicitly referred to in China's 1982 constitution. It was being intensively studied at over sixty institutions in the mid-1980s. Chinese delegates to the WHO emphasised that it was placed on an equal footing with Western treatments in Chinese medical practice. Traditional medicine became one of several priority areas of collaboration between the WHO and Chinese research centres. Seven collaborating institutes were recognised in China in the area of traditional medicine – about one third of the world total supported by the WHO – out of a total of approximately fifty Chinese centres designated overall.[29] Chinese public-health officials also took a leading role in securing a place for traditional medicine in the WHO's planning priorities for the 1990s.

More conspicuous in practice, however, was the convergence between broad Chinese and WHO health-care goals, and the use made by Chinese health authorities of WHO data, educational materials, monitoring criteria and definitions of priorities. The first rested on a shared commitment to the goal of 'health for all by 2000'.[30] More specifically the Chinese government used WHO global health indicators as a basis for its own system of monitoring the provision of primary health care in rural areas. Many of the objectives defined for the 1990s by the Ministry of Public Health and other agencies converged with the WHO's general priorities for the Third World. These included reductions in infant mortality and deaths from the major infectious diseases, more effective control of schistosomiasis, expanded immunisation programmes and improvements to rural drinking-water supplies. Much of the activity directed towards these objectives overlapped with projects funded by UNICEF, especially in relation to the delivery of services in remote and minority areas of China.[31] Chinese agencies were also responsive to a variety of specific problems identified as growing priorities by the WHO during the 1980s and 1990s. China initiated research on AIDS in 1987 and set up a national AIDS committee three years later. Close links were maintained with the WHO's global coordinating and monitoring role in the area.[32] Similarly, with WHO support, China in the late 1980s instituted a programme for the eradication of poliomyelitis by the end of the century.

Speaking as president of the World Health Assembly in 1989, Professor Chen Minzhang, China's minister of public health, underlined both the WHO's and China's conviction that many health problems of the 1990s were rooted in human behaviour. The 'real weapon' to combat disease and promote health, therefore, was information and communication.[33] Chinese health officials promoted the work of the WHO inside China and made extensive use of the organisation's information materials in a variety of educational campaigns. The WHO's fortieth anniversary in 1988, for example, was marked in China with special events, media coverage, stamp issues and a national PHC knowledge contest. The media were similarly mobilised to highlight WHO-related 'days', including World Health Day, World No-Tobacco Day and World AIDS Day. Of these areas work on tobacco and health, and a campaign against cigarette smoking, formed an increasingly important priority of public-health officials in the early 1990s. The Chinese Association on Tobacco and Health was created in 1990 to bring together health professionals, officials and educators, and to liaise with the WHO's personnel.

Chinese delegates were reluctant to stray beyond this kind of technically defined agenda in the WHO. This hesitation reflected the organisational culture of the WHO, China's compartmentalising approach to the work of IGOs and the professional backgrounds of the personnel on Chinese delegations to World Health Assemblies. While China insisted that its health-care problems, and therefore its need for assistance from the WHO and other member-states, were rooted in its economic underdevelopment, officials did not take this appeal as a cue to use the WHO as an instrument of larger campaigns for the restructuring of the international economy. They explicitly criticised the Soviet penchant for importing issues of peace and disarmament into the WHO and other UN technical agencies, arguing that these were questions for other forums. Where choice of a policy position on a 'nonhealth' issue was unavoidable, China tended to resort to a for-the-record statement. In the debates on Palestinian membership in the late 1980s and early 1990s, for example, China supported both the 'just struggle of the Palestinian people' and the establishment of a Palestinian state with membership of the WHO.[34] Delegates were not directly involved in the lobbying and negotiations surrounding the question, however, and for the most part were content to allow it to be handled through informal US–Soviet talks.

In the WHO, then, China periodically cast itself as a representative of developing countries, but at the same time it carefully restricted the range of topics it would address in this role. Chinese support for a greater regional voice for the Western Pacific in the WHO grew during the 1980s. Delegates engaged in informal exchanges with representatives of other member-states from the region, and occasionally made formal statements in World Health Assemblies on behalf of the group. China also actively worked for institutional support for a headquarters and staff for the region, and lobbied for a constitutional amendment that would allow greater representation for the Western-Pacific region on the WHO executive board.

The contrasting tone of many international labour conferences – more politicised, prone to conflicts spun off from Soviet–American confrontation, and frequently preoccupied with constitutional disputes and the hidden agendas of power struggles – evoked another aspect of China's multilateralist personality. Delegates to the conferences were vocal foes of apartheid and defenders of South African workers and unions. The atmosphere of the ILO was also more receptive to the spread of NIEO values. It was, according to China at the 1986 sessions, 'imperative to change the current unfair and irrational order of international economic relations, so as to create a favourable international environment for the development of Third World countries'.[35] The means to these ends were those repeatedly stressed by China in UNCTAD forums: the reduction and rescheduling of debt, the lowering of interest rates by wealthy countries, greater ease of access to their markets for developing countries, and extended technical assistance and aid free of conditionalities. Chinese delegates were staunch supporters of Arab positions on Middle East resolutions and unequivocally shared in the identification of Israel as the 'root cause' of tension in the region. More specifically China called for more active interim measures by the ILO and the international community in occupied Arab territories in order to 'effectively protect the personal safety and fundamental rights' of workers and residents in those areas.[36]

China was itself the target of criticism by the ILO following the Tiananmen events of 1989. The attack was launched by US labour-union delegates at the seventy-sixth session that year. It provoked an immediate Chinese protest against interference in its internal affairs. AFL–CIO representatives kept up the pressure on China across a wide variety of issues being debated in ILO circles, for example by condemning the 'despots who rule China' in discussions of the early 1990s on global warming and fossil-fuel use.[37]

Throughout this period, however, China's attention to ILO expertise and convention work was steadily mounting as a result of its modernisation and industrial reorganisation programmes. Chinese delegates showed little interest in attempts to renovate ILO structures and practices, even though China's own employers' constituency was assuming growing importance as a result of reforms and the opening up of the economy.

Indeed the changes China was undergoing had major implications for its orientation towards the ILO. The 'iron rice bowl' (jobs for life for workers) and the practice of 'eating out of the same big pot' (equal wages for all workers) were disappearing. The move towards a more diversified economy, with various types of state and autonomous enterprises operating in parallel, created considerable Chinese interest in the ILO's work in such areas as labour standards and workplace safety. The influx of Western capital into the SEZs reinforced this inclination. Thus whereas the ILO's tripartite structure had been praised in the 1970s primarily for its recognition of the rights of labour unions, in the 1980s the 'unique' principles of tripartism prompted greater interest in the capacity of the ILO to represent the growing number of small and medium-sized enterprises in China. The

ILO was also of value to China as a source of assistance. It helped in the establishment of training centres in the late 1980s, including, through funding from the UNDP and other donors, projects to support advanced vocational training in Shanghai and Tianjin.[38]

China's general approach to environmental issues as a member of the governing council of UNEP tended to be more cautious and detached than was true of its role in either of these two specialised agencies. Delegates made few interventions at annual or special council sessions. China often had little stake in the topics addressed. UNEP meetings and resolutions usually generated fewer contentious issues than other UN bodies in which China participated. Thus apart from one minor amendment (on the question of the transfer of environmentally sound technology to developing countries), China had little difficulty approving the package of subjects drawn up at the second special session in 1990 for consideration by the preparatory committee for the UNCED.[39] Chinese delegates tended to support, with little or no comment, consensus decisions on such questions as sea-level rise, ozone-layer protection, toxic chemicals, the need for greater UN coordination of environmental activities and the ecological consequences of the Gulf War. China also routinely supported the Arab-sponsored draft decisions of the late 1980s and early 1990s on environmental conditions in Israeli-occupied territory. In UN General Assembly second-committee debates, however, it specifically criticised the Soviet Union for bringing issues of the arms race into the work of UNEP.

Chinese officials occasionally took part in the related work of UNEP governing-council sessions, for example in the small-group decision-drafting process. Thus China was a member – with Australia, Finland, Gambia, Ukraine and Yugoslavia – of the working group at the 1987 meetings that focused on the activities of INFOTERRA and drafted the decision to strengthen it.[40] However this kind of participation tended to be more the exception than the rule. One constraint for some Chinese delegates was language. During the 1980s China raised this issue as a matter of both practicality and prestige on several occasions, both with the secretariat and in council sessions. It argued strongly for equal treatment of all six official and working UN languages throughout UNEP, and made clear its opposition to any reduction of language services resulting from budgetary restraints in the secretariat.[41]

This generally low-key Chinese approach did not reflect a disinterested attitude towards environmental questions, however, or indeed a lack of commitment to UNEP itself. Beijing was increasingly aware of the seriousness of China's environmental problems. This recognition grew in part out of a number of World Bank studies of the Chinese economy during the 1980s that had drawn attention to pollution in urban areas as an important and neglected question. The traditionally defined requirements of growth, however, were paramount for China's economic planners. Extensive environmental controls were viewed as beyond the resources of a developing country. As Premier Li Peng put it, 'The reason we lay emphasis on environmental management is that, on the one hand, our country is still very poor and cannot possibly afford to allot money on environmental control; on the other hand, there are indeed many problems which can be solved immediately and practicably just through management'.[42] China expanded its legal and administrative frameworks during the 1980s and 1990s. A major environmental protection law was passed by the standing committee of the Eighth National People's Congress in December 1989. This was designed to protect the environment and control pollution 'in order to safeguard human health and promote the development of socialist modernisation construction' (Article 1).

China viewed UNEP, then, as one element of its overall international environmental policy. With the exception of some important bilateral programmes, particularly that with the US, this had a predominantly Third World slant. China aimed, first, to secure wider recognition of the special needs of developing countries in relation to internationally agreed environmental protection measures, and, secondly, to deflect mounting Western criticisms of inadequacies in its domestic record. In the late 1980s the latter were directed particularly at the consequences for global warming and ozone-layer arrangements, respectively, of China's extensive use of coal and chlorofluorocarbons (CFCs). The need for technology transfer was a key theme in China's approach to ozone-layer negotiations. China joined the Vienna convention in 1989 and the following year announced its intention of acceding to the Montreal protocol. However delegates criticised the obstacles blocking Third World access to relevant technologies, and urged much greater financial assistance from the North to facilitate transfers.[43]

Further, China took an active role regionally and in meetings with developing countries on international environmental questions, especially in connection with preparations for UNCED in 1992. The highlight of this period of environmental diplomacy was the Third World conference held at ministerial level in Beijing in June 1991, at which Li Peng acknowledged the need for 'greater efforts' by developing countries on the environment, but also pointed to the need for funds and technology from the international community.

The Beijing Declaration agreed at the meeting was important for defining a consensus G77 view of sustainable development in the lead-up to the UNCED. It affirmed developing countries' commitment to environmental protection, but placed strong emphasis on the principle that environmental problems 'must not be viewed in isolation, and need to be addressed together with the process of development, by integrating environmental concerns with the imperatives of economic growth and development'. In particular, this meant recognition of the 'right to development of the developing countries'.[44] These principles shaped China's own approach to the UNCED. In the preparatory committee in 1991–2, China, in line with G77 representatives, argued that international environmental conventions should incorporate adequate provisions for financial assistance to developing countries. Delegates also supported the concept of a special fund to finance sustainable development projects in the South.[45]

SECURITY AND DEVELOPMENT: THE DUBIOUS CHARMS OF GREAT POWERHOOD

Less directly engaged than the Soviet Union in the multilateral exchanges surrounding Security Council sessions, and, with the exception of Cambodia, often with fewer immediate interests at stake, China in the 1980s tended to approach many questions of international peace and security facing the UN from general theoretical or philosophical perspectives. Adversaries and perpetrators were condemned: the USSR or Vietnam, South Africa or Israel. Possible routes to settlement were situated in the context of the five principles of peaceful coexistence. Self-imposed ideological constraints, reflecting differences of capabilities and interests, deterred China from aspiring to great-power status. It had serious misgivings about being seen as too eager or compliant a participant in Soviet and American UN practices of consultation and coalition-building. As the only developing country among the permanent member-states of the Security Council, China saw its task in large measure as being to stay alert to the concerns of elected G77 member-states.

The 1980s nonetheless saw a number of significant changes in China's approach to the UN. As peacekeeping forces began to be grudgingly accepted as legitimate by Beijing following policy shifts in the Security Council in the late 1970s, and as UN contributions to the peaceful settlement of disputes came to be viewed more favourably, its delegates were inexorably drawn into a broadening network of policy commitments in relation to international conflicts. Responses to the situations in southern Africa and the Middle East reveal different aspects of this cautious evolution of Chinese thinking.

For much of the decade the Chinese position on Southern African questions in the Security Council followed a consistent path of denunciation of Pretoria's internal policies, denial of the validity of its claims to be edging towards reform and change, and attacks on its continued occupation of Namibia and strategies of destabilisation and intervention in other states. As Li Luye stated in the Security Council in early 1987, 'apartheid cannot be reformed. It can only be destroyed'.[46] The specifics derived from this general approach were increasingly compatible in the middle and late 1980s with the emerging consensus of a number of Western delegations. They included a demand for the lifting of the state of emergency in South Africa, the release of Nelson Mandela and other political leaders, a lifting of the ban on the African National Congress, and firm evidence on the part of the South African authorities of a commitment to the dismantling of apartheid and the independence of Namibia.

Chinese views on mandatory sanctions were tempered, however, by realistic appraisals of the likely degree of support for various options by the US, Britain and other Western council members. The risk of supporting measures that might indirectly serve to enhance Soviet influence in Africa was also at times a concern for Beijing. On Namibian independence, for example, China argued in June 1986 that the Security Council 'should truly discharge its duties', and called for the enforcement of mandatory sanctions against South Africa under Chapter VII of the UN charter.[47] Similar stands were taken by the OAU and the Non-Aligned Movement at their later summits. The South African linkage of the Namibian situation with the withdrawal of Cuban forces from Angola was denounced by China as another instance of Pretoria's obstructionism and procrastination.

China's position shifted somewhat, however, in light of both the dynamics of the Namibia process and growing attention to the indirect Soviet connections with it. Thus in October 1987 Ambassador Yu Mengjia said that the Security Council should give the secretary general the mandate to work towards a Namibian settlement based on Security Council resolution 435 of 1978; if the South African authorities were again to 'arbitrarily obstruct' the process, the Council should then 'consider' mandatory sanctions under Chapter VII.[48] Chinese officials similarly did not exploit setbacks in the US 'constructive dialogue' with Pretoria to attack its underlying assumptions. China occasionally drew the attention of the Security Council to troubling developments – for example the continued presence of South African security personnel in the South-West Africa Police in 1989 – but it was not a lead player on Southern African questions.

Middle East issues had greater salience for China. Beijing had supported the creation of UNEF in 1956, but the special circumstances of that situation made it inapplicable, in the Chinese view, as a precedent for the institutionalisation of a UN peacekeeping role. In cautiously advocating this role in the 1980s, Chinese diplomats appreciated the restraints under which such forces operated. Having joined in the general UN condemnation of Israel for its invasion of Lebanon in June 1982, for example, China maintained that a continuing and effective UN role was a key to the stabilisation of the area. By the mid-1980s the presence of UNIFIL was still seen as 'necessary,' but officials claimed that continuing difficulties were mounting to 'crisis' proportions. China repeated its call for Israel to withdraw its military personnel from all Lebanese territory and dismantle its security zone in the south of the country, conditions which would allow the deployment of UNIFIL forces along Lebanon's borders. Renewed Israeli activity in south Lebanon in 1988 revived Chinese concerns.[49] Chinese officials also expressed criticism of the rising costs of the operation.

On the central issues of the Arab–Israeli conflict China moved steadily towards a posture of more unequivocal support for the UN. This did not mark a reversal of its traditional stance, characterised by recognition of the PLO, support for Arab-sponsored resolutions on the Middle East in the General Assembly and in the specialised agencies, and condemnation of Israel's continued occupation of the West Bank and other Arab territory. Thus Chinese commentary made much of the fact that a UN seminar on Palestine held in Beijing in 1985 was the first such meeting to take place on the territory of one of the five permanent members of the Security Council.[50] China remained a steadfast defender of the diplomatic privileges of the PLO's mission in New York, particularly in the context of the vulnerability of Palestinian officials to shifting interpretations of their position in US law. The Chinese view was increasingly contained, however, within the ample framework afforded by successive Security Council resolutions. This allowed criticism of Israeli actions, especially in the occupied territories, while at the same time encouraging China's search for a lasting settlement.

Thus in the late 1980s Chinese delegates increasingly addressed both the long-term need for a 'comprehensive, just and lasting settlement' of the Middle East question, and the more immediate requirement of the cessation by Israel of its oppression of Palestinians in the West Bank.[51] On the latter issue, Chinese officials were particularly responsive to the PLO and Arab member-state view that the situation on the West Bank justified Security Council examination. They accepted too the argument that Israel was violating its responsibilities under the international law governing the protection of civilians by occupying powers.

Pursuit of the idea of an international conference under UN auspices, however, with the participation of all five permanent members of the

Security Council together with all parties to the conflict, involved tempering rebukes with recognition of the legitimate security needs of the state of Israel. Qian explained his country's support for this route, and for the prerequisite of Israeli readiness to negotiate with the PLO, at his UN meeting with Shimon Peres in September 1988.[52] The Palestinian *intifada* confirmed for Chinese officials the urgency of a conference directed towards a comprehensive settlement of the Arab–Israeli conflict. China stated in the Security Council in May 1990 that the 'only way out lies in continued pushing for the development of the peace process and in a fair settlement of the Palestinian question', a process which Israel was urged to support. Indeed the fact that the issue was still on its agenda meant that the council had, in China's view, 'failed to play its proper role' in a Middle East settlement.[53] The vigorous Soviet campaign for a Middle East conference, and the prospect of its using such an event to extend its influence in the region, was a further motivating factor for the Chinese.

The road to Madrid was temporarily obstructed by the 1990 Gulf crisis. China's first response at the beginning of August was to echo its earlier line in the Iran–Iraq war, when it appealed 'time and again'[54] to the parties to reject the use of force and to negotiate seriously. Noting that China maintained 'friendly relations' with both Iraq and Kuwait, Li Daoyu reiterated the principle that disputes should be settled peacefully and expressed 'regret' at the 'incident.' A fuller statement shortly afterwards likewise recalled the principles of peaceful coexistence and the UN charter, and expressed support for Arab mediation efforts.[55] Although it was left unclear, Beijing evidently saw the charter more in its Chapter VI than in its Chapter VII guise.

This position was later modified to take account of Iraq's refusal to comply with Security Council resolutions. Qian said in September that China 'understood and respected' the defensive measures taken by Saudi Arabia and other Gulf states. It remained opposed, however, to great-power military involvement in the situation.[56] China's dilemma was sharpened as a combination of international condemnation, UN sanctions and conciliatory Arab approaches failed to produce Iraqi flexibility, and as US opinion and the Western consensus moved towards seeking Security Council authorisation for the use of force. Abstention on this resolution (678) was the only way Beijing could reconcile the conflicting pressures of Washington's need for Security Council voting support and the shared goal of bringing about an Iraqi withdrawal from Kuwait, with its sensitivity to the diverse currents of Arab opinion on the issue and its long-standing condemnation of the use of force in international politics. Chinese officials rejected the view that the resolution made war inevitable. As Qian said in a

German interview in 1992, 'Some countries, but not China, understood this as a justification for war'.[57] Indeed China maintained that its stand was consistent throughout the situation, and that while it was 'gratified' when the ground war ended, the eventual result of military action by coalition forces was in line with China's own desire for Iraqi withdrawal.[58]

Many of these problems, and China's way of responding to them, persisted in the early 1990s. China abstained on the Security Council resolution of April 1991 on Iraq's suppression of the Kurds. Although acknowledging that the situation had significant international aspects, including the refugee flow to Turkey and Iran and the threat of armed conflict spreading beyond Iraq's borders, Chinese officials held that these did not outweigh the principle of noninterference in the internal affairs of member-states. During 1991–3 China also increasingly questioned, on humanitarian grounds, the need for continued sanctions against Iraq. The government argued that barriers to the sending of food, medical supplies and other basic necessities should be lifted and other sanctions phased out. China also opposed (and abstained in the vote on) the Security Council's decision of October 1992 to seize Iraqi overseas assets. Beijing nonetheless adhered strictly to the position that Baghdad should comply with Security Council resolutions, including cooperation with the UN inspection team over the destruction of weapons of mass destruction.[59]

By the start of the 1990s, then, China's qualified recognition of the value of a UN role in relation to international conflicts, including the deployment of peacekeeping forces, had been successfully tested in several situations. This support came under increasing strain. Chinese officials were concerned, first, that a confident and resurgent post-Cold-War and post-Gulf-War UN might financially and logistically outreach itself, and, secondly, that a capacity to meddle in the domestic affairs of countries might come to be defined as a criterion of UN efficacy in the resolution of conflicts.

The deteriorating situation in Yugoslavia presented China with concerns on both counts. By the early 1990s some strands in China's earlier policies towards that country – for example, ideological criticism of its revisionist route to socialism, praise of its historic role in the formation of the NAM and implicit acknowledgment of its security value as an opponent of Soviet power in south-Eastern Europe – had either disappeared or been significantly eroded by events. Some constraints, including trade, particularly in the energy sector, remained and reinforced the ingrained Chinese wariness about UN interference. Other factors, such as the presence of Moslem minorities and the intensifying Western examination of military options, drew China more closely into UN debates.

The spreading violence at first affected China only minimally. In 1991 China supported Security Council efforts to bring the UN more directly into the situation in the wake of EC mediation efforts among the contending parties. However as a 'friend of Yugoslavia' China formally insisted on respect for the principle of noninterference. Thus UN involvement was acceptable in the 'special circumstances' of the 'explicit agreement' of the government of Yugoslavia that it could discuss the situation.[60] Chinese diplomacy was later aimed at supporting mediation efforts and restraining signs of Western impulsiveness. For example, in criticising calls for tighter pressures on Serbia, China unsuccessfully tried to delay Security Council voting on sanctions in May 1992 and abstained in the air-exclusion-zone-enforcement vote of March 1993.

CHANGING THE TIMES: INSTITUTION-BUILDING WITH CHINESE SKETCHES

The pathways of China's engagement with the UN system were diverse, then, but some linked up to take a common direction. In general appraisals from the mid-1980s Beijing maintained that the UN was working well: it had become 'important'. Applying the criterion of a lessening of tensions in regional conflicts led to this conclusion. So did Chinese evaluations of the UN against other yardsticks, particularly the state of North–South relations, though here rather more weaknesses were detected. Viewed in this light – and from the broader perspective of analyses of tendencies in international politics and the world economy – the UN did not require structural renovations. As Confucianists China's foreign-policy elites sought to understand the times; as incrementalists they discreetly shunned contact with Marx's injunction to change the world.

Chinese assessments of the place of the UN in a changing international system nonetheless relied on some traditional socialist tools. First, while, according to Qian at the end of 1988 the world was 'turning from confrontation to dialogue', conflicts between nations were still 'inevitable'. Since war could not be eliminated, disputes had to be settled 'correctly' when they broke out.[61] Even so the Chinese could still point to impressive evidence in the late 1980s to support the thesis of diminished international tensions: steady improvements in Sino–Soviet relations, for example, and moves towards settlements in Southern Africa, in the Iran–Iraq conflict and in Cambodia. Secondly, the division of the world into two systems – socialist and capitalist – continued to be the framework within which many Chinese analyses were situated.[62] The growing appeal of Western vocabularies of interdependence indicated a flexible adaptation of Chinese concepts to changing circumstances. In itself, however, this usage did not necessarily imply a rejection or downgrading of older two-camp models. An understanding of the political and security interdependence of nations was after all an integral characteristic of the theory of peaceful coexistence; and at least some recognition of economic interdependencies was required to give theoretical justification for China's new linkages with IFIs and G7 states.

What inadequacies the UN manifested were thus a product of the constraints put on it by certain member-states. This factor had, in the Chinese view, prevented the UN from acting effectively during the first half of the 1980s. Its achievements were attributed in large measure to Third World diplomacy and to China's own patient prodding. In the early 1990s the UN was actively involved in a growing number of situations, from central America to Yugoslavia to Somalia. Chinese officials had themselves acquired first-hand experience of a variety of UN activities, including the Western Sahara referendum, Namibian independence, UNTSO, Cambodia, and the Iraq–Kuwait observer mission. At the same time the extent of this engagement by the UN gnawed at China's confidence in the organisation.

The task of structuring the UN's future in ways that might make it a more effective instrument in relation to regional conflicts and the clashes of post-Cold-War nationalisms, while ensuring that it did not thereby become dangerously interventionist, posed some inescapable dilemmas. The superpower collusion that Beijing fretted over in the 1970s had gone; but the new situation of a sole superpower supported by a complaisant former adversary was hardly an improvement. Thus in discussions of reform, Chinese delegates stressed the importance of the consent of states as a prerequisite of any form of UN activity. This principle applied to fact-finding in conflicts, for example, an area where China maintained the UN had nonetheless a useful role to play.[63] UN bodies were criticised when they failed, in the Chinese view, to live up to these standards. UNDP staff, for example, were censured in 1992 for using human-rights data in policy documents and statistical reporting.[64]

When juxtaposed with the Western debates of the early 1990s on the UN and world order, these kinds of criteria likewise revealed defects. Washington's conceptions in 1991–2 seemed to observers in Beijing to call for a US leadership role indistinguishable in practice from hegemony.[65] Institutional change in UN structures derived from such perspectives was clearly regressive. Nonetheless there were also points of constructive contact between Chinese and US views of the new international order: for example on the appropriateness of seeking an enhanced UN role, and in overlapping approaches to the peaceful settlement of disputes. Where Washington's world-order views connected with its traditional human-rights agendas, however, or with Western objections to China's arms sales and nuclear-power supplies, they began to clash both with Chinese interests and with the conceptions of world order based on the principles of peaceful coexistence articulated by Deng in 1988.

Part III

Conclusions and Prospects

8 The UN System and World Order

The experiences of Russia and China with twentieth-century experiments in international governance have been mixed. Both states have often been isolated from major trends or detached from the political forces nurturing them. Each has at times treated IGOs with hostility and suspicion. Each has also occasionally greeted them with qualified approval, laced sometimes with an exuberant spirit of rediscovery.

Their own situations in relation to IGOs have undergone many twists and turns. Indeed one of the ironies of the early 1990s was not so much that noted by Yeltsin – the reemergence of Russia out of the collapsed framework of the Soviet Union – as the historical slide of Russia into something akin to earlier Chinese circumstances. China for the League of Nations was in some ways what the Soviet Union (and in turn the Russian Federation) eventually became for the UN: a country wracked with disintegrative tendencies, a struggling economy and political divisions, simultaneously seeking out and fending off foreign economic entanglements. A chronic source of apparently insoluble problems for IGO member-states and secretariats, it was an object rather than a subject of policy.

Realities, of course, are more complex than even the more adroit of images can adequately capture. This final chapter returns to the questions raised at the outset. How can we best characterise the kinds of changes that took place in the 1980s and early 1990s in Russian and Chinese relations with the UN system? What were the main factors that precipitated these developments? And how are we to assess their significance in terms of their effects on each of these countries and on the UN system? Are there implications here for our understanding of the character of late-twentieth-century global institutional order?

RUSSIA AND CHINA IN THE UN SYSTEM

World politics, as Keohane has put it, are institutionalised as well decentralised.[1] Political leaders are constrained by the nature of the systems their countries inhabit. IGOs are among the features of the international system that define limits to the manoeuvrability of the states that governments steer. They offer states a variety of inducements and penalties that enter into the choices governments make among strategies and actions. The way in which IGOs carry out these operations is subject not only to structural and policy variations in the organisations themselves, but also to differential perceptions of their importance by national political actors. In studying the approaches states adopt towards IGOs, then, we need to look not only for those factors that sustain the momentum of longer-term stable relationships – whether cooperative or conflictual – but also those that foster change.

Perceived from Moscow or Beijing, the UN system historically tended to remain firmly relegated to the distant perimeters of national analyses and policies. Their respective judgments of its salience altered in the 1980s, however, as the Cold War died and as the economic opportunities associated with IGOs became more apparent. Yet underlying continuities are also evident. Like other states they made use of the UN as an ideological justification of policies.[2] The foreign-policy elites of the late Soviet Union and the Russian Federation were as insistent as their predecessors on structural continuity in the composition and powers of the UN Security Council. Cooperative responses in social and technical areas of UN activity were also a recurrent, if less visible and more fragile, feature of both countries' approaches. China's persisting definition of itself as a developing country reinforced similarities in response to technical agencies between the Maoist early 1970s and the Dengist early 1990s.

During the 1980s, however, Russian and Chinese perspectives on the UN system changed. IGOs were seen to be more significant actors in the international system. They were also viewed more as practical instruments for self-betterment than as gladiatorial arenas. The new political acceptability of aid had profound implications for China's outlook on IGOs. So, for Moscow, did the schemes for refurbishing the Soviet economy that took shape there in the mid-1980s. Unlike China, it approached the Bretton Woods system in part by constructing a 'deideologised ideology' of activist multilateralism. This served several purposes. It provided a possible means of revitalising trade relations with Western states and removing the barriers to their growth; it offered opportunities for criticising a West still alleged to be mired in Cold-War thinking, and for turning IGO attention to arms-race issues; and it allowed Gorbachev both to put his own stamp on socialist history and Marxist–Leninist conceptual development and, increasingly, to create a network of lifelines for threatened state and party structures in the USSR.

In part this shift reflected a secular trend of the growing importance of IFIs in the world economy generally and in the increasingly constrained circumstances of developing countries more specifically. Partly, too, changing views were a product of the economic disparities of the socialist states with the capitalist world. Appreciation of this gap, and anticipation of its widening, became a powerful motivation for change in Russia from the early 1980s. The prospects of narrowing such inequalities had also traditionally provided PRC leaders with material for inspiring and mobilising domestic publics and setting growth targets, from both revolutionary and 'four-modernisations' perspectives. There were few ideological obstacles to fitting Chinese participation in IFIs into this traditional picture. Apart from a largely reactive deployment of 'five-principles' theory, China displayed little interest in coating its reconstructed IGO policies with new ideological varnish. Beijing's approach also conspicuously lacked the element of domestic political restructuring and democratisation – in its multiple definitions – that was a critical component of Russian experimentation.

Viewed instrumentally, IGOs have certain assets. Because of the inter-state links on which they are grounded, they can to a limited extent assist in the pursuit of goals such as the import of capital or the transfer of technology. But they also have major structural drawbacks.[3] IGOs could not in themselves modify the ground rules or the structure of East–West trade in ways sought by the USSR in the 1980s, or advance it to significantly higher levels. They could not guarantee China the threat-free trade relationship it wanted with the US. Nor could the UN enhance qualitatively, and perhaps not even incrementally, the security – traditionally defined – of Russia or China.

Yet both countries came to rely more heavily on the putative benefits of deepening engagement with the UN system. Their doing so arose in a sense from an admission of structural weakness. The multiple strategies used by different types of Western industrial states for coping with change in the global economy[4] were not available to them. Particularly for the Soviet Union, international economic policy objectives – for example in relation to foreign capital, advanced technology and access to Western markets – were also inseparable from Cold-War-generated strategic and political restraints on economic relations with the capitalist states. Cultivation of the UN system was thus a relatively costless method for an increasingly option-poor state to pursue objectives at both levels. Reduction of bipolar tensions through such means also served the traditional Russian diplomatic goal of stabilising the external environment to facilitate domestic change or consolidation. This kind of engagement was viewed as part of a de facto process of integration with Western economic, political and security structures.

The origins of these changes in orientation to IGOs, then, can be traced primarily, though not exclusively, to the deterioration of domestic economic conditions in the Soviet Union, and in its trade relations with capitalist countries, that was becoming apparent from the early 1980s. Viewed from this perspective many of the uses the USSR had traditionally made of IGOs had a sharply diminishing marginal utility. First, there were other, and better, means for it to attack adversaries, form coalitions, acquire information, forge contacts and promote its prestige. Secondly, the UN had already reached the modest limits of its exploitability as a domestic mobilising tool for the rhetoricians of peace, internationalism and socialism. Thirdly, the practical (as well as the prestige) benefits of hosting intergovernmental scientific and technical conferences faded in comparison with those that might be secured through a transformation of Soviet relations with IFIs.

During much of the 1980s the policy repercussions of Soviet analyses of this worsening economic situation competed in IGOs with the implications of a quite different analysis of world trends. According to this the central political and strategic fact was the ebullience of the Reagan administration, and its apparent readiness to wage the Cold War with much greater intensity in multilateral forums, in the arms race and in its approach to regional tensions in the Middle East, Southern Africa and elsewhere. If this interpretation was valid, then the appropriate response in IGOs was heightened confrontation tempered by the element of caution dictated by nuclear bipolar logic. Much the same policy conclusion followed if perceived conjunctures were subjected to ideological filtration: the acuteness of the crisis of capitalism in the 1980s, that is, indicated the need for invigorated political struggle, qualified by an understanding of the security risks posed by capitalist states approaching their final stage of internal contradictions.

This conclusion, however it was arrived at, conflicted with that suggested by the emerging theoretical framework of the 1980s. In this the Soviet Union's own economic plight – together with the inadequacy of traditional planning methods for alleviating it and the role of conventional CPE structures in precipitating it – was the central issue. The policy logic derived from this genre of analysis pointed, among other things, to the need for constructive working relationships with IFIs. It was a line of argument that led inexorably to the judgement that Russia should itself become – in the structuring of its economy and political system and in its membership of institutions such as the IMF and the G7 – a Western state. This verdict, painful to reach and far from universally accepted among Russian elites, was subject to increasingly critical reevaluation in the 1990s.

Up to a point, however, much of the content and style of traditional Soviet and Chinese approaches to the UN can also be accounted for if we graft a sociological explanation on to this argument. Because of Cold-War politics, according to this interpretation, the USSR and China were traditionally compelled to play certain roles in relation to the UN. Until the early 1970s China was an excluded outsider. It was formally (in 1950) branded an outlaw by civilised society and was allowed to make its views known only through a disreputable interlocuter (Albania). The USSR traditionally occupied a permanent minority role in the Western-led Security Council. In the General Assembly it was the enemy of the first dominant coalition, controlled by the US until the mid-1950s, and an awkward cheerleader of the second, comprising the growing weight of Third World states from the mid-1960s.[5] Variations of one or other of these patterns dominated politics in the specialised agencies. Of these the USSR remained outside the most important: the World Bank and the IMF. In all these microsocieties in which Russia participated, accordingly, we see Soviet delegates behaving in a sociologically predictable fashion: relishing confrontation, leaping quickly to the supposed higher moral ground of ideology and imbued with a prickly concern for formal standing.

This image of the sources of Russian and Chinese UN behaviour is weakened, however, by two considerations: first, the sometimes marked differences of approach of the two states, and, second, the evidence of considerable variation in approach by each country over time.

Despite its past dealings with the UN, a long history of denunciation of that organisation's manipulation by the US and the glistening anti-Western and anti-UN tints of the Cultural Revolution, China in the early 1970s quickly became a cautiously supportive participant in UN security and technical forums. Not long afterwards, and despite the domestic political turbulence of that decade, it moved to establish firm ties with IFIs and came to accept much of the UN conventional wisdom on peacekeeping. It rejected the high-politics linkage manoeuvres often favoured by Soviet delegates in technical agencies.

Similarly the Soviet Union's own approach varied considerably during the Cold War. The shoe-banging veto-wielding persona had disappeared long before Gorbachev turned his attention to the UN.[6] Indeed in the continued shifting of the gears of national diplomatic style in the UN system, there was far more continuity in successive ways of dealing with the UN system than either Gorbachev or Yeltsin was prepared to concede. Under the latter, Russia continued and deepened the consensus-seeking style of the late 1980s; under the former, Soviet delegates maintained their predecessors' love of the heroic, their conviction that nothing succeeds like excess and their belief that ideas, dexterously formulated, have a determining impact on events.

INTERNATIONAL INSTITUTIONS AND NATIONAL DISCOURSE: THE POLITICS OF LEGITIMACY

These changes in their attitudes towards IGOs had a variety of consequences for Russia and China. They went beyond the modification of declaratory positions and of voting tendencies on issues on IGO agendas, or the access that policy shifts gave to UN agency funding programmes. The effects of these shifts, and the changes of foreign policy they reflected, were felt across a wide range of issue-areas and policy processes. Whether directly or indirectly through the mediation of externally influenced economic variables, they had an impact, too, on internal political activity. In so doing, changes of approach to IGOs generally, and IFIs specifically, brought the question of relations with the UN system before a broadened array of domestic actors. The extent and significance of the latter development was constrained, however, by the traditionally elite-bound character of UN policy in both countries, and by the persistence of statist restraints on policy discourse in the case of China. Several dimensions of such effects can be detected.

First, there was an expansion of the range and influence of external actors accepted as legitimate participants in the *formulation of economic policy.* Approaches to reforms in China, for example in relation to prices, exchange rates, private-sector creation and the informal economy, were formulated in close association with IFI secretariats and consultants. IMF and World Bank thinking on the workings of market economies and the dysfunctionality of state structures also indirectly influenced that of Chinese officials and economists. As a result the boundary between externally nudged and domestically initiated policies became blurred, especially since the roots of Chinese modernisation debates lay deep in communist history. In the late 1980s the USSR's pursuit of IFI memberships likewise brought to light a set of externally defined neoliberal conditions for its participation. From inside these organisations in the 1990s Russian Federation publics and government actors found the price of access to benefits unexpectedly high.

Secondly, a similar process was evident in the *making of foreign policy.* This was more true of Russia than China. Soviet interactions with Western states during the Cold War formed the basic context in which its UN policies were made. These environmental factors shaped its resort to 'politicisation' and linkage strategies in technical forums.[7] As bipolar thinking gave way to notions of security interdependence,[8] the types of external influences on Soviet behaviour in the international system altered. The UN was a crucial conduit for this transition. From being embedded in the iron logic of intense conflictual relationships, Russia's UN policy was transformed in effect into a cooperative venture. Western states, and also China, became de facto co-partners in its formulation. Yet, as in the UN's handling of Middle East or Yugoslavian issues, this clearly did not rule out Moscow's use of the Security Council as a means of pursuing its own interests in relation to regional conflicts. China's response, of abstention or non-participation in key council votes, was explicitly rejected by Moscow as ill-befitting a state that had made a commitment to join the Western club.

Thirdly, changing approaches to the UN system were part of, and fed back into, the larger circular process of adaptation and ferment in the *political ideas* that shaped them. This was constrained in the case of China by the traditional shielding mechanisms that deflected IGO and other external influence attempts away from ideologically sensitive questions of democratisation. Growing academic interest in Western, especially US, scholarship nonetheless influenced the course of research on world history and other aspects of China's study of international relations and political economy.

In the case of the Soviet Union there were several dimensions to intellectual change. The altered orientation towards the UN system helped promote a continuing process of adaptation of thinking at policy-making levels from the mid-1980s. Later in the decade, for example, theorising about the origins of the Cold War and the events precipitating its demise increasingly converged with prevailing US interpretations. The wider policy changes resulting from these kinds of cognitive shifts were more evident in the field of foreign policy than in domestic economic policy, where arguably the interplay of powerful organised interests was more significant.[9]

Soviet IGO policies also had repercussions on debates in the media and specialist publications. To the degree that this activity was comprised more of explorations and elaborations rather than critiques of policy, however, this tended to serve a comparable function of rationalisation and justification to that found in earlier Soviet periods. The decline of the view that the foreign policies of Western states were conditioned by the presumed class interests of their ruling circles, for example, can be seen as a functional adjunct of the official pursuit of enhanced relations with these countries. This tendency merged, however, with the rise of a pluralist contest in policy debates on Russia's future in the international system among a variety of competing and autonomous domestic viewpoints. Much of this, of course, can be attributed to factors other than shifts in UN policies, particularly the continuing centrality of the bilateral relationship with the US.

Fourthly, changes of policy towards IGOs reinforced a process of change in the *structure and workings of government.* Some Soviet policy changes – for example on the treatment of nationals working for the UN secretariat – were designed in part to demonstrate a wider seriousness of intent to skeptical Western audiences. Public-administration changes aimed at bringing Russian procedures more into line with those of Western countries presented more difficulties. Until 1990 there was little of the practice, commonly found in Western states, of routine horizontal interdepartmental consultations among IGO-related bureaucracies in Moscow. More thorough analyses of the institutional capabilities of Russian bureaucracies for handling relations with IFIs and UN agencies only got seriously under way after the breakup of the USSR. In China there was a continuing process of institutional adaptation and agency creation to meet the requirements of dealing with IGO staffs and agendas.

Fifthly, the deepening Russian and Chinese involvement with the world of IGOs exerted various interconnected effects on their *domestic economies and politics.* These simultaneously reinforced, but also brought into question, the long-term direction of external policies. In both countries IFI-sanctioned policies had macroeconomic consequences – particularly in terms of the novel phenomena of significant levels of unemployment and inflation – which in turn had social and political repercussions.

Up to a point the domestic political costs of adjustment could be more effectively contained by Beijing. Party-led state structures were resilient. The multiplier effects at local and regional levels of foreign investment capital, expansion of the foreign-trade sector and the buoyancy of autonomous commercial and industrial enterprises, also in practice defused possible tensions. The juxtaposition with other factors, however – the resurfacing of the mesmeric image of an alternately seductive and repellant West, for example, and social and political spillover from expanding relations with the US – made for a periodically volatile mixture. Indeed Beijing's commitment to IFIs and development assistance from Western donors prompted a domestic questioning of reform policies for not going far enough. In its role as inspirer and critic of government, the Communist Party, hoist temporarily on its own Westernist petard, had first to scramble hurriedly to combat the perceived threat of bourgeois liberalisation and then to suppress forcibly the politically challenging form taken by the pro-democracy movement. While it was able to recover much of the lost ground in relations with the West and IFIs in the early 1990s, costs remained evident in relations with the US in particular, for example over the question of GATT accession and in the annual political battles in Washington over its MFN status.

Dual sets of tensions – external as well as domestic – were more pronounced in the case of Russia. On the one hand the application of IFI formulae, particularly on price reform, triggered or worsened domestic social unrest, including the rise of politically oriented strikes in key sectors, that had been increasingly evident from the late 1980s. On the other hand failures to implement programmes systematically, for example in the area of credit restriction, provoked external criticisms of government actions. These led in turn to enforced delays in the introduction of key elements of assistance such as the IMF rouble-stabilisation fund. Further, the Russian experience – unlike that of China – was compounded by domestic protest at the degree of dependence on the West and on IFIs that the government's policies entailed: a dependence that critics found doubly humiliating since it appeared to be unaccompanied by tangible evidence of economic improvement.

For the most part the specific inclusion of IGOs in such attacks was fuelled more by the programmatic critiques of rival Russian elites than by immediate reactions to economic hardship. Problems were exacerbated by inadequacies in the funding of government social programmes as a result of pressures to reduce deficits. Reconstruction efforts were also hampered by the slow pace of development of social formations to fill the gap left in civil society by the erosion of the state- and party-regulated organisations of the Soviet past. A backlog of official retardation or suppression of domestic groupings capable of exercising semi-autonomous transnational roles thus created significant difficulties of transition to a post-socialist society.

This also had implications for Russia's capacity to operate effectively in the contemporary UN system. In practice NGOs carry out important agenda-setting, data-gathering and lobbying functions. They are an integral part of the complex processes of coalition-making and consensus-formation that lie behind Western-state approaches to IGOs. Without such functioning systems, as both Russia and China have tended to be, states are relatively disadvantaged in promoting their interests and pursuing leadership roles in policy areas important to them.

ORDER, INSTITUTIONS AND CHANGE

These events have had continuing significance for change and evolution in world institutional order. This can be seen in the context of two interrelated sets of developments: first, the broader sectoral trend evident in the 1980s and 1990s of expanded institutionalisation in international relations, and, second, the impact on this trend of broader changes in the structures of international politics and the world economy. In particular the end of the Cold War and the transformation of Eastern Europe and the USSR had profound implications both for the UN system and for Russian and Chinese strategies within it.

First, it removed the automatic Soviet counter to Western, and especially US, conceptions of regional and global security issues and North–South relations. This did not so much create as confirm tendencies evident earlier. Soviet attacks on the impact of Western and IFI policies on Third-World economies were already beginning to lose their vigour in the early 1980s, despite the rightward ideological shift of the US and British governments. Such criticisms of externally fostered structural adjustment had a negligible impact. Moscow's growing concern with domestic economic issues, the unimpressive Soviet performance compared with Western economies and stagnation in East–West trade edged North–South issues out of Soviet IGO priorities. Acknowledgement of the failure of earlier strategies in UNCTAD and elsewhere to foster reliable East–South alignments within a NIEO restructuring process reinforced this tendency. The removal of Cold War incentives to engage in strategies of confrontation with Western states in IGOs confirmed it.

For its part China remained a standard-bearer for Southern interests in the UN system. Its criticisms of Western positions on debt, protectionism, development funding and other questions were reinforced by its own stake in these issues, for example in the North American and European textile markets. At the same time, however, Beijing took a discriminating and critical line in IFIs in relation to some Third World positions, for example on debt management and structural adjustment.

Secondly, Russia was transformed from a donor into a competitor with the South for regional IGO and UN funds. The process of terminating Cold War relations served to legitimise, though not render fully respectable to domestic critics, the role of demandant in the international community. The simultaneous collapse of CMEA-based economic relationships significantly reduced the probability of Moscow finding a viable regional alternative to the former hierarchical, and beneficial, division of labour. The magnitude of the task of post-socialist reconstruction in Russia – in infrastructure projects, institutional development, the private sector, environmental clean-up, nuclear safety and other areas – strained Western agendas. These were already overburdened with a variety of post-Cold-War transition and conversion problems and the policy predicaments generated by economic recesson. There was the added prospect of East and South-East European ethnic conflicts generating recurring cycles of demands for preventive aid programmes and enhanced conflict resolution and enforcement capabilities. As a result some problems of the South receded to a lower plateau of Western attention. The elimination of the perceived Soviet factor in Third World conflicts and regional instabilities also removed a motive for assistance on the part of some Western donor agencies.

Thirdly, the continuing regional and global reverberations of change in Central and Eastern Europe, and the former Soviet Union, constructed UN post-Cold-War agendas around issues of regional armed conflicts. IGOs still addressed the kinds of questions that had characterised the 1970s and 1980s: resource issues, economic development, energy, oceans management, the environment. But these increasingly lost ground in the largely Western-adjudicated competition among issues for high-urgency designation. The tendency was reinforced by the temporary absence of the kinds of conditions, such as any threat to the continuing oil glut, that had earlier compelled attention to other global problems.

Fourthly, residual tripolar strategic perceptions were a further casualty of the winding down of Cold War tensions. These had earlier formed one of the elements in the IGO calculations of the US, China and the USSR. The extent to which an economically buoyant and Western-tilted (or at least not anti-Western) China, buttressed by IFI ministrations, served US security interests was debatable. It had limited use as a card in Washington's tacit negotiations with Moscow in the 1970s and 1980s, not least because of Beijing's refusal to cast itself in the role of coconspirator. China was perhaps marginally more reluctant in such circumstances, however, to transform its foreign-policy commitment to a balanced accommodation with the Soviet Union into a self-driven process of deepening economic and political engagement.

A variety of considerations – for example the continued lure of the Chinese market, the comparative advantage of the SEZs in labour costs, the importance of China in East Asian systems and the requirement of avoiding Beijing's opposition in UN Security Council votes – kept up the momentum of Washington's policies. These were maintained even after the imperatives of US–Soviet détente, followed by the opportunities presented by Soviet decline, eroded the remaining elements of the tripolar calculus. With the approach of the mid-1990s, however, economic and security threat perceptions were again becoming more characteristic of US dealings with China in IGOs.

In the late 1980s and early 1990s, then, the UN system was again subjected to the glare of high expectations. Such intervals, historically rarer than prolonged bouts of relative indifference, are standard features of the life-cycles of IGOs. How it emerges from this period of intense scrutiny depends on several factors. Just as Russia and China were both central actors in producing this particular twist in its fortunes, so their respective actions are likely to have a significant bearing on its outcome.

Having taken a crucial role during the previous decade in getting contemporary debates on the UN's future rolling, Russia itself was not in a strong position in the early 1990s to play a major role in driving them forward. The requisite economic basis for the performance of such a role was absent. So was its political acceptability. Further, on many questions Russia lacked the various issue-relevant capabilities required for the different kinds of leadership roles played by state actors in UN agencies.[10]

At the other end of the spectrum, a Russian withdrawal into passivity in IGOs was likewise not a viable option. Despite the changes in the interim, many of the conditions that had prompted the rise of Soviet interest in the UN system in the 1980s were still present. There were no solid bilateral alternatives. The prospect of a renewed alignment with China, for example, even if negotiable, lacked the trade and investment incentives of Western and IFI links. A successful lurch towards Japan required among other things the return of the four island groups occupied in 1945. Unlike other former CMEA states, Russia was not in practice a realistic contender for eventual EC membership.

Other visions of its UN future competed with each other. The immediate post-Soviet role, caricatured as that of a pliantly cooperative US ally, proved increasingly irksome. The Russian Federation's first use of its Security Council veto, on the UNFICYP mandate in May 1993, was a reminder to external audiences – and a means of reassuring domestic ones – that the government was aware that Russia had interests of its own to promote in the UN. These increasingly focused on issues in the several regions in which Russia is an actor. Attention to problems in the Central Asian republics mounted from late 1992. Together with concern about a variety of intra-CIS conflicts, both within and across state boundaries, this encouraged more urgent exploration of the prospects of Russia's assuming a UN-approved regional security role. The philosophical groundwork for such a role was already present in Russian support for the principle of UN intervention to protect human rights, and in the exploration of dispute-settlement mechanisms in CSCE talks. Given much of the tenor of domestic debates on Russian foreign policy, however, and particularly nationalists' unease with Russia's confinement within its post-Soviet borders, this definition of the country's security predicaments was fraught with the risks of quagmires.

For Russia, then, the UN remained in large measure what it had always been: a club for great powers to deliberate on the world's conflicts from the relative safety of veto-protected armchairs. For China, judgments of the UN's worth continued to be structured primarily by development assistance criteria. Yet the prospect of a future China acting like any other great power had also been discreetly raised with Western visitors by Zhouist modernisers as early as the 1970s, partly as a tactic for discrediting domestic political rivals. The security implications of its rapidly changing economic situation affected Beijing's roles in IGOs in the 1990s. These could not be isolated in practice, for example, from Western criticisms of its arms-export policies and regional territorial ambitions, and charges of its role in the proliferation of weapons of mass destruction.

Often frustrating for the powerful, and sometimes little more than necessary evils for the weak, IGOs are rarely congenial settings for states. This form of institutionalised multilateralism exploits their reserves of patience and their readiness to compromise. There are reciprocal benefits in the form of security, economic and other goods. The significance of this exchange, however, depends on their costs, inequalities in their distribution and the differential value recipients attach to them. Russia and China each made conservatively sound, though different, investments in the UN system in the 1980s and the early 1990s. The protracted learning exercise that each engaged in during this period also afforded them a measure of leverage over future IGO developments affecting their interests. But a greater capability to direct the course of UN events still lay with other nations.

Notes and References

The following abbreviations have been used:

CD(P)SP	Current Digest of the (Post-) Soviet Press
FBIS	Foreign Broadcast Information Service
GAOR	UN General Assembly, Official Records
GC	Governing Council (UNEP)
ILC	International Labour Conference (ILO)
JPRS	Joint Publications Research Service
MEMO	Mirovaia Ekonomika i Mezhdunarodnye Otnosheniia
RFE/RL	Radio Free Europe/Radio Liberty
RMRB	Renmin Ribao
S/PV	UN Security Council, Verbatim Records
WHA	World Health Assembly (WHO)

1 Introduction

1. See for example Peter Ferdinand, *Communist Regimes in Comparative Perspective: The Evolution of the Soviet, Chinese and Yugoslav Models* (Hemel Hempstead: Harvester Wheatsheaf, 1991).
2. Benjamin Miller, 'A "New World Order": From Balancing to Hegemony, Concert or Collective Security?', *International Interactions*, 18(1), 1992, pp. 3–4; and 'Explaining Group Cooperation in Conflict Management', *World Politics*, 45(1), 1992, pp. 43–5.
3. John Gerard Ruggie, 'Multilateralism: The Anatomy of an Institution', *International Organization*, 46(3), 1992, pp. 56–7.
4. These and other types are discussed in Samuel S. Kim, *China in and out of the Changing World Order* (Princeton: Center of International Studies, 1991).
5. For example, S. Haggard and B. A. Simmons, 'Theories of International Regimes', *International Organization*, 41, 1987, p. 491.
6. K. J. Holsti, *The Dividing Discipline: Hegemony and Diversity in International Theory* (Boston: Unwin Hyman, 1985), Ch. 2.
7. See for example the review article by Steve Smith, 'The Forty Years' Detour: The Resurgence of Normative Theory in International Relations', *Millennium*, 21(3), 1989, pp. 489–508.
8. Robert Boardman, 'Approaching Regimes: Australia, Canada, and Environmental Policy', *Australian Journal of Political Science*, 26(3), 1991, pp. 450–3.

2 Historical Ironies

1. S/PV.3046, 31 Jan. 1992, pp. 46–8.
2. C. Dale Fuller, 'Lenin's Attitude toward an International Organization for the Maintenance of Peace, 1914–17', *Political Science Quarterly*, 54(2), 1949.

3. Quoted by Robin Edmonds, *Soviet Foreign Policy 1962–1973: The Paradox of Superpower* (London: Oxford University Press, 1975), p. 152.
4. Donald S. Birn, *The League of Nations Union, 1918–1945* (Oxford: Clarendon Press, 1981), p.18.
5. F. P. Walters, *A History of the League of Nations* (Oxford University Press, 1960), pp. 94–6.
6. C. Howard-Ellis, *The Origin, Structure and Working of the League of Nations* (Boston: Houghton Mifflin, 1928), p. 169.
7. Walters, op. cit., pp. 354–5, 358, 370–1.
8. Alexander Dallin, *The Soviet Union at the United Nations: An Inquiry into Soviet Motives and Objectives* (New York: Praeger, 1962), p. 18.
9. Walters, op. cit., pp. 580–4.
10. Kazimierz Grzybowski, *Soviet Public International Law* (Leyden: Sijthoff, 1970), p. 355.
11. Andrei Gromyko, *Memories*, trans. Harold Shukman (London: Hutchinson, 1989), p. 115.
12. I. Deutscher, *Stalin: A Political Biography* (London: Oxford University Press, 1967), p. 525.
13. Grzybowski, op. cit., pp. 359–60.
14. J. E. Johnson, 'The Soviet Union, the US and International Security', *International Organization*, 3(1), 1949, p. 3.
15. J. M. Mackintosh, *Strategy and Tactics of Soviet Foreign Policy* (London: Oxford University Press, 1962), pp. 65–7.
16. Grzybowski, op. cit., p. 53.
17. Ruth B. Russell, *A History of the UN Charter: The Role of the United States, 1940–1946* (Washington: Brookings, 1958), pp. 533–9; Robert C. Hilderbrand, *Dumbarton Oaks: The Origins of the UN and the Search for Postwar Security* (Chapel Hill: University of North Carolina Press, 1990), p. 235.
18. See for example, Konstantyn Sawczuk, *The Ukraine in the UN Organization: Study in Soviet Foreign Policy, 1944–1950* (Boulder: East European Quarterly, 1975), p. 140; V. V. Aspaturian, 'The Union Republics and Soviet Diplomacy: Concepts, Institutions and Practices', *American Political Science Review*, 53, 1959, pp. 388–411.
19. L. O. Leshchenko, *Ukraina na mizhnarodnii areni, 1945–1949* (Kiev: Naukova Dumka, 1969), pp. 30–46.
20. Rupert Emerson and Inis L. Claude Jr, 'The Soviet Union and the UN: An Essay in Interpretation', *International Organization*, 6, 1952, pp. 18–19.
21. Dallin, op. cit., p. 28.
22. Cited by A. Stepanov, 'Soviet Foreign Policy and the Restructuring of International Relations', *International Affairs*, 1, 1974, p. 8.
23. Sh. Sanakoyev, 'The UN and the Security of Nations', *International Affairs*, 12, 1972, pp. 20–1.
24. Sir William Hayter, *Russia and the World: A Study of Soviet Foreign Policy* (London: Secker and Warburg, 1970), p. 101.
25. D. Dmitriyev and E. Shakunov, 'Definition of Aggression and the UN Charter', *International Affairs*, 5, 1973, p. 59.
26. V. Yelizarov, 'National Contributions to the UN Budget', *International Affairs*, 4, 1979, pp. 58–60.

27. Jonathan Haslam, 'The UN and the Soviet Union: New Thinking?', *International Affairs* (London), 65, 1989, pp. 678–80.
28. Cited by Richard F. Starr, *USSR Foreign Policies after Detente*, rev. ed. (Stanford: Hoover, 1987), pp. 96–7.
29. Christopher Andrew and Oleg Gordievsky, *KGB: The Inside Story* (London: Hodder and Stoughton, 1990), pp. 420–1.
30. *Pravda*, 12 March, 1986; CDSP XXXVIII(10), pp. 21–2.
31. *Pravda*, 16 Sept. 1975; CDSP XXVII(37), pp. 10, 23.
32. *Pravda*, 10 Sept. 1982; CDSP XXXIV(36), p. 16; 'Enhancing UN Effectiveness', *New Times*, 38, 1982, p. 1.
33. Philip E. Mosely, 'The Soviet Union and the UN', *International Organization*, 19, 1965, pp. 666–7.
34. *Izvestiia*, 19 Dec. 1974; CDSP XXVI(51), p. 22.
35. *Pravda*, 19 Sept. 1972; CDSP XXIV(38), p. 25.
36. Petrovsky, cited at FBIS-SOV-87-181, 18 Sept. 1987, p. 5. See further Edward C. Luck and Toby Trister Gati, 'Gorbachev, the United Nations, and US Policy', *Washington Quarterly*, 11, 1988, pp. 19–35; Gunther Unser, *Die Sowjetunion in den Vereinten Nationen* (Koln: Bundesinstitut fuer Ostwissenschaftliche und Internationale Studien, 1990), pp. 38–48.
37. V. Petrovsky, 'Postkonfrontatsionnaia perspektiva OON', *MEMO*, 4, 1990, pp. 16–24.
38. See further Elena N. Nikitina, 'New Soviet Environmental Policy: Approaches to Global Change', *International Studies Notes*, 16(1), 1991, pp. 31–6.
39. See for example, Eduard Shevardnadze, 'Ecology and Politics', *International Affairs*, 11, 1990, pp. 3–15.
40. FBIS-SOV-87-174, 9 Sept. 1987, p. 8.
41. Gerasimov, cited at FBIS-SOV-90-221, 15 Nov. 1990, pp. 7–8.
42. *Izvestiia*, 11 Sept., 1991, p. 7; FBIS-SOV-91-178, pp. 15–16. See further V. Petrovsky, 'OON i gosudarstvennye prioritety SSSR', *MEMO*, 5, 1991, pp. 23–4, 29.
43. FBIS-SOV-92-014, 22 Jan. 1992, p. 30. One commentator identified the confirmation of Russia as the legal successor of the Soviet Union as the 'primary achievement' of Russian foreign policy during 1992. See Andrei Kortunov, quoted at CDPSP XLV(1), 3 Feb. 1993, pp. 16, 24.
44. FBIS-SOV-92-014, 22 Jan. 1992, p. 29.
45. *Izvestiia*, 2 Jan. 1992; FBIS-SOV-91-001, p. 79.
46. FBIS-SOV-92-181, 17 Sept. 1992, p. 7.
47. Cited by Haslam, op. cit., pp. 679–80.
48. A. Kortunov, in *Literaturnaia gazeta*, 11 July 1989, at CDSP XLII(30), pp. 9–10.
49. Allen Lynch, *The Soviet Study of International Relations* (Cambridge University Press, 1987), pp. 124–5.
50. Margot Light, *The Soviet Theory of International Relations* (New York: St. Martins, 1988), pp. 40–1, 67.
51. For this interpretation, see for example Jerry F. Hough, 'The "X" Article and Contemporary Sources of Soviet Conduct', in T. L. Deibel and J. L. Gaddis (eds), *Containing the Soviet Union: A Critique of US Policy* (Washington: Pergamon-Brassey, 1987), p. 143.

52. Light, op. cit., pp. 228, 278, 292.
53. Ibid., pp. 268–72, 281–6.
54. Grzybowski, op. cit., p. 53.
55. Stephen Clarkson, *The Soviet Theory of Development: India and the Third World in Marxist–Leninist Scholarship* (University of Toronto Press, 1978), pp. 42–3.
56. Light, op. cit., p. 133.
57. Lynch, op. cit., p. 103.
58. G. I. Morozov, *Aktualnye problemy deiatel'nosti mezhdunarodnykh organizatsii: teoriia i praktika* (Moscow, 1982), pp. 1–3.
59. Ibid., pp. 25–37.
60. A. P. Baryshev, *Strategiia Belogo Doma i OON* (Moscow, 1972), pp. 6, 22–3, 257 ff.
61. *Organizatsiia Ob' 'edinennykh Natsii: sbornik dokumentov* (Moscow, 1981), pp. 7–8.
62. Morozov, op. cit., pp. 10–12; E. L. Kuz'min, *Mirovoe gosudarstvo: illiuzii ili real'nost'? Kritika burzhuaznykh kontseptsii suvereniteta* (Moscow, 1969).
63. V. I. Markushina, in *Problema okruzhaiushchei sredy v mirovoi ekonomike i mezhdunarodnykh otnosheniiakh* (Moscow, 1976), pp. 347–8.
64. P. A. Novikov, in G. I. Morozov and P. A. Novikov, eds, *Global'naia ekologicheskaia problema* (Moscow, 1988), pp. 157–8.
65. Morozov, op. cit., p. 8.
66. *Organizatsiia Ob' 'edinennykh Natsii*, p. 8.
67. A. Ye. Nesterenko, in *SSSR v ekonomicheskikh nauchno-tekhnicheskikh organizatsiiakh OON* (Moscow, 1983), p. 39.
68. Ye. D. Lebedkina, *Mezhdunarodnyi sovet nauchnykh soiuzov i Akademiia Nauk SSSR* (Moscow, 1974), p. 202.
69. V. I. Markushina, *OON i mezhdunarodnoe nauchno-tekhnicheskoe sotrudnichestvo* (Moscow, 1983), p. 33.
70. Morozov, op. cit., p. 262.
71. Morozov and Novikov, op. cit., Chs 1, 2.
72. Ibid., p. 185.
73. Haslam, op. cit., p. 679.
74. Lynch, op. cit., p. 67.
75. Kortunov, op. cit., pp. 9–10.

3 Bretton Woods and After

1 V. Gerasimov, in *Pravda*, 27, June 1992; CDPSP, XLIV(4), p. 11.
2. F. P. Walters, *A History of the League of Nations* (Oxford University Press, 1960), pp. 316, 425–6.
3. Jozef M. van Brabant, *The Planned Economies and International Economic Organizations* (Cambridge University Press, 1991), pp. 45–6.
4. Ibid., pp. 26, 32, 34.
5. Joseph Gold, *Membership and Non-membership in the IMF* (Washington, DC: IMF, 1974), p. 124. This was in the fourth draft of the Keynes plan; there was no comparable reference in the final version.
6. Ibid.

7. Ibid., pp. 133–4; Valerie J. Assetto, *The Soviet Bloc in the IMF and the IBRD* (Boulder: Westview, 1988), p. 59.
8. Brabant, op. cit., pp. 45–6.
9. Ibid., pp. 46–7; Assetto, op. cit., p. 60.
10. Assetto, op. cit., p. 58.
11. Gold, op. cit., p. 134.
12. Assetto, op. cit., p. 63.
13. Brabant, op. cit., pp. 41–2, 174.
14. Ibid., pp. 52–3.
15. UNCTAD, 6th Sess., 1983, vol. II (New York: UN, 1986), p. 170.
16. Brabant, op. cit., pp. 47–8, 175.
17. Assetto, op. cit., pp. 63–4.
18. Brabant, op. cit., p. 35.
19. V. Panov, 'International Financial Organizations: Their Role in Neocolonialist Policy', *International Affairs*, 7, 1973, pp. 65–9; Yu. Nechaiev, 'What Aims does the IMF Serve?', *New Times*, 19, 1978, pp. 14–16.
20. *Izvestiia*, 22 Oct. 1976; CDSP XXVIII(42), p. 20.
21. *Izvestiia*, 17 Sept. 1982; CDSP XXXIV(37), p. 18. In general see G. Matiukhin and V. Shenaev, 'Novaia valiutnaia sistema i uroki Bretton-Vudsa', *MEMO*, 6, 1978, pp. 43–52.
22. *Izvestiia*, 2 Dec. 1982; CDSP XXXIV(48), p. 16.
23. Panov, op. cit.
24. *Izvestiia*, 19 Feb. 1972; CDSP XXIV(7), p. 24.
25. *Izvestiia*, 22 Oct. 1976; CDSP XXVIII(42), p. 20. See further Yu. Osipov, 'Problema perestroiki mezhdunarodnoi valiutnoi sistemy i razvivaiushchiesia strany', *MEMO*, 11, 1983, pp. 57–72.
26. G. Yuriev, in *International Affairs*, 10, 1973, p. 121.
27. S. Otreshko, 'Mezhdunarodnaia torgovaia sistema kapitalizma i peregovory "Tokio Raund"', *MEMO*, 4, 1980, pp. 70–82.
28. ECOSOC, Official Records 1984 (New York: UN, 1988), vol. II, pp. 29–30.
29. A/C.2/39/SR.4, 15 Oct. 1984, pp. 9–10.
30. Brabant, op. cit., p. 175.
31. *Pravda*, 12 Dec. 1974; CDSP XXVI(50), p. 15.
32. ECOSOC, Official Records 1984, vol. II, p. 30; I. Yegorov, 'Bor'ba razvivaiushchikhsia stran za ekonomicheskuiu samostoiatelnost'', *MEMO*, 5, 1983, pp. 70–83.
33. ECOSOC, Official Records 1984, vol. I, pp. 82–3.
34. *SSSR v ekonomicheskikh nauchno-tekhnicheskikh organizatsiiakh OON* (Moscow, 1983), pp. 285–6.
35. Y. Kolosov, 'The Mass Media and International Law', *International Affairs*, 7, 1973, pp. 55–7; V. Sivtsev and V. Saidov, 'Informatsionnyi imperializm i bor'ba za novyi mezhdunarodnyi informatsionnyi poriadok', *MEMO*, 3, 1983, pp. 51–63.
36. *Izvestiia*, 29 June 1976; CDSP XXVIII(26), p. 25.
37. *Pravda*, 15 April 1972; CDSP XXIV(15), p. 15.
38. A. Dostal, in *Ekonomicheskaia gazeta*, 31 July, 1977; CDSP XXIV(31), pp. 4–5.
39. UNCTAD, 6th Sess., 1983, vol. I (New York: UN, 1984), Doc. TD/323, pp. 152–3.

40. Ibid., pp. 56, 152–3; and statement of Group D at p. 76.
41. Helmut Faulwetter, 'The Socialist Countries' Conception of the NIEO', in Brigitte H. Schulz and William W. Hansen (eds), *The Soviet Bloc and the Third World: The Political Economy of East–South Relations* (Boulder: Westview, 1989), pp. 78–9.
42. *Pravda*, 6 June 1972; CDSP XXIV(23), p. 19; *Pravda*, 19 August 1976; CDSP XXIX(33), pp. 19–20.
43. UNCTAD, 6th Sess., 1983, vol. I, p. 52, and vol. II, pp. 170–1; A/C.2/40/SR.3, 15 Oct. 1985, pp. 12–13; P. Khvoinik, 'Tupiki dialoga "Sever-Yug"', *MEMO*, 7, 1983, pp. 60–7.
44. A/C.2/39/SR.5, 17 Oct. 1984, p. 8; A/C.2/40/SR.23, 12 Nov. 1985, p. 9.
45. A/C.2/40/SR.43, 5 Dec. 1985; A/C.2/40/SR.3, 15 Oct. 1985, pp. 12–13.
46. ECOSOC, Official Records 1985 (New York: UN, 1989), vol. I, p. 31.
47. *Izvestiia*, 11 Aug. 1989; CDSP XLI(32), p. 21.
48. Schultz and Hansen (eds), op. cit., p. 2; Andre Gunder Frank, 'The Socialist Countries in the World Economy', ibid., p. 14; Peter W. Schulze, 'Socialist Transformation and Soviet Foreign Policy in the Gorbachev Era', ibid., p. 70.
49. 'USSR: New Management Mechanism in Foreign Economic Relations', UNCTAD/ST/TSC/10/Rev. 1, 1988.
50. David M. Kemme, Appendix, in A. M. Solomon and A. Aganbegyan (eds), *Managing the Transition: Integrating the Reforming Socialist Countries into the World Economy* (New York: Institute for East–West Security Studies, 1989), pp. 51–4.
51. Ibid., pp. 54–6.
52. Judy Blatt, *Economic Reform and Political Change in Eastern Europe: A Comparison of the Czechoslovak and Hungarian Experiences* (London: Macmillan, 1988), p. 277.
53. Brabant, op. cit., p. 48.
54. A working party was set up in 1989. See further *GATT Newsletter*, 62, June 1989, p. 5.
55. Viktor Gerashchenko, 'Global Economic Institutions', *European Affairs*, 3, 1990, p. 55.
56. A/40/PV.6, 24 Sept. 1985, p. 51.
57. A/41/PV.6, 24 Sept. 1986, p. 61.
58. From the Political Report of the Central Committee, in *Pravda*, 26 Feb. 1986; CDSP XXXVIII(8), pp. 31–32.
59. I. Ivanov, of the Ministry of Foreign Affairs (International Economic Relations), in *Pravda*, 1 Sept. 1986; CDSP XXXVIII(35), p. 14.
60. Nikolai Shmelev and Vladimir Popov, *The Turning Point: Revitalizing the Soviet Economy* (London: I. B. Taurus, 1990), p. 245; Ye. Primakov, in *Pravda*, 15 Sept. 1987; CDSP XXXIX(37), p. 14.
61. John H. Jackson, *Restructuring the GATT System* (London: Pinter, 1990), pp. 84–7.
62. *GATT Newsletter*, 17, Nov. 1982, p. 1.
63. 'USSR: New Management Mechanism in Foreign Economic Relations', op. cit.
64. Shmelev and Popov, op. cit., p. 246.
65. UNCTAD, 7th Sess., 1987, vol. I (New York: UN, 1989), annex VI, p. 122.
66. ECOSOC, Official Records 1988, vol. I (New York: UN, 1991), p. 21.

67. UNCTAD, 7th Sess., 1987, vol. I, annex VI, pp. 124–8; ECOSOC, Official Records 1988, vol. I, p. 154; A/C.2/44/SR.11, Oct. 16, 1989, p. 4.
68. Kemme, op. cit.
69. *The Economy of the USSR: Summary and Recommendations* (Washington, DC: IMF, IBRD, OECD, EBRD, 1990), pp. 4–8.
70. ECOSOC, Official Records 1988, vol. I, p. 22; ECOSOC, Official Records 1989, vol. II (New York: UN, 1992), pp. 29–30; Ivanov, cited at FBIS-SOV-89-199, 17 Oct. 1989, p. 11.
71. *GATT Newsletter*, 67, Dec. 1989, p. 1.
72. *Izvestiia*, 17 May 1990; CDSP XLII(20), p. 22.
73. Anders Aslund, *Gorbachev's Struggle for Economic Reform* (London: Pinter, 1991), pp. 226 ff.
74. *Journal of Commerce*, 12 Feb. 1991, p. 6B; OECD, *Economic Outlook*, 48, Dec. 1990, p. 31. Windfall gains on gold were later checked by substantial reported 'losses'.
75. FBIS-SOV-90-211, 31 Oct. 1990, p. 2; FBIS-SOV-91-051, 15 March 1991, p. 1.
76. FBIS-SOV-91-045, 7 March 1991, p. 5; 'Communication from the USSR', GATT Doc. L/6864, 20 June 1991.
77. A. Ustinov, in *Sovetskaia Rossiia*, 5 June 1991; FBIS-SOV-91-113, pp. 2–3. Britain, France and West Germany later liberalised their own lists of prohibited items.
78. The EC favoured specific programmes to support such areas as infrastructure development, banking and credit, technical assistance, and currency reform. On the background, see in particular European Parliament, Economic and Social Committee, 'Corrigendum to the Information Report...: Soviet Union', EXT/74, 3 July 1990, p. 14; First Meeting of EEC-USSR Mixed Committee, 10/11 May 1990, Moscow (Brussels, 1990).
79. *The Economy of the USSR*, op. cit., pp. 1–2.
80. *Common Issues and Interrepublic Relations in the Former USSR* (Washington, DC: IMF, 1992), p. 2.
81. Richard E. Feinberg, *The Soviet Union and the Bretton Woods Institutions: Risks and Rewards of Membership* (New York: Institute of East–West Security Studies, 1989), pp. 2–10.
82. V. Shcherbakov, in *Izvestiia*, 19 July 1991; CDSP XLIII(29), p. 7.
83. IBRD, Annual Report 1992, p. 135; *Russian Federation* (Washington, DC: IMF, 1992), p. 36.
84. FBIS-SOV-92-008, 13 Jan. 1992.
85. Interview cited at FBIS-SOV-92-159, 17 Aug. 1992, p. 10.
86. RFE/RL, Oct. 28, 1992. Cf. his criticism of the 'modish postulates drawn from Western macroeconomic textbooks', and their applicability only to countries that already had market economies (CDPSP XLV[13], 1993, pp. 17–18).
87. *Pravda*, 27 Jan. 1992; CDPSP XLIV(4), p. 11.
88. IMF, 46th Annual Meeting of the Board of Governors, 1991, pp. 152–3; IMF, *Russian Federation*, op. cit., p. 21; Gerashchenko, cited at RFE/RL, 28 Oct. 1992.
89. IMF, *Russian Federation*, op. cit., pp. 4–5.
90. Michel Camdessus, cited at RFE/RL, 6 Nov. 1992; and his criticisms of Central-Bank policies at CDPSP, XLV(5), 3 March 1993, p. 16. IMF staff in

Moscow were particularly critical of the budget deficit (CDPSP, XLV[13], 1993, p. 26).

91. Assistance in 1992 totalled $18.4 billion (RFE/RL, 6 Nov. 1992).

4 Interesting Diversions

1. Inis L. Claude Jr, *Swords into Plowshares: The Problems and Progress of International Organization*, 4th ed. (New York: Random House, 1971), p. 398.
2. C. Dale Fuller, 'Lenin's Attitude toward an International Organization for the Maintenance of Peace, 1914–1917', *Political Science Quarterly*, 54(2), 1949, p. 261.
3. Chris Osakwe, *The Participation of the Soviet Union in Universal International Organizations: A Political and Legal Analysis of Soviet Strategies and Approaches inside ILO, UNESCO and WHO* (Leiden: Sijthoff, 1972), pp. 3–4.
4. A/C.2/39/SR.5, 17 Oct. 1984, p. 7; *SSSR v ekonomicheskikh nauchno-tekhnicheskikh organizatsiiakh OON* (Moscow, 1983), p. 305.
5. Ibid., p. 319.
6. R. Panteleimonov, 'ILO Falsifiers', *New Times*, 10, 1984, p. 26.
7. Osakwe, op. cit., p. 64. In general see H. K. Jacobson, 'The USSR and ILO', *International Organization*, 14(3), 1960, pp. 402–8.
8. *Ten Years of World Cooperation* (Geneva: League of Nations, 1930), pp. 264, 269–70; F. P. Walters, *A History of the League of Nations* (Oxford University Press, 1960), pp. 165, 265, 757.
9. V. I. Markushina, *OON i mezhdunarodnoe nauchno-tekhnicheskoe sotrudnichestvo* (Moscow, 1983), p. 213.
10. *SSSR v ekonomicheskikh nauchno-tekhnicheskikh organizatsiiakh OON*, op. cit., p. 313.
11. *OON i mezhdunarodnoe ekonomicheskoe sotrudnichestvo* (Moscow, 1970), pp. 287, 289. There is a more favourable view of the FAO's 'useful work' in Africa at ECOSOC, official records 1985, vol. I, p. 62.
12. A. E. Nesterenko, in *SSSR v ekonomicheskikh nauchno-tekhnicheskikh organizatsiiakh OON*, op. cit., p. 39.
13. WHA 41/1988/REC/2, p. 22.
14. *The Work of WHO. Biennial Report of the Director-General* (Geneva: WHO, 1982), p. 16.
15. Figures from World Health Assemblies, 1984–90.
16. WHA 34/1981/REC/3, Co. A, p. 208; WHA 36/1983/REC/3, Co. A, p. 23.
17. WHA 43/1990/REC/2, p. 138.
18. WHA 34/1981/REC/3, Co. B, p. 327.
19. WHA 38/1985/REC/3, Co. B, p. 230; WHA 40/1987/REC/3, Co. B., p. 235.
20. Denisov, WHA 44/1991/REC/2, p. 40.
21. WHA 34/1981/REC/3, Co. B, p. 310.
22. *SSSR v ekonomicheskikh nauchno-tekhnicheskikh organizatsiiakh OON*, op. cit., p. 319.
23. L. Fyodorov, 'ILO: Changes Needed', *New Times*, 18, 1985, pp. 18–20. See also the socialist states' letter to the ILO director general, *Pravda*, 1 Dec. 1984; CDSP XXXVI(48), p. 13.

24. *SSSR v ekonomicheskikh nauchno-tekhnicheskikh organizatsiiakh OON*, op. cit., p. 322.
25. Kostine, ILC, 70th Sess. (1984), p. 8/14; ILC, 68th Sess. (1982), p. 5/3.
26. Declaration by socialist states, at ILC, 71st Sess. (1985), p. 12/21.
27. ILC, 72d Sess. (1986), p. 10/5.
28. 'Joint Statement of the Government Representatives of the Socialist Countries...', Working Group on Structure, ILC, 68th Sess. (1982), app. II, pp. 3/18–19.
29. ILC, 73d Sess. (1987), p. 16/30.
30. ILC, 74th Sess. (1988), p. 24/15.
31. ILC, 77th Sess. (1990), p. 18/4.
32. He was not able to attend. See FBIS-SOV-90-195, 9 Oct. 1990, pp. 7–8.
33. FBIS-SOV-90-221, 15 Nov. 1990, p. 6.
34. The USSR had been absent at the founding conference in Stockholm in 1972 (because of the issues surrounding representation of the Germanys), though in practice its embassy there maintained close touch with developments and indicated a positive attitude towards the proposed organisation.
35. UNEP, GC, 8th Sess. (1980), at GAOR, 35th Sess., suppl., A/35/25, p. 94.
36. UNEP, GC, 11th Sess. (1983), at GAOR, 38th Sess., suppl. A/38/25, p. 11.
37. *SSSR v ekonomicheskikh nauchno-tekhnicheskikh organizatsiiakh OON*, op. cit., pp. 303–4, 308.
38. B. Asoyan, 'WHO Conference for Africa', *New Times*, 47, 1976, pp. 29–30.
39. WHA 34/1981/REC/3, Co. B., p. 294; WHA 37/1984/REC/3, Co. A, p. 66.
40. WHA 41/1988/REC/3, Co. A, p. 72.
41. Savel'ev, WHA 35/1982/REC/3, Co. A, p. 39.
42. WHA 39/1986/REC/2, p. 245.
43. WHA 37/1984/REC/3, Co. A, pp. 62–5.
44. WHA 37/1984/REC/2, p. 32.
45. WHA 42/1989/REC/2, p. 256; WHA 43/1990/REC/2, p.160; WHO Doc. A 43/3.
46. WHA 36/1983/REC/3, Co. B, pp. 314–5.
47. WHA 35/1982/REC/2, p. 65.
48. WHA 44/1991/REC/2, p. 42.
49. Kostine, ILC, 67th Sess. (1981), p. 12/15.
50. ILC, 68th Sess. (1982), pp. 5/3, 11/10, 13/16.
51. Ibid., p. 11/11; ILC, 70th Sess. (1984), p. 8/13.
52. A. Sergeyev, 'In the Spirit of Cooperation', *New Times*, 47, 1979, pp. 8–9.
53. Asakwe, op. cit., p. 100, n. 119.
54. ILC, 71st Sess. (1985), p. 22/12.
55. ILC, 75th Sess. (1988), p. 13/28; ILC, 76th Sess. (1989), p. 8/23.
56. ILC, 77th Sess. (1990), p. 15/9.
57. UNEP, GC, 8th Sess. (1980), at GAOR, 35th Sess., suppl., A/35/25, pp. 16–17; UNEP, GC, 9th Sess. (1981), at GAOR, 36th Sess., suppl., A/36/25, pp. 7, 24; UNEP, GC, Sess. of special character and 10th Sess. (1982), at GAOR, 37th Sess., suppl., A/37/25, p. 22.
58. UNEP, GC, 11th Sess. (1983), at GAOR, 38th Sess., suppl., A/38/25, p. 12.
59. UNEP, GC, 12th Sess. (1984), at GAOR, 39th Sess., suppl., A/39/25, p. 14; UNEP/GC.13/16 (1985), pp. 14–15.
60. UNEP/GC.15/12 (1989), pp. 14, 30–9.

61. UNEP, GC, 2nd Special Sess. (1990), at GAOR, 45th Sess., suppl. A/45/25, p. 15; UNEP, GC, 16th Sess. (1991), at GAOR, 46th Sess., suppl., A/46/25, p. 21.
62. Delegation of the Netherlands for the EC, ibid., p. 22.
63. UNEP, GC, 3rd Special Sess. (1992), at GAOR, 47th Sess., suppl. A/47/25, p. 40.
64. UNEP, GC, 14th Sess. (1987), at GAOR, 42d Sess., suppl., A/42/25, annex ii, pp. 96–7, 122–3; cf. the earlier socialist countries' statement in the General Assembly Second Committee on the arms race, A/C.2/40/SR.50, 11 Dec. 1985, p. 10.
65. WHA 35/1982/REC/3, Co. A, p. 65.
66. WHA 34/1981/REC/3, Co. A, pp. 132–3.
67. WHA 42/1989/REC/3, Co. A, p. 88.
68. WHA 43/1990/REC/2, p. 137; ECOSOC, Official Records 1988, vol. i, p. 143.
69. *The International Chernobyl Project: Proc. of an International Conference* (Vienna: IAEA, 1991), pp. 9–10, 13.
70. From *The Work of WHO. Biennial Report of the Director-General*, op. cit., various years.
71. Sergeyev, op. cit., pp. 8–9.
72. ILC, 69th Sess. (1983), p. 39/10; *Pravda*, 8 June 1983, at CDSP XXXV(23), p. 16.
73. Kostine, ILC, 71st Sess. (1985), p. 12/21.
74. ILC, 73rd Sess. (1987), p. 8/9.
75. ILC, 77th Sess. (1990), p. 11/5.
76. Asakwe, op. cit., p. 76.
77. *International Labour Conventions and Recommendations, 1919–1991*, vol. II (Geneva: ILO, 1992), pp. 1222 ff.
78. UNEP, GC, Sess. of special character and 10th Sess. (1982), at GAOR, 37th Sess., suppl., A/37/25, pp. 22–3; A/C.2/42/SR.21, 27 Oct. 1987, p. 3.
79. V. Prokudin and G. Rzhanova, 'The Main Trends in Scientific and Technological Cooperation in Environmental Protection within the CMEA Framework', in *Contributions of CMEA Member-Countries to Environmental Protection* (Moscow: CMEA, 1982), pp. 7–15; A/C.2/39/SR.20, 31 Oct. 1984, p. 2.
80. E. Chossudovsky, *East–West Diplomacy for Environment in the UN: The High-Level Meeting...* (Geneva: UNITAR, 1989), ch. 1. On the importance placed on ECE work, see Soviet remarks at UNEP, GC, 8th Sess. (1980), at GAOR, 35th Sess., suppl. A/35/25, p. 81.
81. *Inter-governmental Conference on Environmental Education: Final Report* (Paris: UNESCO, 1978); UNEP/GC.13/16, pp. 18, 54; A/C.2/40/SR.13, 25 Oct. 1985, p. 11.
82. UNEP/GC.15/12, p. 20; UNEP, GC, 16th Sess. (1991), at GAOR, 46th Sess., suppl., A/46/25, p. 29.
83. *Report of the UNCED, Rio de Janeiro, June 3–14, 1992*, vol. II, A/CONF.151/26, p. 90.

5 Beyond Common Security

1. S/PV.2641, 13 Jan. 1986, p. 21; S/PV.2676, 16 April 1986, p. 13.
2. *Proc. Symposium on Global Security for the 21st Century, Dec. 1986, Florence* (New York: UN, 1987), pp. 44–5.
3. S/PV.3046, 31 Jan. 1992, pp. 43–8.
4. *Izvestiia*, 29 Jan. 1992; CDPSP XLIV(4), p. 19.
5. *Izvestiia*, 14 Feb. 1992; CDPSP XLIV(7), p. 15. There were possible advantages to this arising from Western attacks on China's human-rights record, but Moscow had earlier urged restraint in IGO criticisms of Beijing.
6. See further Robert Boardman, 'The Middle East in the New International Order: Gorbachev, the Russian Federation, and the Rediscovery of the United Nations', in Paul Marantz and David Goldberg (eds), *The Decline of the Soviet Union and the Transformation of the Middle East* (Boulder: Westview, 1993).
7. Alexander J. Bennett, 'The Soviet Union', in Bernard Reich, (ed.), *The Powers in the Middle East: The Ultimate Strategic Arena* (New York: Praeger, 1987), pp. 111–2.
8. Arthur Lall, *The UN and the Middle East Crisis, 1967* (New York: Columbia University Press, 1968), p. 31.
9. On the earlier period, see Anthony Stacpoole, 'Energy as a Factor in Soviet Relations with the Middle East', in Adeed Dawisha and Karen Dawisha (eds), *The Soviet Union and the Middle East: Policies and Perspectives* (New York: Holmes and Meier, 1982), pp. 85–102.
10. Ramesh Thakur, *International Peacekeeping in Lebanon: UN Authority and Multinational Force* (Boulder: Westview, 1987), p. 136.
11. Shahram Chubin, 'Soviet Policy in the Middle East', in S. F. Wells Jr and M. A. Bruzonsky (eds), *Security in the Middle East: Regional Change and Great Power Strategies* (Boulder: Westview, 1987), p. 255.
12. See further Istvan S. Pogany, *The Security Council and the Arab–Israeli Conflict* (New York: St. Martins Press, 1984), pp. 42–3, 45.
13. Rosalyn Higgins, *United Nations Peacekeeping 1946–67. Documents and Commentary, vol. 1* (London: Oxford University Press, 1969), p. 261, n. 5.
14. Ibid., pp. 235, 262, 264, 300, 426.
15. Wayne S. Vucinich, 'Soviet Studies on the Middle East', in Ivo J. Lederer and W. S. Vucinich (eds), *The Soviet Union and the Middle East: The Post-World War II Era* (Stanford: Hoover, 1974), p. 205.
16. Lall, op. cit., pp. 114–28, 231–2, 256.
17. Cited by Safronchuk, S/PV.2659, 11 Feb. 1986, p. 22.
18. Ibid., pp. 14–15.
19. Belongov, S/PV.2737, 20 Feb. 1987, p. 32.
20. S/PV.2721, 18 Nov. 1986, p. 43.
21. Doc. S/18571; S/PV.2737, 20 Feb. 1987, pp. 39–40.
22. R. Boardman, 'From Windhoek to Lome: A Canadian Perspective on Namibia's European Connection', in L. A. Swatuk and T. M. Shaw (eds), *Prospects for Peace and Development in Southern Africa in the 1990s* (Lanham: University Press of America, 1991), pp. 251–68.
23. S/PV.2918, 17 April 1990, pp. 23–24. Cf. *Pravda*, 17 Nov. 1989; CDSP XLI(46), p. 30.

24. On Soviet UN policy, see further Robert O. Freedman, *Moscow and the Middle East: Soviet Policy since the Invasion of Afghanistan* (Cambridge University Press, 1991), pp. 206–7.
25. S/PV.2725, 8 Dec. 1986, p. 43.
26. S/PV.2776, 18 Dec. 1987, pp. 31–6. The preferred phraseology shifted later towards variations on 'peaceful and secure existence within internationally recognised boundaries'.
27. CDSP XLI(27), 2 Aug. 1989, p. 1.
28. S/PV.2923, 29 May 1990, pp. 109–11.
29. S/PV.2784, 18 Jan. 1988, p. 36.
30. Vorontsov, S/PV.3026, 6 Jan. 1992, pp. 36ff.
31. Andrei Kozyrev and Gennadi Gatilov, 'The UN Peace-making System: Problems and Prospects', *International Affairs*, 12, 1990, p. 80.
32. See articles by Ye. Primakov in *Pravda*, at FBIS-SOV-91-048, 12 March 1991, pp. 18, 21; and his press briefing, *Izvestiia*, 13 Feb. 1991, at CDSP XLIII(7), p. 4.
33. 'Gorbachev Advances Settlement Plan for Gulf', Press Office of the USSR Embassy, Ottawa, 18 Feb. 1991.
34. 'Saddam Hussein is Testing the World Community', *International Affairs*, 11, 1990, p. 52.
35. The *Economist*, 23 Feb. 1991, p. 22; and the article by G. Vasilyev, *Pravda*, 20 Sept. 1990, at FBIS-SOV-90-191, p. 10. See further Olga Alexandrova, 'Soviet Policy in the Gulf Conflict', *Aussenpolitik*, 42(3), 1991, pp. 231–2.
36. For example, Mehran Nakhjavani, *After the Persian Gulf War: The Potential for Economic Reconstruction and Development in the Persian Gulf Region* (Ottawa: Canadian Institute for International Peace and Security, 1991), pp. 14–15.
37. Yeltsin, FBIS-SOV-92-173, 4 Sept. 1992, p. 11; Kozyrev, FBIS-SOV-92-202, 19 Oct. 1992, p. 11.
38. S/PV.2978, 3 March 1991, p. 46.
39. A. S. Grachev, in *Novoye Vremya*, 17 April 1991, p. 22.
40. S/PV.2928, 15 June 1990, p. 12.
41. Belongov, S/PV.2919, 20 April 1990, pp. 15–17.
42. S/PV.3009, 25 Sept. 1991, p. 53.
43. FBIS-SOV-92-105, 1 June 1992, p. 11; FBIS-SOV-92-164, 24 Aug. 1992, p. 7; FBIS-SOV-92-168, 28 Aug. 1992, p. 8; *Economist*, 19 Dec. 1992, p. 45.
44. ITAR-TASS report, at FBIS-SOV-92-173, 4 Sept. 1992, p. 11. This tone later became more critical of the US, for example for trying to 'dictate terms' to Russia on the Security Council's handling of the situations in Yugoslavia and Iraq. See Yeltsin at CDPSP XLV(4), 24 Feb. 1993, pp. 9–10.
45. FBIS-SOV-92-180, 16 Sept. 1992, pp. 11–12. Russia insisted that the decision to suspend Yugoslavia's participation in the General Assembly did not affect its 'possible participation' in other bodies, especially the Security Council (Vorontsov, at S/PV. 3116, 19 Sept. 1992, pp. 4–6).
46. A/C.1/42/PV.8, 20 Oct. 1987, pp. 26, 33.
47. A/C.1/43/PV.4, 20 Oct. 1988, p. 73; A/C.1/45/PV.4, 23 Oct. 1990, p. 7.
48. FBIS-CHI-91-106, 3 June 1991, p. 3.
49. Andrei Kozyrev, 'The USSR's New Approach to the United Nations', *International Affairs*, 7, 1990, pp. 13, 16; V. Petrovsky, article in *Za Rubezhom*, 39, 21–7 Sept. 1990, at FBIS-SOV-90-192, p. 12.

50. FBIS-SOV-89-065, 6 April 1989; FBIS-SOV-89-072, 17 April 1989, p. 9.
51. S/PV.3046, 31 Jan. 1992, pp. 46–8.
52. Ibid., p. 48.
53. GAOR, 47th Sess., suppl., A/47/33, 1992, pp. 4–5.
54. GAOR, 43rd Sess., suppl., A/43/33, 1988, p. 4; GAOR, 44th Sess., suppl., A/44/33, 1989, pp. 42–5.
55. 'New Issues for Consideration in the Special Committee. Working Paper submitted by the USSR', Doc. A/AC.182/L.65, 1990.
56. Ibid.
57. GAOR, 46th Sess., suppl., A/46/33, 1991, pp. 16–18.
58. Doc. A/AC.182/L.65, Corr. 1; and Russian Federation, 'Draft Declaration on the Improvement of Cooperation between the UN and Regional Organizations' (Doc. A/AC.182/L.72).
59. GAOR, 47th Sess., suppl., A/47/33, 1992, pp. 26–7.

6 From Periphery to Pole

1. Yongjin Zhang, 'China's Entry into International Society: Beyond the Standard of Civilization', *Review of International Studies*, 7(1), 1991, p. 16; and *China in the International System, 1918–20: The Middle Kingdom at the Periphery* (London: Macmillan, 1991).
2. F. P. Walters, *A History of the League of Nations* (Oxford University Press, 1960), pp. 184–5, 718.
3. Ibid., pp. 332–3.
4. Gerald E. Bunker, *The Peace Conspiracy: Wang Ching-wei and the China War, 1937–1941* (Harvard University Press, 1972), p. 34.
5. Samuel S. Kim, *China, the United Nations and World Order* (Princeton University Press, 1979), p. 99n.
6. Robert C. Hilderbrand, *Dumbarton Oaks: The Origins of the United Nations and the Search for Post-war Security* (Chapel Hill: University of North Carolina Press, 1990), p. 229.
7. Kim, op. cit., p. 100.
8. Zhai Qiang, 'China and the Geneva Conference of 1954', *China Quarterly*, 129, 1992, p. 108, n. 21.
9. Byron S. Weng, *Peking's UN Policy: Continuity and Change* (New York: Praeger, 1972); and 'Communist China's Changing Attitudes toward the UN', *International Organization*, 20, 1966, pp. 677–704.
10. Kim, op. cit., p. 101.
11. RMRB editorial, at SCMP-71-44, no. 5004, 1 Nov. 1971, p. 221.
12. Chinese government statement, NCNA, 29 Oct. 1971; SCMP-71-45, no. 5009-13, 8–12 Nov. 1971, p. 50.
13. See further Kim, op. cit., pp. 194–241.
14. Ibid., pp. 282–333.
15. Ibid., pp. 334–404.
16. Gerald Chan, *China and International Organizations: Participation in Non-governmental Organizations* (Hong Kong: Oxford University Press, 1989).
17. For example, *Beijing Review*, 27(43), 22 Oct. 1984, p. 4.
18. Michael Yahuda, 'China's Foreign Relations and the Modernization Programme', in Jack Gray and Gordon White (eds), *China's New*

Development Strategy (New York: Academic Press, 1982), p. 41; Robert Kleinberg, *China's 'Opening' to the Outside World: The Experiment with Foreign Capitalism* (Boulder: Westview, 1990).

19. Nicholas R. Lardy, 'Chinese Foreign Trade', *China Quarterly*, 131, 1992, p. 694.
20. Ibid., pp. 695–6.
21. David Shambaugh, *Beautiful Imperialist: China Perceives America, 1972–1990* (Princeton University Press, 1991). In general see Harry Harding, *A Fragile Relationship: The United States and China since 1972* (Washington, DC: Brookings, 1992).
22. See for example Fu Yaozhu, in *Shijie Zhishi*, 14, 16 July 1991, at FBIS-PRC-91-152, pp. 2–3; and the study by Dorothea A. Martin, *The Making of a Sino–Marxist World View: Perception and Interpretation of World History in the People's Republic of China* (Armonk: M. E. Sharpe, 1990).
23. Shaun Breslin, 'The Foreign Policy Bureaucracy', in Gerald Segal (ed.), *Chinese Politics and Foreign Policy Reform* (London: Kegan Paul International, 1990), pp. 122–4.
24. See for example statements by Li Daoyu, S/PV.2933, 6 Aug. 1990, pp. 28–9; Qian Qichen, S/PV.2943, 25 Sept. 1990, p. 49; and comments on world trends of multipolarity, at A/C.1/44/PV.9, p. 53.
25. S/PV. 2943, 25 Sept. 1990, p. 51.
26. Report on the Gulf War symposium, at *Beijing Review*, 34(28), 15–21 July 1991, pp. 8–10. Chinese participants to a major international academic conference held in Beijing later in 1991 also emphasised the postwar relevance of the five principles.
27. Articles by Shu Zhong and Hu Ping in *Shijie Zhishi*, 5, 1 March 1991, pp. 5–6, 13; and Xi Shugang in *Gongren Ribao*, 19 March 1991; at FBIS-PRC-91-066, pp. 1–2, and -067, pp. 2–3.
28. Yitzhak Shichor, 'China and the Role of the UN in the Middle East', *Asian Survey*, 31(3), 1991, p. 261.
29. *Beijing Review*, 27(46), 12 Nov. 1984, p. 12.
30. Wu Xueqian, in *Beijing Review*, 27(41), 8 Oct. 1984, p. 23; A/C.2/40/SR.14 (1985), pp. 14–15.
31. FBIS-PRC, I/189, 28 Sept. 1983, p. A1.
32. Liang Yufan, at FBIS-PRC, I/176, 11 Sept. 1985, pp. A1–2.
33. Wu Xueqian, FBIS-PRC, I/188, 27 Sept. 1985, p. A2. Cf. the defence of charter principles by the Chinese UNGA 1st Committee delegate at A/C.1/42/PV.56, p. 11.
34. Guo Chuanling, 'Present World Economy: Basic Features and Trends', *Contemporary International Relations*, 4, 1990, pp. 8–15.
35. Chen Xiong, 'The Intention and Elements of Gorbachev's Theory of "New Thinking"', *International Strategic Studies*, 2, 1988, pp. 27–33; Gao Wenmei and Luo Renshi, 'Reflections on the Soviet Readjustments of Asia-Pacific Strategy', ibid., pp. 1–7.
36. Jin Dexiang, 'The World in the 1990s: More Unrest, More Turmoil Ahead?', *Contemporary International Relations*, no. 6, Feb. 1991, p. 9.
37. Zou Keyuan, 'Building a New International Political and Economic Order: A Chinese Perspective', mimeo., 1991.
38. FBIS-CHI-91-211, 31 Oct. 1991, p. 2.

7 Understanding the Times

1. FBIS-PRC, I/191, 30 Sept. 1983, pp. A6–7.
2. Xie Qimei, at FBIS-PRC, I/066, 5 April 1985, p. A1; and Chinese comments on the 3rd UN Development Decade, at A/C.2/40/SR.14, pp. 14–15.
3. Jin Dexiang, 'The World in the 1990s: More Unrest, More Turmoil Ahead?', *Contemporary International Relations*, no. 6, Feb. 1991, p. 9.
4. FBIS-PRC-91-129, 5 July 1991, pp. 1–2.
5. FBIS-CHI-92-025, 6 Feb. 1992, p. 1.
6. Marc Williams, *Third World Cooperation: The Group of 77 in UNCTAD* (London: Pinter, 1991), p. 71.
7. FBIS-PRC-89-074, 19 April 1989, p. 2.
8. FBIS-PRC-90-058, 26 March 1990, p. 1; and -084, 1 May 1990, p. 6.
9. H. K. Jacobson and Michel Oksenberg, *China's Participation in the IMF, the World Bank, and GATT: Toward a Global Economic Order* (University of Michigan Press, 1990), pp. 61–2.
10. Ibid., p. 70.
11. Ibid., pp. 75–80.
12. Meeting between Li Peng and Barber Conable, reported at FBIS-PRC-88-058, 25 March 1988, p. 1.
13. Figures from FBIS-PRC-88-049, 14 March 1988, p. 1; Jacobson and Oksenberg, op. cit., pp. 118–19, 155.
14. Ibid., pp. 121–6.
15. FBIS-PRC, I/076, 19 April 1985, p. A1; Qiu Qing, at the 1988 meetings, FBIS-PRC-88-187, 27 Sept. 1988, p. 3; and the evaluation of the Brady plan in RMRB, 12 April 1989, at FBIS-PRC-89-073, p. 1.
16. IMF, Proc. 46th Annual Meeting of the Board of Governors (1991), p. 49.
17. Jacobson and Oksenberg, op. cit., p. 140.
18. Ibid., pp. 140–50.
19. Meetings of Michel Camdessus in Beijing, at FBIS-PRC-89-070, 13 April 1989, pp. 4–5; and the summary by Li, at IMF, Proc. 46th Annual Meeting, p. 50.
20. FBIS-PRC-90-011, 17 Jan. 1990, p. 5; Xinhua report, at -019, 29 Jan. 1990, p. 1.
21. FBIS-PRC, I/034, 20 Feb. 1987, pp. A3–4.
22. Robert Boardman, 'Guns or Mushrooms: Relations between the European Community and China, 1974–1980', *Politica. Tidsskrift for politisk videnskab*, 13(1), 1981, pp. 50–79.
23. Feng Yushu, 'When will China return to GATT?', *Liaowang* (Hong Kong), 6–13 Feb. 1989; FBIS-PRC-89-029, 14 Feb. 1989, p. 1.
24. Li Lanqing, interview, FBIS-CHI-92-053, 18 March 1992; RMRB, 13 Feb. 1992, at FBIS-CHI-92-031, p. 1; 'China and GATT', *The Economist*, 6 March 1993, pp. 25–6.
25. WHA 36/1983/REC/2, p. 119.
26. WHA 44/1991/REC/2, p. 81.
27. WHA 42/1989/REC/2, p. 105.
28. *Zhongguo Xinwen She*, 31 Aug. 1983; FBIS-PRC I/71, p. A1.
29. WHA 36/1983/REC/2, p. 130; WHA 40/1987/REC/2, pp. 87–8.

30. 'The World Economic Situation and the Prospects for Health for All by the Year 2000', WHO Doc. A42/Inf.Doc./1 (1989).
31. WHA 44/1991/REC/2, p. 80; JPRS-CPS-87-037, 15 May 1987, p. 7; A/C.2/44/SR.38 (1989), p. 19; *Beijing Review*, 26(43), 24 Oct. 1983, p. 25; *China Daily*, 14 May 1991, p. 1.
32. 'Global Strategy for the Prevention and Control of AIDS,' WHO Doc. A43/6 (1990); WHA 44/1991/REC/2, p. 79.
33. WHA 42/1989/REC/2, p. 317.
34. Ibid., p. 261; 'Study of the Director-General on the Application of Palestine for Membership of WHO', WHO Doc. A43/25 (1990).
35. ILC, 72nd Sess. (1986), p. 15/8.
36. ILC, 77th Sess. (1990), pp. 15/17–8.
37. ILC, 76th Sess. (1989), pp. 24/31–3; ILC, 77th Sess. (1990), p. 22/25.
38. *China Daily*, 15 March 1988; FBIS-PRC-88-052, p. 3.
39. UNEP, GC, 2nd Special Sess. (1990), at GAOR, 45th Sess., suppl., A/45/25, p. 17. China also criticised the Soviet-style linkage of environment with disarmament issues. See A/C.2/40/SR.50 (1985), p. 9.
40. UNEP, GC, 14th Sess. (1987), at GAOR, 42nd Sess., suppl. A/42/25, p. 16.
41. UNEP, GC, 15th Sess. (1989), at GAOR, 44th Sess., suppl., A/44/25, 1989, p. 14.
42. Qu Geping, 'Work Report to the Third National Conference on Environmental Protection', in *Chinese Environmental Protection* (Beijing, 1990), p. 90.
43. FBIS-PRC-90-126, 29 June 1990, pp. 1–2.
44. 'Beijing Ministerial Declaration on Environment and Development', *Environmental Policy and Law*, 21/5/6 (1991), pp. 267–9; *Beijing Review*, 34(27), 8–14 July 1991, pp. 9–13.
45. FBIS-CHI-92-046, 9 March 1992, p. 1.
46. Li Luye, S/PV. 2736, 19 Feb. 1987, p. 23; S/PV. 2659, 11 Feb. 1986, pp. 5–6; Liang Yufan, S/PV. 2685, 23 May 1986, p. 14; S/PV. 2795, March 7, 1988, p. 17.
47. S/PV. 2692, 17 June 1986, p. 26.
48. S/PV. 2757, 29 Oct. 1987, pp. 40–1.
49. S/PV. 2708, 23 Sept. 1986, p. 32; S/PV. 2813, 9 May 1988, pp. 17–18.
50. FBIS-PRC, I/078, 23 April 1985, p. A4.
51. S/PV. 2787, 28 Jan. 1988, pp. 50–1.
52. FBIS-PRC-88-188, 28 Sept. 1988, p. 1; S/PV. 2849, 17 Feb. 1989, p. 31.
53. Ding Yuanhong, S/PV. 2923, 29 May 1990, p. 114; Li Daoyu, S/PV. 2946, 8 Oct. 1990, p. 43; S/PV. 2965, 5 Dec. 1990, p. 9.
54. Li Luye, S/PV. 2712, 7 Oct. 1986, p. 18.
55. S/PV. 2932, 2 Aug. 1990, p. 23; S/PV. 2933, 6 Aug. 1990, pp. 28–9.
56. S/PV. 2943, 25 Sept. 1990, pp. 49–50.
57. FBIS-CHI-92-053, 18 March 1992, p. 1.
58. For example, Li Daoyu, at S/PV. 2978, 3 March 1991, p. 51.
59. FBIS-CHI-92-049, 10 March 1992, p. 4. This was combined with approaches to Gulf states. See John Calabrese, 'Peaceful or Dangerous Collaborators? China's Relations with Gulf Countries', *Pacific Affairs*, 65(4), 1993, pp. 471–85.

60 S/PV. 3009, 25 Sept. 1991, p. 50; S/PV. 3114, 14 Sept. 1992, pp. 9–10; S/PV. 3135, 13 Nov. 1992, p. 15. China was particularly critical of the appearance of references to Chapter VII of the charter in resolutions. See Chen Jian at S/PV. 3174, 19 Feb. 1993, pp. 19–20.

61. Qian Qichen, in RMRB, 16 Dec. 1988; *Beijing Review*, 31(52), 26 Dec. 1988–1 Jan. 1989, pp. 14–16. See also Wang Qiwen, article in *Shijie Zhishi*, no. 24, 16 Dec. 1989, at JPRS-CAR-90-021, 20 March 1990, p. 1.

62. Peng Naidian and You Wen, 'The Challenge of Competition in Global Reform', *Gaige* (Chongqing), 20 Jan. 1990; JPRS-CAR-90-020, 14 March 1990, p. 1.

63. *Special Committee on the Charter of the United Nations and on the Strengthening of the Role of the Organization*, Report, GAOR, 45th Sess., suppl., A/45/33 (1990), p. 18. Such comments were often set in the context of criticisms of more ambitious Soviet plans for the UN (A/C.1/42/PV.56, p. 12).

64. FBIS-CHI-92-029, 12 Feb. 1992, p. 1.

65. Ye Ruan, 'Conception of World's Future', *Shijie Zhishi*, no. 13, 1 July 1991; FBIS-CHI-91-140, pp. 2–3.

8 The UN System and World Order

1 Robert O. Keohane, *International Institutions and State Power: Essays in International Relations Theory* (Boulder: Westview, 1989), p. 1.

2. Cf. Hans J. Morgenthau, *Politics among Nations: The Struggle for Power and Peace*, revised by Kenneth W. Thompson, brief edition (New York: McGraw-Hill, 1993), p. 110.

3. Peter R. Baehr and Leon Gordenker, *The United Nations in the 1990s* (London: Macmillan, 1992), p. 155. Some weaknesses from the perspective of institution-building, however, may also be viewed by states as assets if they protect sovereignty.

4. See in particular Peter J. Katzenstein, *Small States in World Markets: Industrial Policy in Europe* (Ithaca: Cornell University Press, 1985), pp. 23–4, 201–2.

5. See further M. J. Peterson, *The General Assembly in World Politics* (Boston: Unwin Hyman, 1986), p. 254.

6. On the decline of the use of the veto generally, see further Anjali V. Patil, *The UN Veto in World Affairs, 1946–1990* (London: Mansell, 1992), p. 463, and Appendices.

7. Cf. H. K. Jacobson, *The USSR and the UN's Economic and Social Activities* (University of Notre Dame Press, 1963), pp. 278–9.

8. For a discussion of the related concepts of common security, classical security, security interdependence and economic security, see Robert Boardman, 'Ecological Security, the Oceans, and Common Security', paper presented to the XVII Conf. Pacem in Maribus, Moscow, June 1989.

9. James Clay Moltz, 'Divergent Learning and the Failed Politics of Soviet Economic Reform', *World Politics*, 45(2), 1993, pp. 301–25.

10. On this capability, see further Ernst B. Haas, *When Knowledge is Power: Three Models of Change in International Organizations* (Berkeley: University of California Press, 1990), p. 128.

Index